One Room in a Castle

ONE ROOM
IN A CASTLE

Letters from Spain,
France & Greece

by

KAREN CONNELLY

TURNSTONE PRESS

Turnstone Press gratefully acknowledges the assistance
of the Canada Council and the Manitoba Arts Council.

Cover photograph: Karen Connelly

Design: Manuela Dias

This book was printed and bound in Canada by
Friesens for Turnstone Press.

Second printing: November 1995

Canadian Cataloguing in Publication Data

Connelly, Karen, 1969–

One room in a castle

ISBN 0-88801-194-6

1. Connelly, Karen, 1969–   - Correspondence.
2. Connelly, Karen, 1969–   - Journeys - Europe.
3. Europe - Description and travel.   I. Title.

D923.C65 1995   914   C95-920191-2

for Angela and Al Pallister
who lent me a room in their small castle
and
for those who do not have a map

The forest is everywhere. It is in every man, just as in every man is his own prison.

Once you have escaped your prison, and gone through the forest and ocean of yourself, you do not need a retreat. You do not need a church or a monastery.

The world is open before you.

All you need to do—and want to do—is walk through it.

—Kenneth White
Letters from Gourgounel

Whatever we have been given is supposed to be given away again, not kept . . . The only essential is this: *the gift must always move.*

—Lewis Hyde
The Gift

Contents

Jamais Avignon

Acknowledgements

I would like to thank Angela and Al Pallister, who provided me with a room in their castle, and a roof over my head for two years.

Many, many people made this book. Some gave me their stories. Others freely offered me their light, their anger, their sadness, their beauty. Many read parts of the manuscript while it was still in one of its earlier forms—often its original, letter form, in fact. I would like to thank each of you for your generosity, your comments, and, in many cases, the letters you wrote in reply. Among these people, I would like to thank certain individuals in particular: Nancy Holmes, who knows the whole story; Tariq Hussain, who knows the other whole story—*shi! daim;* the Ramos and the Aracama families in the Basque country; Tiff, who told me to stop whining; Noemi, *mi bruja preferida;* Carola Hahnel and George Tyler, for their encouragement and cooking in France; Marie-Claude

Tavernier and the Gypsy community of Montclar, Libby Oughton, the muse; my various, generous extended family in Greece, especially Panagos and Mireille, for their kindness and electricity; Jackie Henry, a tireless forwarder-of-mail, financial administrator, and great mother.

I would like to acknowledge the literary journal *Exile,* where "My Father's Country" was first published; the *Malahat Review,* where "The Day Mandori Died" was first published; and *Poetry Canada,* where the Greek poems were first published. Thanks are also due to the University of New Brunswick, where I worked on parts of this book during my residency. The contents and physical structure of two excellent books aided me in writing this one: *Mère Méditerrannée,* by Dominique Fernandez, published by Éditions Bernard Grasset, and *Gypsies of the World,* by N.B. Tomasevic and R. Djuric, published by Henry Holt and Company. I gratefully acknowledge the generosity of two funding agencies: the Canada Council and the Alberta Foundation for the Arts. These organizations allowed me to eat and travel while I was writing parts of this manuscript and others that are still in progress.

And thank you, the reader, for entering this book.

Letter to the reader

A STRANGE NIGHT. Strange because it's warm for late November, even on the island. Strange because I'm looking after a friend's house, experiencing its night sounds for the first time. Three in the morning. Sleep is a foreigner in this hour. The surf keeps me awake: waves ten feet high on a sea they usually call smooth as oil. The rhythmic crash of the water is like my own heartbeat amplified in my ear, inescapable. And it's a strange night because I let the kitten out earlier, and he disappeared from the locked courtyard. The children who live in this house will be heartbroken.

A foreign bed, the Aegean pulse, guilt for a gray, blue-eyed kitten: these things keep me awake. . . . And you, whoever you are, reading these words. You, whom I have never met, never seen. Yet now, through incomprehensible stretches of distance and time, we touch here, on the page.

This is the peculiar magic of a letter. Of words, received.

I've been writing and receiving letters since I was a small child. They are my favourite way to write, my favourite thing to read. When I started to travel and live for long periods away from Canada, I realized we can live entire histories on paper. Our friendships and loves, even our vaguest contacts, strengthen, weaken, erupt, entangle, but always transform, through words. Words received, when we are far away, become very powerful.

This is a book of letters. I wrote some of them to close friends; some of them were entries in notebooks and journals, letters to myself. Many of them were written specifically to you, the reader I've never met. As I sifted through old correspondence and reworked the writings I found there, I thought about you. I tried to imagine who you are, who you might be. I envisioned a multitude of people and occupations, a thousand possible lives, kitchens and bedrooms and living-rooms inhabited by objects that continually whisper your history. I saw you in strange countries, in different cities, walking in fields and streets, on lakesides, in restaurants, coffee shops, waiting, waiting for the bus. What a strange, what a unique, position to be in: to wonder, from this distance, from any distance, who you are.

I was imagining you because I was thinking about what happens when we write *to* a person. One person. Not an audience, but a human being. I thought, Wouldn't it be wonderful to write a book the same way you write a good letter? The letter as a literary form invites a rare, sometimes funny, sometimes jarring intimacy. Its truth is selective and highly personal. I wanted to file off the edges, loosen the constraints of chronology (no dates, just headings), and place my writing in its true setting: with my letters, inside my own voice and experience.

When we travel in different provinces, or on separate continents, even when we simply seek a different light, we lose each other over and over again. Then a letter arrives, and we are found. I dislike and sometimes do not live in easy reach of a telephone. I am still coping with my suspicion of fax machines. But I take my envelopes like gifts to the post office, where they are weighed and stamped and checked once more, again, because I must be careful, must care for these folded messages. The words in an envelope are as valuable as the words in a mouth.

Everywhere in the world, people are writing letters. On thin or heavy bond paper, on lined and unlined sheets, before the eerie blue and gray and green glows of computer screens. The light in the rooms where we write is harsh (a kitchen full of unpacked boxes); it is honey and sunflowers (the porch at the farm); it is too strong (the new lamp in the living-room, while the children down the hall read their books in bed).

Our letters sometimes fail us, because words are imprecise tools, no matter how fervently we believe in them. Sometimes we cannot say exactly what we mean; sometimes we lie. But letters—and this is their great power—always bear testimony to the simple, astonishing fact of our days. Even a postcard does this. Words are invisible bridges in a world of chasms. They span foreign territories, political jungles, entire oceans, even the erratic tides of our own lives.

So. Slip Montreal's first red leaf of autumn into the envelope. Enclose the ticket stubs from the museum in Madrid, or from the one in Fredericton. Fold in the dried petals of a flower whose name remains unknown. Press oregano and sweet basil between the pages. Send any talisman that will fit into the narrow pocket of an envelope. Send words.

No matter what it actually says, every letter proclaims, *I am alive here, in this place, now.* And you are also here, on the page, in my pen, in my imagination. On the other side of the country, over the waters, past the mountains, you are also here, alive, in our torn and remarkable world.

K.C.
Greece

The House on Hope Street

Strange to be travelling back
through darkness, too, desiring
everything I am afraid of . . .
                    —Susan Musgrave

The house on Hope Street

MY INTENTION IS to tell everything.

I already know Everything does not fit on a page, even a thousand pages. Let me give you a detail for the beginning, a detail for spring: as soon as I left the bustling excitement of the airport and drove into the green fields, I could hear them. The frogs. Late May, the frogs are in love, and I am home.

Home. The city where my mother lives. Streets I know like old songs, songs I'm embarrassed to know, but do, and secretly love. Or not so secretly. I smile and smile. I've already cleaned up Lorca the bicycle, and ridden through the city, singing, laughing over bridges, tearing too quickly along the path by the green river. Home. Stone blue mountains to the west. Even as I write, Cimmeron, the bay horse, gets fat in the foothills. Christine's hair has grown longer; she's made an enormous dragon puppet to add to her collection. Gabriel has bought a motorcycle with the money he owes me. My cousin is in love. My brother is in jail. My sister won second place in the first women's rodeo of the season. I am in Calgary, Alberta, and I am laughing and laughing, because I'm happy, because I love this place, because the Greek cook at Paros on Fourth drops his handful of tomatoes, wipes his hands on his apron, and hugs me until I have no breath.

I am home.

For a while. Until the wind changes.

I went two days ago and booked my ticket to Amsterdam. I will leave at the beginning of September.

But wait, a small interruption: a black squirrel undulates over the red roof shingles, pauses, looks in the window at me, shakes its tail. A peanut? A piece of bread? It hops to the rain gutter beside the window, jumps down to drink at the shallow puddle of rainwater on the porch roof. Almost every day since I've arrived, I crawl out my bedroom window and sit on this roof to take the sun and read. Usually in my underwear. The porch below is walled by lilacs. When I am up on the roof, dozens of lilacs are at my feet and enormous bees buzz intently through a white and purple feast.

This house! I looked after it last summer while the owners were away in Italy. They are back this year, but they will spend most of the season at their cabin on Silvan Lake. So I am living here again, tending the plants, the ghosts, and the garden.

I have never loved a house before. I am still and always leaving that place in the suburbs, the house I grew up in—but I never loved it. Though I cared for some of them, none of the rooms I've rented since has exerted any great power over me.

But this house took me into itself gently, with

such a powerful, deep grace—like the grace of certain cathedrals—that I was very quickly overcome. The owners—Angela and Al Pallister—have taken care of the ghosts here. They remain, calm, gentle even, moving through the halls like Angela's family in old England still breathes in black and white photographs.

The photographs are in her bedroom, an elegant, simple room, pale yellow and blue wallpaper, a pale, pale blue lake of bed, a high dresser adorned with a small mirror, ropes of turquoise and glass beads looped over its edge, half a dozen tiny Chinese essence bottles, perfume bottles, a silver box, a wooden box, a porcelain figurine.

And a wall of old photographs. Her mother is there, a beautiful, slender woman with black hair and blue eyes, a woman born in China, as Angela was. Photographs of her brothers when they were small boys. Photograph of a girl with a face as soft as a ripe peach. Photographs of new babies and weddings, a dozen bridesmaids with flapper haircuts and floppy hats, every one of them white-skinned, lovely, squinting against the sun. Every one of them old or dead now, gone over.

The most intriguing image shows a man and a woman standing on a porch. Late nineteenth century? The man has a short, serious beard, small round glasses. He is on the left, turned away, pretending the photographer is a fence post. Clearly it's an insult to this gentleman's dignity to be photographed. His hands are deep and clenched in his pockets. We see the watch chain curve over his trim waistcoat. But the woman beside him turns her face, her whole body, to the camera, like someone waking to a lover. Broad bands of light fall in uneven sections across her white, high-necked blouse, across her long dark skirt. She smiles disarmingly, straight into the lens, open-mouthed, hand held to her throat to feel her own voice starting there.

It is clear, looking at her, that she is about to speak, or laugh.

Why, why will she laugh? What is she about to say?

Photographs place the moment in your hand like a stone, a stone turned and rolled and worn impossibly thin by the crashing, silent waves of time.

Curmudgeon

MR. PALLISTER was a map-maker for the United Nations. More than a map-maker, he was a kind of scientist. He measured entire coastlines and continental basins. East Africa, Afghanistan, and Italy. He flew in planes and calculated the heights of mountain ranges, foothills, valleys, then translated all of it to paper. Isn't that remarkable? He insists it isn't. "It's mathematics," he says. "The uninitiated are always using words like *remarkable,*" he adds in a curmudgeonly, unimpressed tone. "And words like *magical.*" He clears his throat. I laugh and sip some of the Scotch he's poured into my glass.

Mr. Pallister has come into the city to pick up some building supplies for the boathouse. Angela called from the lake before he came and said in her most concerned English gentlewoman's voice, "I'm so sorry, but you'll have to put up with him for a couple of days. I know he's dreadful, absolutely dreadful, but there's nothing I can do. I hope he behaves himself." Mr. Pallister is cantankerous. Old. "Irascible" is the sound that comes from him when he clears his throat. But I've discovered it's a front, created in part by his mischievous sense of humour. He wants to see how far he can go in his caricature of an ornery old coot. He's crusty on the outside but soft on the inside, like a fresh Italian pastry. Over coffee, we have lumbering elephant conversations about living in Canada, living abroad, returning. He pauses a long time between words sometimes and I have to control myself from interrupting. "When you come back," he says, "you realize you know nothing . . . about the place where you were born. . . . And it knows . . . nothing . . . about you. . . . I've been back for ten years. . . . I still can't fathom precisely . . . what is . . . going on."

He and Angela met nearly forty years ago in Africa. They stayed in Kenya for two years, married in England, restationed in Afghanistan, lived in Italy for almost a decade. Mr. Pallister worked for the United Nations. Last year, when I looked after the house, I spent much more time with Angela, swooning about the Mediterranean, exchanging travel enthusiasms. We drank gin and tonics and laughed and leaned together over her beautiful books. But I didn't often talk to Mr. Pallister. I was a little frightened by him.

Not now. He's impossible, grumpy, he growls at the apple-faced boys who work in the produce department ("The tomatoes . . . are too ripe! How . . . do you justify . . . these bruised grapes?"), but the other day he insisted I eat one of his fresh croissants for breakfast. We have a date to go together to the farmers' market. We've discussed homosexuality and hammers (it's hard to find a really good hammer in southern Europe: Canada can be praised without restraint for good tools). Despite Angela's warnings, and his grumpy exterior, Mr. Pallister is sane, liberal, kind. Lonely white tufts of hair wander his head. He often wears a very beaten-up beret from his days with the Russian engineers. The creases of his old hands are black with oil and numerous kinds of dirt, and he often forgets to wash them before he eats. I like this very much. The other day, over dinner, I noticed the top knuckle of his right middle finger is gone. I would like to know how he lost that bit of finger, but I'm afraid to ask. The same day I noticed it was missing, he said, out of the blue, "I don't care for inquisitive people."

He spends his time restoring antiques, building things, taking care of the garden. He made me pesto for lunch; I made curried eggplant for supper. We discussed politics. He says Alberta is unbelievable, Ralph Klein ruins his appetite, he wishes he never left Italy. The cheese there was magnificent and you could always get fresh basil. The Italians, for all their faults, were civilized. Canadians don't know how to eat properly.

The magic thread

MR. PALLISTER HAS left for the lake.

Now I am alone again. I can walk around without trousers on and read under the sun in the garden and write letters at the antique dining-room table. I can be a ghost, almost, in this dwelling of ghosts.

Angela told me the first owner of this house was a woman, Julia. The house was hers in 1906, when it was rare for a woman to own anything but her knickers. Angela also told me a strange family grew up here. The eccentric daughters used to hide caches of food under the planks in their bedroom closets, apparently frightened by their father's stories of famine in India. One of them became a sculptor and travelled the world, studied with Balinese mask-makers and actors of Comedia Dell'Arte. She ended up in Paris (didn't they all?) where she bought a theatre. Why do other people's lives sound so improbable?

Is she still alive, going for Sunday walks in

Luxembourg Gardens, wrinkled, with henna hair and green sparks for eyes? If she is still alive, does she have any teeth left? I don't know. But I know she lived and walked in these rooms, and her essence left its dust in the century-old dining-room curtains, in the wood grain of the wainscoting, in the brass light fixtures.

I believe that the people of the past live beyond us. Isn't that what history is? Isn't that the first law of thermodynamics? When I say ghosts, I am not talking about white figures and rattling chains, but neither am I speaking metaphorically. A thread stretches from the present into the past, just as it casts forward into the future, and we are connected to it. It pierces and runs through our hearts.

The creation of distance

I WAIT NOW for a letter that does not come. A letter from a good friend who visited, recently, from far away. Why doesn't she send me something, a sign, a clue?

I ask out loud in the room, and silence whispers something inaudible to itself.

I have no idea of her, and she has not been gone so long. See how quickly it happens? A month, almost two months, and a great silence between us. The human race has been confused for centuries. Miles or kilometres or even light years do not make distance. What creates and imposes distance is not physical space. Sometimes we are farthest away from the man or woman we are sitting beside. What creates distance is silence.

When we hear something, some sound—the bird call, the piano singing underhand, the floor giving way under weight and creaking upstairs—we know someone is there, some presence or person, we know they are close, close. (That is why the telephone is a useful but ultimately hurtful invention.) When there are no sounds—and of course I think of her letters as her living voice—there is immense distance. It will not matter when she arrives in France next year, when we finally wake on the same continent. She will be hours and worlds closer to me in kilometres travelled by plane, but it will make no difference until I hear her voice in the bathroom, her voice behind me, coming through the hair that falls over my ear. If silence creates distance, a living voice brings us home.

The story I've written for her isn't finished yet. I still don't know how it ends. Why couldn't the Russian pianist stay in Canada? And if she leaves, how do I describe it without getting all sweet and sticky? I envy the ease of painters. A realistic painting could tell the story with precise edges, every colour exact, the entire image: two women sit on a piano bench, with their backs to the piano. One of them rests a hand on a sheaf of music; the other has her face turned to the window as if to look outside, but her eyes are closed. And anyone who sees the painting knows that the closed eyes signify *no*.

I hope to receive words from her soon. Or smoke signals. Or a sign in the stars.

A tiger on the roof

I SIT ON THE roof in my underwear.

From here, I see the nearby shining angles of downtown, a brick high school in a green field, old row houses, the busy traffic of Seventeenth Avenue. (Seventeenth Avenue, where I buy wine, bagels, books; where, under the cover of night, I leave empty beer bottles for the raggedy men.) I receive this view of the city through white and purple lilacs, because I am lying on my stomach, elbows pressed into the fine roof gravel. An earth mover ploughs over the sidewalk on the next block. Squirrels trapeze the trees.

The wind pushes marble slabs of cloud away from the sun; heat leaps down. The sun stretches now against my side, down my side, my left side more than my right, which is close to the shade. The sun is heavy against my ribs, a warm animal. The sun is a great cat, a tiger lying here on the roof with me, panting. He's one of the living artefacts the Pallisters brought home from India.

What's the tiger's name?
Tell me.

Hailstorms and hunger

MY GREAT FRIENDSHIPS are accompanied by hail-storms. The most savage hailstorm started up as I finished reading a letter from a friend, anxious, laughing, talking aloud to myself, holding the paper and photographs in my hand. As I write, I turn my head away from the screen and watch the white crash of hail, breathe crushed leaves and torn bark. White stones fall in the open window, the blind trembles, rattles. Cold wind pours in, along my back, over my bare neck onto my chest. The sky to the east is so dark, so dark, but even as I write it lightens and the hail falls into rain.

The blind rattles, the door slams. This wind!

My friend Marcus sends a photograph of a thin, black-eyed girl with fresh bread in her hands, a serrated bread knife tucked under her left arm. A large cut on the outer curve of her thumb repeatedly draws my eyes. This small, dirt-filled cut becomes the focus of the photograph. Marcus writes about hunger.

It is right to make a life out of our hunger? If you are always hungry, you always have to eat, and nothing satisfies completely. You remember that tremendous meal from two years ago, on the *paseo* of San Sebastian, in an old port on the East Coast, at that restaurant in Strasbourg, or was it actually in the Chinese food place in Claresholm, after you went to see your first rodeo? Or was it, in fact, right here in Cowtown, on Sandra and David's balcony, when you were drunk and happy, close to good people, feeling the warm night air on your face? You want every meal to be as delicious as that one, the one you ate so long ago, but no meal ever quite equals it, the lost one, the feast from before. So you keep eating, you travel in order to eat, more bread, more rare cheese, more dishes tendered with spices whose names you can't pronounce.

Odd that I write about hunger on a day when I I have no appetite. I am drinking Scotch. More hail this afternoon, a street festival in Calgary, and something that upset me terribly: a phone call from an old lover. Our voices filled the space of two years, filled the distance between this smiling red-neck town and Montreal, filled my body. Later I cried and cried, sobbed, a phrase from my adolescence: her body racked with sobs. Because he reminded me that I am very much alone. More difficult: that I have chosen this solitude on purpose. Again. Suddenly I could not face a solitary supper at the antique dining-room table, under the old, coloured-glass lamp. And I write now to fend off my aloneness, to remind myself that some connections will endure through time, no matter where I live on this earth.

Sadness today. The sky half light, half cloud.

Smell of crushed lilacs after hail, after rain. I am tired, unable to sleep most nights, thinking all the time about returning to Europe. Why do I always leave?

Before I go away, I usually feel this way. Freakish. Like a monster. Oh, you know: a troll, a gnarled forest creature, never anything nice, like a mermaid or a fairy. Why am I going away? What am I doing? Is this any way to live? This flight, my life in boxes, my life spreading, crashing into other places, a glass of milk spilled again and again. Don't cry over spilt milk! But I do, I do. It's ridiculous, stumbling through languages and over suitcases, backpacks, boxes full of notebooks and poems and candlesticks and old slippers.

My mind overflows its own banks at night, that's why I can't sleep. I swim through images from three continents, I drown in memories, in possibilities. Then I get angry, to be so full, to be so unsure of where I want to live because I want, it seems, to live everywhere. Virginia Woolf said, "It is the women in their gardens who are happy." I don't have a garden of my own. I don't even have a bed.

Spilled Koolaid

REAL JOY LIVES in the garden, even if the garden isn't mine. Purple clematis flowers on the trellis. While Nancy makes coffee, she tells me her life and listens to mine. Because we fall in love with the wrong people and make other bad investments, we regularly look at each and burst out laughing. "You are so stupid!" we howl at each other, over and over again, while a troop of shouting children and barking dogs manoeuvre in the backyard. The days flood with lake water and the pleasure we take in each other's company. I have so many good people to visit before I go away again.

How to hold so much life? How to convince someone that it must not be forgotten?

Already the words and hours and spilled Koolaid of the week are washed away.

There is so little room in a life: how to get everything in? If you are building a house, you must put on an addition. How to fit all these trunks, shoes, letters, books, toys, poems and countries into the narrow chambers of the heart? And people, where to put the people we love?

I walk into and out of the necessary, powerful lives of my friends. Their worlds are so various, full of such pain, such daily laughter, so many carrot sticks and so much gossip from the college and a hundred papers and love, love, love. It's the oldest theme and source. We push shopping carts around and pick raspberries for it. It compels us to write poetry and turn to each other, stunned, suddenly awake. And it is why we go to far-away places, and return.

The return is always most mysterious and crucial to me when I am about to leave. I wonder when I will be satisfied with what is here, instead of desiring the possibility of more. Different light, new colours, the skin of an unknown face.

Where are the mornings I imagine, and why do they dawn in another country? Let me write for one thousand hours, about long nights under incomprehensible stars, about a braid of words and stories and tangled dreams as long as a continent, wider than the Atlantic, a song that loops and grows and laps along the Spanish coast into the still-bluer waters of the Aegean.

I look at my hands, that are not broken in any way. Miraculous. I splash water on my face and stick my head out the window to inhale the night.

It's late. I still haven't eaten. I have to eat, or go outside, or walk, or calm myself, because I feel wrought, wound up, full of fear or desire: I can't tell the difference. I may start to laugh or cry hysterically if I don't *do* something.

So. I close the window. The blue night sky rains cold wind, and I am shivering.

There will be a partial eclipse of the moon tonight. Will you see it?

Inside a name

THE MOCK-ORANGE blossoms arrived this morning, so suddenly, like a flock of white birds alighting on the bushes in the backyard. Mock-orange, for no real oranges grow in the yards of Calgary. The sun is so bright this morning that the green leaves shine with a purple sheen.

If only you could smell those orange blossoms.

It's quiet here, in the backyard of the old house. I'm hidden from the street by a dark wall of pines.

I will be unsuccessful if I search for the words that might give you this moment on paper. There are no such words. This moment is closed off, sealed from you: the welcome coolness of the shade under the pines, the faint taste of raspberry and coffee in my mouth, the sun melting a chocolate darkness into my hands.

It is difficult to believe that we own nothing but our own breath, the moment, the moving vision in front of us. True, the connections spiralling out behind and before us are endless, but our very own is *now*. Your eyes on these words. The paper in your hands. The clutter and noise, ignored, around you, the silence, ignored. And even now (as you read this) I am somewhere else.

What is on the other side of this letter? This season? What is on the other side of leaving the Pallisters' graceful old house?

It is impossible to know. Not only is it impossible, it would be wrong to know. The other side is there, like the other side of the moon, in darkness, waiting. What we have now is this day, this light. Our hands. Our names.

INSIDE A NAME is a kind of fate. We can be sure of this. I will always try to escape my name (my drunken Catholic father, my red-neck upbringing, the girl howling in the basement). On the other hand, some men and women will always try to enter their names more completely. I have a friend who was born in South America, but never lived there. Yet he lives in his Spanish name as if he's living in a country; that armadillo eaten by his parents, a tango pulsing on an old record player, his horsebreeding grandfather who did not believe in cars.

In foreign languages, my name never sounds the way it does in English. Often, I am not even called by my name: I am given a local name that has a similar meaning or sound to Karen. Kanika. Kalen. Carmen. Katrin. Katerina. My middle name, Marie. Maria.

With the metamorphosis of the name, the self is transformed through language. In a different country, when I hear myself called by a new name, I leave the old one somewhere behind me. This is an alteration as subtle and powerful as one shaft of light falling in a dark stable. My friend tells me that when he finally returned to South America to visit, people spoke his name correctly, without stumbling or missing the accent. He believed, for a wild moment, that he was finally home.

Is it as impossible to fully enter a name as it is to fully escape one?

Lightning wine

TARIQ COMES OVER tonight with a bottle of smoky Italian wine. We drink in the living-room on the ivory-coloured chesterfield and talk about all the things we've lately fucked up, how we didn't know, how it wasn't so simple. It is still not simple, in fact, but the room we sit in embodies such a perfect balance of elegance and comfort that we're inspired to conclude, by the bottom of the bottle, that we will not make the same mistakes again. After I open my cheaper bottle of Chilean wine, we drink to the new and different mistakes we will make in the future.

We are inspired, too, by the storm that comes almost without warning. Lightning brightens and blues the entire room, our faces, his brown hands. The crash of thunder makes the windows shudder, rattles the silver on the shelves, brings down a torrent of rain.

After Tariq leaves, the house is quiet and breathing, alive, as only loved houses are. I walk around in the absence of our voices, looking at the house as if at a woman who is asleep. A peacock screen stands in front of the fireplace. Every rug comes from Afghanistan or Turkey. Mr. Pallister takes care of his accounts and reads his mail at a scroll writing desk. Clearly the house lived in England in a previous incarnation. Even the paintings hang in the old way, from hooks on the oak wainscoting. The picture rail. A hundred books about Italy and ancient Greece line the low shelves in the sitting room.

I walk through the rooms, remembering. The heavy velvet curtains that separate the living-room and the dining-room are almost one hundred years old. The silver teapot on the mantelpiece comes from Morocco. All the small secret boxes—boxes of wood, silver, brass, ornamented and plain, small chests from China and Turkey—they contain rose petals, single stones, the clear essence of the world.

There is even a chaise longue stuffed with real horsehair in the study. But it's more than the orna-ments and furnishings that give the place its spirit. The rooms themselves rouse contemplation and a deep sense of peace. As if the walls and curved windows will protect and offer you more solace than a concrete apartment building ever could. I don't think it's a house I would choose, if given the choice. It's too big and I know nothing about antiques. A house like this must have antiques. But that doesn't matter. The house chose me.

Caruso

IT IS HARDLY surprising that Angela Pallister loves the Mediterranean. Her eyes took their colour from that sea. She arrives from the lake, carrying sacks of fresh market vegetables, a load of dirty clothes, and the latest *Guardian*. If a rose could speak, it would sound like Angela. That is why it's always a surprise to see her when she comes home from the cabin, wearing a threadbare T-shirt and dirty blue jeans, her hair uncurled. As soon as she comes in the door and puts down her various bags, she asks me, "My dear, is Caruso still alive?" As if she already knows that I almost killed him a couple days ago.

Caruso, the overwrought canary. From the sitting room, where the canary lives in a delicate bamboo cage, I hear Angela's inquisitive, gentle voice, "Where are his tail feathers, my dear?" And so I am forced to tell the story, casting myself in the most innocent position possible. Caruso lost his brilliant yellow tail feathers when a friend's puppy romped into the sitting room and immediately tried to eat him, bamboo cage and all. The cage crashed from the window box to the floor, Caruso screamed in his chirpy falsetto, the white puppy barked and leapt on the cage with true doggish joy. A kaleidoscope of seeds and feathers and bird shit sprayed the room. In the next hour, as I vacuumed sunflower seeds and bird gravel out of the Afghani rugs, Caruso's tail feathers fell out one by one.

But, yes, Caruso is still alive. A trauma victim, but alive. With Angela here, he has even started to sing again.

The Greek writer Kazantzakis had a canary when he was a child. "My father gave me a canary and a revolving globe. . . . I used to open the cage and let the canary go free. It developed the habit of sitting at the very top of the globe and singing for hours. For years, as I wandered insatiably over the earth, greeting and taking leave of everything, I felt that my head was the globe and a canary sat perched on the top of my mind, singing."

Extrah-dinary

THOUGH I'M STILL waiting for a letter from my far-away friend, I've finished the pianist story I wanted to write for her.

That's what I've been doing. I'm not here just to drink all of Al Pallister's excellent Scotch. No! During the days, I dust off the antiques, try not to kill Caruso, commune with the ghosts, and write.

Angela read the story before she returned to the lake. She said, "Extrah-dinary!" in her most English way. "How heartwarming that these sorts of things happen in Alberta."

"Angela," I said, "it's just a story. It isn't exactly *true.*"

"Yes, but you've written it. If you can imagine it, it has happened. Flaubert—or was it Proust?—one of them said that everything we invent is true. Or was it Celine? Anyway, whoever said it was right. There is no such thing as fiction, my dear." (One of the things I love about Angela is that when she calls you "my dear", you know it's not just some English affectation. She really means it.)

Angela may be right, but even if what we invent is true, it's also still invented. *Created.* Esmeralda *is* a story, designed and told as a fiction. Fiction is a peculiar medium to me. Like swimming in a pool when you are used to the sea! The architecture of real life is so rich that the lives I create in fiction seem almost superfluous. (The critic would say that's just because I'm a lousy fiction writer. Possibly; but then again, the critic so often misses the point.) For me, the question about fiction is, "Why create another story when so many are being lived?" Angela herself is a breathing, speaking novel, with her tales of sailing to Africa and meeting sea captains and corrupt Italian cardinals.

No fiction could be enough to hold her even now, in the garden, when she closes the newspaper, shakes her head, and asks in her flawless syllables, "How can people be so evil? When does one begin to understand it?" Angela's eyes are rain-washed sky and water, blue blue blue. How old is this woman, and why is her voice still so pure? After mourning the newspaper, she is silent. She rubs the top knuckles of her fingers; they are already hooked by arthritis. She spreads her hands out, palms upward, and scrutinizes them intensely. But I know she doesn't wish to read her own future in the deep lines of skin. No; Angela is trying to read the future of the world.

I want to write her stories down and give them back to her and say, Look, I agree, I agree with you, it really *is* extraordinary. And, of course, people are far more than their words and stories. Their complexities rival those of galaxies. The firmest conviction gives over to a foolish heart. We lie because we are too implicated by the truth. What we want most, a friend once told me, is a secret that no one can tell us. In a short story or novel, how is it possible to convey accurately human contradictions, swings of mood, the trapeze act of the mind? It is difficult to get at the truth of one's self; how much more difficult to create an imaginary world and reveal *its* truth.

The story is called "Esmeralda." *Is* it a story, though? Or is it being lived somewhere now, in a different country, with other names?

Esmeralda   a story

SHE HAD AN OUTLANDISH name, and her appearance
was outlandish, too. Esmé, she was called, although
on the inside of her exercise books *Esmeralda* was
printed in small green letters. Had her face not been
so striking, people might have thought she was ugly
because her body was heavy, almost ungainly. If she
walked quickly, her limp was very pronounced; one
knee seemed to have a permanent kink. She'd broken her leg as a child and the village doctor botched
the delicate setting of the bones. Her eyes were the
same amber and honey colour as her hair. In contrast
to her round body, her face was narrow, sometimes
painfully sharp. A long, aquiline nose. If you were
sitting close to her, you could see the complex
lattice-work of veins in her ears. When she played,
her nostrils flared and her face flushed. Even those
who didn't care for her thought she was beautiful
then.

She leaned very close to the piano and did not

coax it to life but demanded that it rise up and make itself heard. Her way of speaking and dealing with people was gentle, although most people never knew it because she spent so much time alone. She loved to sing, and once, after we had become close, I managed to persuade her to sing for us. This surprised the people who thought her aloof, even unkind; her voice was deep and warm as flesh. During the final great snowstorm of the year, when we all gathered to say goodbye and feel the heat burst out of the fireplace for the last time, Esmé told the story of her song, then sang it in a language none of us could understand. It was a time we all have occasionally, fleetingly, when we feel close to the human beings around us, and are filled with hope for them and for ourselves, when we pray quickly and silently, even if we don't believe in a god, that something will keep us safe and help us to become ourselves. The painters, musicians, sculptors, piano tuners, kitchen staff: gathered in a ragged circle of fire-light, faces warm under the red shadows, we listened to Esmé sing as though we were hearing a hymn we had loved since we were children.

BEFORE I WENT to the colony in the mountains, I visited the piranhas at the bank, paid off my loan, and put a thousand down on my Visa card. I flicked paint out from under my fingernails while a woman in pointed shoes thanked me for being such a good customer. As I left, she urged me to continue doing business with the bank. Ha! I thought, and whistled myself through the shiny doors. That very afternoon, free at last, I boarded a bus with a dufflebag stuffed

full of paints, pastels, brushes, and a bag of pow-
dered graphite, which is used to simulate illumina-
tion. I was interested, at that time in my life, in
making light come out of the canvas.

As soon as I arrived at the colony, I lugged my
bag out to my high-ceilinged studio in the woods; I
wasn't interested in seeing my room in residence
because I was only going to sleep there. It was the
first time in my life I hadn't had a money-grubbing
job to do while I painted, and I was determined to
take advantage of every moment of my liberation.
That same afternoon, after twelve hours on a bus, I
set up my rows of paints and the photographs I
wanted to work from. I walked for an hour through
the trees collecting pine-cones and rocks and small,
inspiring twigs—I'd always liked to have things to
touch—then returned to my studio and sketched for
two hours to loosen up my fingers. I gobbled down
the stale muffin I had bought the day before in
Vancouver because I thought going to supper in the
cafeteria would be a waste of time. I was twenty-four
and my favourite phrase was Heinrich Boll's decla-
ration: It's a crime to sleep!

For two weeks I worked constantly, only stopping for a few hours at a time to sleep or rush off to
grab something to eat. I didn't bathe; I ate nothing
before noon. I ran back and forth through the snow
from my studio to the cafeteria, startling hungry
deer. I'd met almost no one in the colony, although
I knew the place was full of other artists. Sometimes
I heard wild piano music pounding through the cold
air. There was a lounge and a beautiful swimming
pool and a famous library, but I hadn't gone anywhere except into my studio and into the trees,

where the shadows of the spruce dropped sharp and dark against the snow. I ignored other people because I didn't have money to spend on drinking, and I didn't want to get roped into boring conversations or have any melodramatic love affairs.

Esmeralda changed my mind about listening to other people. I met her just as my first flush of painter's mania was subsiding and I was returning, a little, to the world of bathtubs and breakfast.

SHE HAD A STRANGE, almost magical way of perceiving the world; people felt nervous around her, intimidated. During a master class, the principal oboist from the Boston Symphony asked, "In your opinion, what does music mean to most musicians?" He was a chubby, laughing man; the atmosphere of the class was conversational. The other musicians and composers were being witty, sharp-tongued, a little stupid, saying that music was a harmonious way to make a buck, or meet rich women in evening gowns. In response to his question, Esmé answered, "Like anything we love, music is salvation." She did not notice the lack of seriousness around her, the giggles, the restless feet.

She acquired the reputation of being too serious, high-minded, possibly miserable, but that was not true. When she was with someone she trusted, she laughed often. She had grown up in a certain darkness, in a country of secrets, and only by great external seriousness was she able to get as far as she had. When I knew her, she was twenty-six, already one of the most talented pianists in the Soviet Union. She was a woman who had come from a village in Moldavia and was without connections of any kind.

At fourteen, playing in a school concert, she interpreted a piece by Prokofiev almost faultlessly, with an unrushed power rarely observed in amateur musicians. One of the people in the audience was a visitor from Moscow, himself a pianist, an instructor at the conservatory. He spoke briefly with Esmé's parents. He said he would do everything in his power. . . . Esmé's father, a pharmacist, and her mother, a worker in a zipper factory, received a call from Moscow. A month later, Esmé was living in a dormitory. She could see the Kremlin walls from her window. She studied music history and theory five hours a day, and received lessons from one of the most famous piano teachers in Europe.

"It was like a huge wind tore through my life, blew everything apart. For longer than a year, I was stunned, well-stunned, like a cow before slaughter. I could not believe what had happened to me. When I had time to wander around Moscow, I had to consciously keep my mouth closed, or else I would have looked like an idiot. After three months, I was allowed to go home for a week of vacation, and though I loved my little town and my people, I suddenly realized, I understood for the first time: I had escaped. I would not grow up to work in the zipper factory. I would not study chemistry. I would play the piano. I would live in music. Do you see what that is? What that means? When I returned to Moldavia, I went back to the little school where I had learned to play. The upright piano with all its chips and forever out-of-tune strings made me weep. In Moscow, I had already been assigned a huge grand piano in a room with a mirror and a window. The piano in my school looked like a broken toy. I was only fourteen years old, but I knew a miracle had befallen me. For the last twelve years, I have tried to understand why. The gifts in our lives are the greatest mysteries we ever know."

WHEN SHE WAS TWENTY-THREE, she attended a music competition in Poland, where she heard from a playwright about a renowned "centre for artists" in Canada. He had spent four months there and told her of the musicians he'd known, how they were given freedom and space and time to work. He gave her the address.

Esmé already had a considerable reputation. She had played abroad, recorded in England, won several major competitions. She was known in Russia as "the dark angel", even though she was pale and almost blonde. Her style was marked by a severity of interpretation rare in someone so young, and her playing, though grave, was surprisingly open and deep. She had a vulnerability, an honesty that most musicians never attain: she gave.

Every few months, since her twenty-third year when she'd heard about the artist centre, she had applied for permission to leave her position at the conservatory and study in Canada. Her teachers and advisors claimed that an extended sabbatical would be the end of her career. In an unstructured program, her discipline would evaporate, people would question her dedication. She would lose a great deal of what she had worked so hard to gain. The director of the conservatory met with her several times to warn her, dissuade her from leaving, remind her of the dangers, the temptations.

But four months later, in the beginning of September, Esmé made her first unaccompanied journey out of eastern Europe. She was twenty-six years old. While flying through darkness over the North Pole, she thought how wonderful it would be if the plane crashed. "Death," she explained, "can be the most potent revenge." She knew that she was to experience freedom for the first time in her life. She could not sleep for fear of nightmares. "The idea of doing whatever I wanted for more than an hour made me very anxious. I began to suspect that they were right, that I would become lazy, lose technique, fail to play well without the pressure of a schedule."

That did not happen. If people went to the colony with a desire to work, they worked. I discovered later that my flurry of creativity was not unique. The heat of creation made that mountainside warmer than others; the snow melted faster there, wildflowers opened sooner. Some of the sculptors began to work in epic proportions. At night they dreamt of bronze mountains high enough to scrape Orion's feet. Painters rushed around with paint on their elbows and foreheads. After they played and played, the musicians saw the faces of Elektra and Stravinsky in the clouds. In the evenings, we went swimming, or drank beer, or recited filthy limericks. Some of us stayed in our rooms and studios and thought about how far we were from creating anything that would live beyond us. We moaned, cried, laughed. We joked about becoming secretaries or zoo-keepers or engineers. I learned there that my life, and Esmé's life, all our lives, were nearly invisible fibres in a long, ancient thread. I tried to be unafraid of being so small. At the tail end of those nights when I had been thinking too hard, I often ventured up the mountain paths until I was compelled to stop and stare up at the sky with an open mouth. At first I was afraid to believe it, but I heard the stars singing.

I once asked Esmé if she had ever heard such a thing. She looked at me curiously, as if I were joking. "Jacqueline, stars don't sing. They never sing. They weep. Sometimes in sorrow, sometimes in joy. That is why they seem to tremble. They are crying."

AFTER MY FIRST few weeks of mad painting, when my inhuman pace had slowed down, I began spending the late afternoon in the library, studying beautiful art books and sketching notes to myself. When I paused at my work, I watched the musicians who came in to listen to music. Often they were so concentrated on the storms and reveries coming out of their earphones that I could sketch their motionless faces and bodies for more than half an hour at a time. Others grew restless, though, listening to the world's great composers. They rubbed their foreheads and hands violently, trying to press comparable music out of their own skin.

I noticed Esmé because she came to the library as often as I did. I did not know she was a musician because she rarely listened to music. She read the newspapers, then flipped through the new photography magazines and literary journals. She had bought a great deal of the turquoise jewellery so popular in those mountains; as she turned pages, her bracelets jangled and rang. Enjoying the silvery disturbance in that quiet place, I often tried to sit close behind her or off to her side, just out of her line of vision. I loved sketching her arms and hands because they were very fine, long, lightly veined and muscled. I came to expect her in the library. If she was not there I felt vaguely disappointed. One afternoon I watched her writing furiously on loose sheets of paper, copying something from one of the books on her table. When she rose and disappeared between the book shelves, I stood up and walked slowly past the books: all writings by Solzhenitsyn. As she was still hidden among the book shelves, I leaned over and looked at what she was writing in her notebook. It was in Russian.

Uneven footsteps thumped up behind me. I was caught in the act. I swung around with an apology in my mouth, but she spoke first. "A reprint of his Nobel Lecture. I am memorizing it," she said. "Incredible, isn't it? Though he wrote it in Russian, I am memorizing a translation of it in English." Solzhenitsyn had won the prize five years before, in 1970. "But I have never seen a copy of this lecture in Russian. And I have read only parts of *One Day in the Life of Ivan Denisovich.* It is very difficult to find that novel. I don't think he has been able to publish anything else in the Soviet Union."

"I didn't mean to . . . I'm sorry I—"

"No, do not apologize. It is nice to meet you finally. My name is Esmé." She put out her hand. "And you?"

"Jacqueline."

"We seem to work here always at the same time. You are a painter, aren't you?" I nodded, I groped for a book, put my other hand in my pocket. Her eyes did not let go of my eyes. "May I ask you a question, Jacqueline?" I nodded again and returned the book to its place. "Why do you always draw just my hands?"

Even as I looked away, I felt the bright flush rising in my cheeks, my jaw. I laughed.

She leaned over and shook my hand again, smiling for the first time now. "Let's go and have a cup of coffee. I'll tell you."

Several days after I'd noticed her, I had left my sketch pads on the table and gone to the bathroom. Esmé, having felt me watching her, did exactly what I had done: she had come over to look at my work, flipped through my sketchbook, where she recognized her own hands, the blue-studded bracelets. "But you did not catch me," she said, sipping her coffee. "Russians are quick like that. I was on the other side of the library by the time you came back." We spent the rest of the afternoon together, and ate supper at the same table. Suddenly I was talking more than I had in weeks.

What is more extraordinary than the unexpected discovery of another human being? We talked so much that first night, of our work, our lives, our beliefs. She had an easy sense of humour, even though we often discussed Vietnam, governments, their abuses of freedom. She talked often of the Soviet Union, but she did not rage or wallow. She smiled. "Who understands these things? There is nothing evil in the world except for human beings. I was eleven years old when I realized that; I wanted to stop being a girl and change into a horse. Then I began to love music, and I was happy. Music, my own hands, taught me that human beings also know what is beautiful and good."

Our greatest similarity was our love of water, the freedom of motion it creates. "It's flying," Esmé said. "It's the closest we'll ever come to being free of our bodies." We began to meet in the change-room before swimming, then we would leap into the pool and do lengths until we felt our arms turning to rubber. We usually swam for about forty-five minutes, then we would play for another ten, walk on our hands, turn over and over like seals in the deep end, try to swim the length of the pool underwater. We would also race. Unless she was being kind, Esmé always won. After hopping out and rinsing off, we usually sat in the sauna for ten minutes, laughing about the swimmers who slapped about like wounded fish, or the ones who did two lengths for every one of ours. These fast, technically flawless swimmers she jokingly called "The Soviet Athletes". We came to recognize them on dry land, too; as they walked by, Esmé or I would whisper to the other, "Ahh, one of the Soviets!"

In the change-room and the sauna alike, Esmé was almost careless about her body. She was not ashamed of it. She never told me exactly how she had achieved that particular freedom, having grown up in a restrictive country. She only said, "Beneath every tough comrade lives a Russian with warm blood." Even "liberated" women who had various lovers still needed to wrap a towel around themselves in the presence of their own sex. Esmé, naked and built like a well-fed Italian duchess, would have none of it.

Sweating in the wet heat, Esmé said, "The atmosphere of the earth was just like this when amoebas decided to become gazelles." She loved the sauna. We usually spent too much time in there and came out feeling light-headed. Once, when we were alone, Esmé began doing a series of elaborate stretches that embarrassed me. She was always embarrassing me in the sauna, either by stretching, or by examining her own body with her hands, or by spreading oil over herself with the careless strength of a groom rubbing down a horse. I had to turn away from watching this, or close my eyes and cross my legs. Esmé never crossed her legs; she said that it was bad for the circulation and didn't fool anybody. "Everyone knows what you have down there, Jacqueline," she once said in a thick sexy voice, and I laughed, uncrossed my legs, then crossed them again the other way. I was thankful for the heat and half-darkness of the sauna because Esmé could never catch me blushing.

At that time, I was working steadily on studies for my paintings, two of which were commissions for a wealthy doctor who had worked years before in India. He had given me a couple of black and white photographs of laughing children wearing raggedy saris, and he wanted two paintings of these same photographs in colour. "I've never seen it since," he said, "the colour I saw there. It made me think I had wasted most of my life by wearing navy blue and gray and hospital green. I still dream about India sometimes. It was a hell of a place to work, but it was beautiful."

I had spent weeks doing studies from the photographs and mixing oils and flipping through various books in search of Asian colours. I was saturated; I needed to begin. One evening in the sauna, I told Esmé I was somehow reluctant to go ahead on canvas. I had a perfect vision in my mind and was afraid I might not be able to release it without doing damage.

"Hmmm, yes," she said, and began to braid her wet hair. "This happens also to composers. They hear the creature singing in their minds, but sometimes they believe writing the notes will silence it, kill it. Strange. When this happens to me, I just begin another work, a playful work, something that does not matter to me, what I call a little mouse piece. Then, when the little mouse comes out, I fool the lion into following it, and suddenly the mouse is devoured and my other work is roaring around the room." She poured more water onto the coals and stood naked over the hiss of new steam. Her back was broad and smooth. "Why don't you paint me first?" she asked, turning around, smiling. "I will be your mouse."

The idea of Esmé being a mouse was preposterous. She knew it, and I knew it, but I agreed to do some work with her as a model. She came to my studio the next day. She walked around touching things lightly, smelling the paint, looking in closets. It was strange to watch her do this, like a cat in a new house. She made the place her own. It was only natural that she should take off her clothes and stand naked for me. I sketched her in charcoal first, then painted in watercolours, then did indeed get some canvas and work over her skin with pale oils. I went very quickly, messily, without much concentration. A thousand times I asked her if her feet were cold, if she was tired, if she wanted to change positions or rest. She always said no, and kept her body perfectly still, one arm raised, hand behind her neck, the other hand on her upper abdomen, her thumb between her breasts. A couple of times we stopped and drank tea. Esmé sat cross-legged on her feet with a blanket draped loosely around her shoulders. She wore a small enigmatic grin on her face. "What are you smiling about?" I asked her.

She raised her eyebrows. "I'm just happy," she said, standing up. The blanket around her fell to the floor. Because I was sitting on a low stool, I was suddenly looking directly at her thighs. I stood up, too. "Can I see what you've done?" She walked over to the easel and flipped through the charcoal sketches, making little sounds of approval when she came to something she liked.

It worked. That night, after spending three hours with Esmé during the day, I began the Indian paintings and stayed in my studio until two in the morning. Before leaving, I flipped through some of the studies on Esmé, looking carefully at what had been in front of me all day. She had a wonderful body, all hills and basins, roundnesses, long lines. I put the sketches up on a shelf and pulled on my boots for the short walk through the trees. That night, in a dream, she came to my studio while I was working on a portrait of her. She ran her hand through the charcoal and smeared the image of her face. "That is not my skin," she said, and reached for my hand the same way she had when we first met, not to shake it again, but to lift it and press the charcoal in my fingers against her cheek. "This is my skin." And the charcoal did not appear black on her face but turquoise blue, like her bracelets, like the water in the pool. "It's flying," she whispered. I heard the sound of her deep, easy laughter, and woke, thinking she had come into my room.

A week later, we sat in the sauna together, alone, inhaling the smell of wood and wet heat. Although I was naked from the waist up, and quelling a

49

powerful desire to cross my arms, I still wore a towel around my hips. After lolling for a few minutes, Esmé stood up in all her pink glory and poured some more water over the coals. She glanced at me and put her hands on the backs of her hips, taking up two handfuls of flesh. "If you can't stand your own naked body, with all its flaws and beauties, then you will never be able to enjoy sex honestly." I was so embarrassed by this that I did cross my arms. Esmé laughed, unpinned her hair, and let it fall over her breasts. "There," she said, looking down at herself. "You can't see mine either."

She laughed at me again and stepped up from the first bench to the second, where the air was hotter. After a few seconds of stillness—my eyes were closed—I felt her manoeuvre herself behind me. She began to massage my shoulders with one hand, then the other, then both. This surprised me at first, but I relaxed under the strength of her fingers. I swivelled my neck around, feeling oiled, pliant as an otter. I thought I felt her breath on my neck. Then she kissed me, very lightly, just under the ear. Before I could say anything, or even absorb the sensation, we were both caught off guard as two other women entered the sauna, laughing and chattering.

Esmé left almost immediately, saying goodbye to all three of us, and I stayed in the heat for ten more minutes, my mind turning somersaults. It was only the heat making me feel so dazed. I left the sauna when I felt sure that Esmé had already dressed and gone. Glowing and glazed with sweat, I immediately stumbled to the washroom taps and drank water like a draught horse, swallowing great slow mouthfuls. Through the routine of showering, drying myself, dressing, I kept thinking about having been kissed (but had I really? was I imagining it?) by a woman, on the neck. I tried to remember that sensation, that rising pressure through the centre of my body, that buoy floating up, pulling the thick net of desire through my skin. Impossible, that flush radiating from just under my belly. I was imagining it. Or I had been thinking of a man. I looked at my flushed face in the mirror, my black hair, still wet, my mouth, my eyes. I looked fine, perfectly normal.

AFTER THAT, TENSION SHIFTED and clicked in between us. We still went swimming together, we still sat in the sauna, but it seemed that everyone sat in the sauna, trying to escape the suddenly brutal cold outside. We were never alone for more than two minutes. We never spoke of what had happened (or not happened) that evening, but I still thought about it. Esmé and I still talked for hours together over coffee and hot chocolate, growing closer, weaving ourselves through each other's lives. Another layer existed, too, a deep, untouchable place that was also the most touchable, because it lived in our very skin, our eyes. But I did not quite believe it existed, and I was afraid to go there.

Sometimes, after talking late into the night, warming our bodies with tea and memory, we walked together down the road towards the little town at the base of the mountain. "We are in Switzerland," she said once, opening her blue-gloved hands to catch the snow. Then, a moment later, we heard someone whistle high and long for a loose dog, and heard him call, his voice lower and less powerful, barely touching us. He whistled again, spearing both wood and stone with one long note. Esmé and I stood breathless in the dark, listening, feeling the nerves pluck and quiver in the backs of our legs. Why does a high whistle through a cold night stir sadness? Without any awkward words we turned and hugged each other.

During the next weeks, she talked so much about Russia that I went back to the paintings of Chagall, hoping to know the colours in Esmé's mind. I returned to graphite, hard charcoal, and bright oils; flowers, mythical monsters, and Indian children's faces inhabited my fingers, came rushing out whenever I worked. I did not sketch Esmé again because I was working easily from the photographs and my own vision; a model would distract me. She did not mention anything about it. I went to her evening and lunch-time concerts. After every one of these recitals, I went backstage and gave her a hug and a kiss and never once did I experience the sensation I had felt in the sauna.

THEN, IN THE middle of December, we had a Christmas party.

Over one hundred people gathered in the common room, laughing, drinking, dancing, saying goodbye. Some artists in the photography and music studios were leaving, returning to their Canadian cities or different countries; others were only going home for two or three weeks, and would return for the second term. Esmé and I went together. When we arrived, we found people crowded around the fireplace at the back of the lounge. A British ceramicist was singing "Walking in a Winter Wonderland" at the top of her lungs, with dirty words substituted for the regular lyrics. She accompanied her song with gyrating hips and shimmying shoulders, making everyone think of nightclub acts in Las Vegas because she wore a red sequined dress.

It was a very good party. Several conversations in the works were neither trivial nor depressing. Esmé did not have her usual mineral water but instead drank screwdrivers with plenty of orange juice, "to drown out the taste of this sad vodka," she said. We danced. I taught her the lyrics to a few Christmas carols. We even stayed after the midnight toast and had a cup of coffee laced with whiskey, chocolate, and cinnamon, topped with whipped cream. A great pot of this stuff brewed in the kitchen, and the entire lounge smelled like a chocolate factory full of Scotch drinkers. The scent of cinnamon lingered in our mouths. Esmé laughed as we drank, saying, "This is dessert, dessert! I want one of these for breakfast! I will become alcoholic!" When we finally left, we were still quite drunk and very happy, leaning on each other, laughing.

Outside, between the lounge and Jackson Hall, we tried to have a snowball fight. Defeated by our poor and somewhat drunken aim, we dropped the snowballs and tried to push each other into the snowbanks on either side of the pathway. When our jaws began to feel numb from laughing in such cold air, we declared a truce and began walking together up the path. Passing a snow-laden pine tree, Esmé could not resist reaching up and shaking it over my head. I was blind with snow for a few seconds and stunned by the icy whips down my neck. I lunged for her with a scream, pushing her right over the snowbank under the great boughs of the pine tree. She disappeared completely in the hole made by the wall of snow and tree. I was breathless and laughing, still scooping snow out of the collar of my coat. "Esmé?" I leaned over the snowbank to peer into the trees. Darkness. I could see the icy soles of her boots. She had fallen upside down.

I heard a moan. "Esmé? Are you all right?" Then I was afraid that she'd banged her head at the base of the tree, or hurt her back. "Esmé! What's wrong?"

She coughed. "I'm so cold," she said, and her feet wriggled beneath my chin. "I think I'm drunk enough to fall asleep like this, but I am freezing." A few warm words of Russian came, a sputtered laugh. "I have snow in my mouth!" She struggled like a turtle knocked backwards on its shell. Kicking away snow, I reached in to pull her out. She was quite heavy; each time I pulled, her coat slid up her back, exposing bare skin. "I'm freezing!" she said a few times. "I have snow everywhere." Rising at last, encrusted in snow and ice, she jogged stiffly towards the hall. I ran along beside her. "I'm sorry, Esmé, I didn't know you were going to drown in there! I'm so sorry!"

When she opened her coat, kerchiefs of snow fell to the floor. I went with her to her room, opened the door for her, ran the bath. She was shivering. "Take off your clothes," I said. Her chattering teeth filled the room with the sound of tiny castanets. "Hop in the bath." She pulled off her damp sweater and pushed her skirt to her ankles, giggling and whispering in Russian as she fell backwards onto the bed in a heroic struggle with her tights. As soon as I drew them off her calves, she jumped up, her naked body blotched red with cold, and ran to the bathroom.

"Aye! Aye! It's too hot! You're trying to kill me." I heard the splash and dance of water as it rose up the sides of the tub. When I went in she was doing a jig, lifting up one foot and the other. I put my hand in. "It's not too hot. It's your skin. Your skin's still cold." She rolled her eyes and, grabbing onto the enamel sides, lowered herself in. She moaned and smiled. "Will you give me the oil?" she asked, pointing to the counter. She did not pour it into the water. She poured a small pool of it into her hand and began to rub it into her chest. I left the bathroom. Beside her bed, I slowly hung up her clothes. I felt the texture of the red sweater, the black skirt, the black tights, Esmé's clothes. Esmé, in the bathtub, the sound of the water still running there, hot over her feet.

I opened the bathroom door and said, "I think I'll go to bed now." She smiled and said, "Come here first." I closed the door behind me to keep the steam in and squatted down beside the tub. She rose up out of the water a little. (The faint perfume of bath oil, the scent of wet heat, wet skin, her breath, her breasts and belly and wide shoulders rising up, an ocean opening, slipping down her hips.) Then she laid her hand on my face—it was wet and very warm—and she kissed me, my mouth. I felt the moist warmth of her lips with my own. Her hands slipped down my neck, eased away the collar of my blouse. The hair on my arms rose. For a moment, I thought I might cry, these touches were so gentle.

WE DID NOT SLEEP until much later, almost dawn. Many times, surfacing from a deep kiss or suddenly feeling the contours of her body against mine, I said, "What's happening?" but, as in a dream, there was no answer, only her face appearing before my own, beautiful and opened as I had never seen it before. She never stopped smiling. I kissed her the way I had kissed the older boys of my adolescence, hopefully, recklessly, in a heady state of joy. But I felt guiltless and sure of myself now, despite my external awkwardness. There was passion, and want, and the anxious way of muscles under skin flexing and tensing, but I was hardly able to name the act a sexual one. It was innocent love-making, not sex. I felt very young, younger than any teenager ever feels in her storm of flesh and emotion.

So soft, so open, so different, to feel breasts where you have always felt a hard chest. We buried ourselves under the covers of her narrow bed and hugged each other. Her hair was still wet. She smelled like flowers. The wall beyond us was speckled and darkened by the shadows of the pines. For a moment, we stopped moving and held our breath to listen to the wind rocking and teasing the trees. Esmé whispered, "The ocean. It sounds like the ocean."

I touched her neck, the white slope of her chest. "Esmé, I don't really know what to do, you know." She laughed. Her neck stretched back; the hollows of her collar-bones became blue pools of shadow, I saw the brightness of her teeth as she lowered her head and traced kisses over my belly.

The sound of my own breath surprised me, as her tongue touched me, as her mouth, like wet satin folding, unfolding, rubbing, braided itself into my own flesh, Esmé's mouth, and the curve of her back rising beyond me in shadow, darkness, my own body falling into the darkness of many colours, the deepest darkness of the body, the blood, where everything disappears but living feeling, pleasure in the skin, and I cried her name.

She glided up to me again, leaned over to wipe her mouth on the covers. She was smiling. Her arms looped over me; her leg rested on my stomach. After a while, I said, "What about you?"

"We have time," she whispered. "We have time. I have been wanting to be with you for so long." We fell asleep on that single bed, holding each other, breathing the perfume of women's sex.

When I woke in the morning, she was not beside me. I sat up and looked around, thinking perhaps I was in my own room: I had dreamt the whole thing. "Esmé?" I whispered. She had made love to me the night before.

Just as I was about to get out of bed, she came in with muffins and coffee. She kissed me. "Hello. How are you? No, no, don't get up. We'll eat in bed." And we did. Then we showered together, washed each other slick and fragrant, leaned together again and again, trying to fit our bodies together. We made love with the hot spray of water pounding our backs and legs and bellies. I could not believe how happy I was, how free I felt with her.

Later we lay in bed, touching each other's backs with our fingertips. Esmé talked about what it was like for her to live in Russia. "Sometimes you can see the faint signs, a certain way of talking that no one would recognize but another lesbian. Homosexuals are considered deviant, abnormal, sick, but lesbians! Lesbians are unthinkable! Lesbians aren't even mentioned in the criminal code because it's assumed they don't exist, unless they are just two women getting together for the pleasure of a man. It is difficult in the world of culture, of restricted culture, to be what I am. And it is such an evil for the privileged, not like beating your wife or children. Much worse than that. So unspeakable. So undisciplined: the greatest of sins. By the time I was about fourteen, I knew that I was different. I struggled with it, cried, made endless promises to myself. I thought about killing myself: there seemed to be no other answer. I was convinced I was the only woman on earth who loved other women. I was so lonely with my self-knowledge that I thought I might as well die. A good friend saved me, an older boy who played the cello. Drawn together because we were both loners, we became close enough to talk about sex. That was when I found out that homosexuals existed, and we convinced each other that there had to be other people like us. Finally I accepted it, accepted my desire, accepted myself. I found out what an orgasm was and nearly went crazy with joy. I watched the ballet classes in the conservatory with such lust that I had to run upstairs sometimes and masturbate under my piano.

"When I was eighteen, a new teacher came from Kiev, a very well-known pianist originally from East Germany. She was very beautiful. Tall, blonde, quite thin. Too thin. Fine, fine bones. I dreamed about her, wrote love poems to her, longed for her, wanted her. This went on for about a year and a half. When I was nineteen, she and my classmates made a trip to Warsaw for a music festival. Our hotel had somehow halved our reservations, so we ended up sleeping four or five to a room. Lena and I were assigned a double

58

bed; there were two other students in the room, sleeping on cots. All through the evening of the first series of concerts, I was terrified that when we went back to the hotel, Lena would ask one of the other girls to sleep with her. But when we prepared ourselves for bed that evening, she just talked and joked in her usual way. We all said goodnight, laid down. One of the other girls turned out the light. The room was so small that if I stretched my arm out of the bed, I could touch one of the other students' cots.

"Of course I could not go to sleep. I breathed in deeply, slowly, smelling the scent of her face cream, her hair. She lay with her back to me but I was close enough to feel the warmth of her body. I could see the shape of her neck in the pillow. I lay absolutely still, trying to hear the pulse of her heart, thinking of the times she had leaned over me when I was playing to see that my posture was correct. I remembered the time I had seen the lace of her bra, the curve of her breast. I was a virgin, but I felt that I would die if I did not touch her.

"I rested my hand close to her back, felt the material of her night-dress, but not the skin beneath. I did not move for over an hour. I heard three bodies breathing regularly. Finally, slowly—it seemed so loud—I shifted, so that the whole side of my hand was pressing against her back. She did not stir at all. I thought she was asleep. I opened my hand, touched her very, very lightly, travelled up towards her neck, her hair. Tears were in my eyes, I was so happy to touch human flesh.

"When she rolled over, I felt my stomach turn in fear. I pulled my hand away and closed my eyes. Then I felt her face come close to my own, her breath on my chin, my neck. She whispered into my ear so quietly that I did not hear every word. I had to piece her sentences together from rhythm and syllable. 'Not here. Wait until we are alone. Yes. I want you.' And she kissed me very lightly. I opened my eyes to see her face but she was already turning over again.

"I did not sleep all night. My mind was full of noise and moving like a train. I imagined everything for us. I lay in bed and hugged myself so hard that I bruised my arms with my own fingers.

"We became lovers. I was dazed with glory. I ran up stairs, I sang in elevators, I stared down the ugliest streets with a foolish smile on my face. She changed my life by allowing me to love her. And she loved me back, I think, although perhaps not in the way I wanted, not as absolutely as I loved her. For a long time, I wondered if she loved her brother more than she loved me, but now I know that something like that cannot be measured or judged.

"It was the happiest time of my life. We became even better friends. My playing grew very strong, energetic, lively. I grew confident; I was placed in several important concerts. Lena's brother was a well-known violinist. I remember him telling me how wonderful it was that I was finding a style. He really liked me. Once, the three of us went to my town in Moldavia to visit my parents.

"It was because of her brother that she left. We had been together for two years when she disappeared. I was twenty-one. Lena was thirty-four. Her brother defected while on a tour of Austria. He went out to buy cigarettes and ended up at the American embassy.

"I don't know what happened to Lena. I don't think she went with him—though she did go with him on tour, because she had friends in Austria and wanted to see them. If she had defected as well, she would have been publicly denounced. And she would have gotten some message to me, somehow. She would have told someone. I still don't know what happened to her. It has been over five years. I've never been able to find out if she aided him somehow, or if she was simply punished—is being punished—for what he did. Or perhaps she is teaching piano in New York. Perhaps she is afraid to communicate with me for my sake. I don't know. I do not like to think that she is wasting her life in some Siberian desert. But I don't know.

"I was sick after her disappearance. I could not play. And then, when I was better, I refused to play. I was so angry, so alone, and no one would tell me what had happened in Austria. All the musicians who had been on the tour had seen nothing, heard nothing. I went to the director. He claimed it was a mystery; no one knew what had happened, where she was. I wrote letters to committees, heads of state, the newspaper. I risked a great deal by being so vocal, so full of questions, so furious. I contacted someone who worked for Amnesty International. I went mad with grief because I could tell no one how much I really needed her.

"The autumn recitals were coming up in Moscow. Much earlier in the year, before Lena's disappearance, I had been chosen to represent the conservatory. I told them my hands were dead. I had stopped playing. I lost over ten kilograms. I smoked. I contemplated suicide but did not have the courage for that. I knew that if I was sent back to Moldavia, my career as a pianist would be over. I would become a chemist, or perhaps I would work in the factory. This thought filled me with sadistic pleasure. I would waste my gift. Like a perverted alchemist, I would turn gold to shit. There is a certain kind of despair which fools you into believing that your pain will weaken if you poison others with it. I was going to transmit my suffering to everyone who had worked with me, encouraged me, moulded me.

"A psychiatrist was brought in. For some reason, perhaps because he was so ugly, I was terrified. I knew what could happen. After a long interview, he asked me to play, surveying me with an eye that showed how pathetic he thought I was, how pale and weak and thin. I said to myself, fuck him, I will play so well that he will fall down on his knees and worship me. And that is how I played. A miserable but vengeful goddess.

"That went on for a long time. My furious interpretations were thought to be a little strange, much too extreme, but I was working again. I was practising for ten hours a day sometimes, straining the muscles in my forearms. I used to crack my nails with playing so hard, and bleed on the ivory keys. If the director and my advisors were horrified, they were also impressed by my new power. I played all the music as if it were a battle, or as if it were dying right there on the page. I interpreted nothing light or glorious. I despised waltzes and gentle pieces— they were sentimental, unworthy. My Mozart sounded diseased. My *allegro vivace* movements were criminal, like a war of butterflies. I loved Rachmaninoff and the lonely music of Bartok and Beethoven's darker works. Everything I played I transformed into the music of sorrow. . . ."

Esmé told me a lifetime, several lifetimes, in the months we were together. Her great-great-grandfather, Philippe Lassaigne Maritain, had been a French professor of European history and literature who taught in Moscow. As a young man in Paris, he had met Victor Hugo many times. Each of his seven children was named after characters from Hugo's books. Sometimes the names were adapted to Russian, sometimes they remained as they had been in French. Esmé's mother, grandmother and great-grandmother were all called Esmeralda, Esmerina, or Esmerazia.

My Esmeralda knew nothing of her namesake's story until she came here. One evening, I came to her practise studio with an English copy of *The Hunchback of Notre Dame*. In candlelight, sitting among five down pillows, a blanket, and a bottle of cheap, sweet Hungarian wine, I read everything there was about Esmeralda, the gypsy woman with her trickster goat. She laughed every time I came to a passage that described the downtrodden Esmeralda. "Aye! What a name, what a gift!" We fell in love with Quasimodo. We spilled wine on the pillows. She reached over to me with both arms, kissed my throat, and whispered, "Have you ever made love under a piano?" Her mouth tasted of fruit. I looked over at the Blüthner grand, polished to a high black gleam. We blew out the candles and rolled under the piano, our mouths already open to each other's skin.

A CERTAIN SADNESS shadowed us now, because it was already the end of February. Esmé would leave Canada in April. We did not talk about it very much. We did not make promises as other lovers do, knowing we had no right to think of promises or pacts.

A few people knew we were in love, simply by the way we spoke to one another. In 1975, there were no other lesbians that we knew of at the colony, but there was a pair of very enthusiastic homosexuals from Chicago who looked like twins. They were photographers who took the most amazing pictures of each other. I became friends with them, but Esmé tended to draw away. Her fear of being discovered or penalized never disappeared, although it diminished while she lived here. She was still afraid of what could happen outside herself, what could be done *to* her, but she was not afraid of her heart. "I sometimes experience moments of such bitterness," she once told me, "and such anger, anger at the way my world has been, because I have not been free. And I do not even mean in a political sense, though I suppose everything becomes political eventually. It is the same for deviants here, I think. There are so many risks, so many lies, so great a denial of the self." She often called herself a deviant: "When I was learning English, I always remembered it by associating it with the word 'devil'."

In late March, Esmé announced one morning that she planned to play "Carnaval" by Schumann for her last concert. She lay beside me in bed stretching one leg, then the other, towards the ceiling. Light poured through the curtains; our window was open. It would still snow in the mountains, but the heat and movement of spring already roiled in the sky and under the ground. The clouds were high, round sometimes, summer clouds. It was warm; new birds returned from the south. We could smell pine sap whenever the wind was blowing.

Esmé said, " 'Carnaval' is romantic, full of light, soft. I haven't played a piece like it since I was with Lena. It's the last time you'll hear me play for . . . a long time. So I want to play something happy for us. We have been happy together, haven't we?" After reaching down to kiss my foot, she jumped out of bed. For a few moments, she turned around and around the room, her body naked and dazzled with sunlight, her hair lit with gold. She had the dignity of a dancer who did not know she was wounded, or simply did not care.

The concert was in April, four days before she was scheduled to go home. It was held at the old hotel on the river, a great stone chateau originally built for the elite travellers who came to the mountains in the early 1900s. Members of the orchestra from the city were going to play, and reviewers came, and most of the rich people staying at the hotel. As I walked through the plush foyer, past the velvet and leather chairs, I heard the sound of a harp, a woman singing in French. I became disoriented, took several wrong turns, circled back and came to the foyer again. The ceiling was very high, domed in places like a cathedral. I felt as if I'd lost myself in a castle. Someone had told me that the concert hall was on the third floor, close to a gallery of old paintings, but when I went up there, I met an acre of round oak tables, where old ladies clinked their wineglasses and laughed beneath enormous chandeliers. I turned and ran all the way down the stairs again, tripping on my high heels, out of breath. I began to whisper Esmé's name. I was afraid she would begin to play without me. I asked one of the busboys where the concert was. He said, "I think it's already started, on the second floor, east wing." I was in the opposite end of the hotel, going up and down the wrong flights of stairs. I ran through the gilded hallways, shoes in my hand, catching glimpses of myself in the grand mirrors. I was afraid I would miss her, or they wouldn't let me in. People turned around to look at me, point; I heard someone say, "Miss, Miss . . ." Then I was pulling my skirt up over my knees to take the stairs two at a time. I begged the doormen to let me sneak into the hall. They asked me to put on my shoes, which I did, then they slivered open the door and I slipped in. I stood at the back for her whole performance, but I could see her face. She had been playing for perhaps two minutes.

Now, years later, I listen to the "Carnaval" whenever I want to remember her. I see Esmé playing gently, expansively, as though the hope hidden in the notes had stretched her fingers. No one has ever played for me as she did that night, with such faith and longing. Her hands were like doves.

I REMEMBER HER beyond me, beyond this world where I live now, my life so various, so busy, so changed. I haven't become a great painter, though I am quite good. I am good enough. These days, when I swim in a river of paint, my small daughter often swims beside me, leaving her smudged fingerprints on big sheets of yellow construction paper, taped to the lower halves of my studio walls. I have been very lucky. I know what is beautiful and good. Esmé and I wrote for almost five years. Then I married. And I had Katrin. Then I left my husband. . . . Everything, my life, happened. Is happening now. Time and distance. Esmé and I lost each other in the translation.

But I remember her voice as she spoke of music the day before she left, when we sat in her studio and the reality of her departure fell on us like part of a mountain. The piano faced the window and both of us sat on the bench. "If only we could *be* the music," she said, "instead of being the vessel for its power. Because it only touches us lightly. It never stays. It isn't the world. It raises us up, doesn't it? But then it finishes. It stops. We fall again, and the silence is even deeper than before.

"Doesn't every musician want to become her music? Can you imagine the freedom of a bird? That is music, Jacqueline, that is flying. But how much of it belongs to us? The notes rise up and turn to light. We can't keep them. Yet if we don't let them go, they stay in our hands and grow silent before us. *That* is why I have to play. To let something *live*."

She closed her eyes, bent herself over the piano, and laid her hands on its black surface. After a while, she raised her head, but her eyes remained closed. Putting my hand beneath her chin, I turned her face to mine. Then I leaned forward and kissed her eyelids. They were very white. Her eyelashes were the colour of doeskin. I felt them against my lips. We sat for a long time, barely touching, our faces turned toward the trees outside. It was a windless day, and the pines were threaded with the flight of birds. Both of us heard the music dance and slip from their small warm throats.

On becoming a rainbow trout

DARK BROWN HANDS. Hands are to the body what eyes are to the face. Fingernails white as the edges of the moon. I spend the day with Alex and Robert, close to the face of the mountain, in the Elbow river valley. We picnic and play at the water, grow cinnamon skin, lose our clothes. The river is cold but irresistible, a blue arm pulling us in, in, deeper, until we are helpless with laughter and drenched. So strong, this force that carries whatever it can to the sea.

I tell them, Open your eyes under water, you can see everything, you become a fish.

The current pulls you, flies you over the round rough stones, through sunlight shattered silver, into the deep green places made for diving. And you know what it is, for an instant, to be a rainbow trout. Alex laughs, What do you mean, a trout! And Robert doesn't believe me, but then they try it and know it's true and we let ourselves be taken again and again by the silver and azure current, our eyes open under the water, our bodies tumbling, spilling through blue, through bubbles of light.

The sun still pulses in the skin of my shoulders, my burnt nose. But now the spill of blue is my robe, sliding off the dining-room table to the chair. Here's the table, the candlestick-holder. Beyond this paper, a crystal bowl of dried rose petals on the Chinese tapestry. Above, the lamp of red and green and yellow glass, glass like candy. A pool of cool shadow, this house, but outside the late day is still hot, still alive.

After such a day, words are the narrowest place. This ridiculous ink and paper: it's not at all what I meant to do with my life. I should have stayed in the river, I should have taken the plunge. Is death the only way to free the living essence of the flesh? After pure hours, what I want most is to get out of my own body, flay away physical and spiritual desire. Tell me where I can find the talisman to return me, with sure violence and speed, to the world of the rainbow trout. Send me a sea witch's herbs. Turn me into a fish.

The frog

YESTERDAY I WAS out at the farm, riding Cimmeron, the mare with a black mane and tail, black ear-tips. After riding I went in for a (drum roll) "family supper". What is usually a difficult, sometimes savagely funny affair became thoroughly depressing. My stepsister noticed that the answering machine had recorded a message earlier in the day when all of us were out. No one had heard it yet. My mother, poised between mashed potatoes and moose roast, turned around and pressed the "play" button.

One of those rare lulls in my family's noisy gatherings happened just then. Each of us heard the stupid computerized operator asking the inarticulate answering machine if it would accept a collect call from "David". "David," my young brother said, speaking his own name in an impossibly deep, cramped voice, so it seemed like one syllable instead of two. David, who is in prison. The answering machine could not accept his call, of course. David said his name again louder through the operator's recorded voice, as though he were waving his arms and ragged shirt in the air but the plane was passing over anyway.

Another rarity in my family: each one of us was at an awkward, painful loss for words. What could be said?

My mother looked at the answering machine as she would a lame horse. Pity, disappointment, real sadness. My stepfather made an angry clatter with his fork.

I thought, Isn't this an impressive example of the failure of modern communication? My brother's phone call began with one impotent machine and ended with another. Nothing human to sustain his hope for connection.

After supper I slipped away for a walk.

I escaped into the fields, along the creek called Jumping Pound, past the beaver dam, away. So green, with splashes here and there of mustard seed, sharp yellow flowers. I came to the place in the hay field where the path disappears, flooded by grasses. Green grows past the knees, past the thighs, up to the chest. The sun was still so hot at six that I took off my shorts and shirt and walked in my bare skin through grass on fire with light. You know it: the slant of late afternoon sun that ignites everything it touches. Mountains before me and a thousand forests around. Deer beds. Hawks above fishing for mice in a burning green ocean. I forgot my dear, monstrous family. I walked until I couldn't go any farther, because the grass was like thick emerald water.

How did we ever think that God did not live on and in the earth? Why did we ever think he lived in some far-away place called heaven? Yesterday I saw the world—a thousand details running into my eyes like clean water—and I thought: all this means something else, or something *more,* than what it actually is. Oscar Wilde once said, in a fit of desperation, "You must not see symbols in everything," but there *are* symbols in everything. How can we *not* see them? All I live and see transmutes into metaphor. Each metaphor connects itself to something else. There is meaning in these endless connections.

Three days ago, I read a depressing article in a science magazine about frogs, who are disappearing slowly from the dirty face of the earth. Yesterday at the farm, when I walked back through the fields, slowly picking up my shed clothing, I felt a shudder in the deep grass and looked. There it was, big enough to cover the larger part of my palm, the colour of wet wood, with dark brown markings over the eyes, gold-dust irises. I followed the frog until the grass thickened into a cage. The frog was still. A fat frog. Bellyful of dragonflies and mosquitoes. I picked her up. We exchanged a long serious look. I carried her back to her original place on the path. As if she knew where she was, she suddenly jumped, pushing my hand down like a springboard. I sang all the way home.

This is an enormous continent, but we are a small people. We forget the land as casually as we forget our livers and kidneys, although without them—land, liver, kidneys—we would not exist.

Surgery

POETRY OVERTOOK ME the other day. I spent hours working on a new prose poem. I am almost super-stitious about looking at my notebook yet, because the work is still too new, too raw with emotion. Poetry is the surgery of language. It is the inner sanctum, the place where the vitals are opened, where the source is seen without shield or pretense, and healing becomes a possibility.

Why healing? Because words, in their pure form, help us bind up what is broken. When we are most alone, most afraid, most pained, what do we crave? The human voice, gentled. Other than a cry, includ-ing a cry, poetry is the essence of the human voice, the pure substance. Small children, with their half-words and their thoughts half-sung, speak in poetry.

In a poem, connections exist absolutely, as the entire body receives its breath from the flow of blood. What has been severed can be rejoined with words. And in the space of a page, that which has been taken from us can be taken back. We don't know this, or we don't remember it, until we have no other choice. When we have the words we need, we take them for granted. But when we don't have them, when they are stolen from us, we know, almost in our skin, that words embody a power verging on magic.

Letter to My Father's Country   *a prose poem*

I COME IN SEARCH OF something else, an artist's studio in the Dominion Bridge Building, an alcove hidden in those sprawling red bricks. The welders next door tell filthy jokes and splay their bear-paws across their tools with the ease of old lovers. But I can't find the Dominion Bridge Building, or the studio, or the welders' shop, I've come the wrong way, I'm lost and pedalling at random down one street and up another. It's a working-class neighbourhood tucked away like a mediaeval village. The industrial dragon lives just over the hill, a belching, snorting monster who swallows people when they pass by the lair.

A common phenomenon. Warehouse buildings make room for artists, cheap rent, poor regulations, high ceilings and toilets like cesspools next to the boiler rooms. You can play drums and whip each other and gut demons in those places, no one ever knows what you do, where your art ends and your own violent nights begin. All the welders think you're out of your mind but that's exactly where they like to meet you.

I'm looking for my mask-maker's studio. I'm all turned around, where does the sun rise in this city? Wasn't I born here, don't I know these streets? My friend's a mask-maker, she's made all my masks these last ten years, and now I want her to make me a new one called

LIAR SWALLOWED UP

WOMAN WHO EATS THE SKY

THIEF WHO STOLE EVERYTHING

But I can't find her hands or her clay or the rooms she hides them in, I can't find the frigging building, it's huge, it spans a city block, and I can't find it. I ride around on my bike like a lost kid without any money for gum.

I don't remember anything from this place, it's summer-green here, a man's mowing his lawn, many men are mowing their square lawns, the air is splashed with flowerbeds and barking dogs. A pitbull with a pushed-in brown face attacks me but the fence nets his teeth over and over, catches his body by the jaws. I pedal on, I pass by.

And turn to the right, to the left, into the traffic, onto a road I've forgotten for years. A road I've forgotten that has not forgotten me because suddenly I hear my name, something's calling me, the concrete itself, under the hot bicycle tires. I look down. I look up and there it is, the orange sign, the black letters, something left over forever from Hallowe'en, the chain-link fence jagged around the whole place. Oh my god. My god—

—my father used to bring me here. I haven't lost

my way, I've found my father's old workplace, he used to be the foreman here, the guy who ran the cement yard. This is where my father worked and lived.

Suddenly, in this excellent Saturday afternoon sunlight, the sky tossed high and blue, I see my father's ghost. I see my father. And I recognize the girl-child standing in front of the huge cement-mixers whose wheels are as tall as she is, ten times heavier. Her shoes are scuffed, blue, on the wrong feet. The girl cradles her arm carefully, looking down, because a grasshopper rests there, on her wrist. The girl can see the grasshopper breathing. Lightly, quickly. This yard explains everything. The jagged fence.

Oh, father. My blind father, your eyes were always ghost-blue, too pale, water from the Dead Sea. Now I remember your clothes, cement dust and mortar, the scent of crushed stone, beaten stone, stones and rocks lifted like sacrificial lambs and gulped down by machines.

You ground up whole mountains to make the street I stand on. Now the purple bicycle is a dead metal pipe in my hands, many metal pipes, like the old weapons used against us. But you beat the earth harder, didn't you? You beat it and reshaped it according to the wishes of rich men.

The last green acre in your heart tried to find a place to hide in the forests of my childhood. Do you remember the long days in those hills, that enormous orchestra of trees? Do you remember the beaver dam, the cabin a treasure of mud and dog and grass, one hundred frogs plié-ing through the pond? You stood on the trail with your hand outstretched,

"There. There, see the deer?" You kneeled down in the living grass, giving to me and giving to me what you stole every day of your life.

My heart almost bursts, now that I understand. Now that I come home to your country, this ugly yard where I knew you in exile from the forest. Where you poisoned the pigeons with sweet anti-freeze, where the gorgeous pheasants gleamed upon the wall.

The waves of these memories are tidal, so powerful they knock me over. My bike's on the ground and I'm sitting in the gravel and my hands are gripping the chain-link fence, ten fingers clutch the hard wire. Salt water splashes the dust on my face into narrow dirt-trails, like the ones where I walked behind you, marvelling at your easy power, your arm just another shaft of your gun.

Now the train goes by, the red-orange CP Rail cars, the brown Canadian, the yellow-assed Government of Canada, the gray ones from Milwaukee. All the boxcars pass, chug along, and the trucks and pick-ups line up to wait. The muscled forearms of the drivers bulge from the open windows, absorbing sunlight. None of those men knows how I love them, how I hate them. No, they look over, pissed off at the train, they notice a bike on the ground, see a girl on the truck-route staring through a fence into the yard. They see she is young enough to be one of their daughters, they realize she's crying uncontrollably, shoulders and chest convulsing, they see her sun-burnt Saturday-afternoon face, but above all they see that she is eminently fuckable, young enough. They do not see the ghost she sees. If they did, they would deny ghosts, they would say they saw old Connelly from Revelstoke, from the Shamrock Inn, they would say they saw a man much like themselves, much like my father.

The black CP Rail cars smell of sulfur, the stock-cars stink of cattle, that shit squeezed from fear, the animals already packed tight and bloody and bawling, meat with the fur still on. But the train has almost passed now, the train's almost gone, and I knew about all that when I was eight years old, from the stockyards over there, across the road. The starving horses to slaughter, the blind billy goats to slaughter, the ponies with rotten hooves to slaughter, the calf with a crooked neck to slaughter. I was a child then, I didn't own the words I own now but it's clear I knew, I knew everything. The memory finally speaks: death was a safe harbour for the deformed and the abandoned. I was a careful child. I knew that every creature in the killing house remembered a green field.

Just like you did. Just like you do.

They never end, these stories of love and destruction.

Your daughter is here, her hands raw against the fence, looking in. Your son is there, on Spy Hill, his forehead raw, rammed like a bull against the fence, staring out. His country, too, cement and concrete and metal pipes clanging in the brain. He knows the inside of that prison like he knows the inside of his mouth, my beautiful brother, my half-twin, another one wasted, gone, a gray and metal clamp of death around his life. The vicious barter of that place has made him a beggar without hands.

Father, how can you ask why I leave, why I'm driven away from the hills you taught me to love, from the songbirds? How can you ask? I hate swallowing the same devastation again and again. To eat so much loss makes you empty, to breathe plague makes you die, to batter and crush the mountain makes dust of your bones.

The train whistles on, the trucks drive by. The yard is empty. You do not work here any more. Even this place and its ranks abandoned you in the end. I release the chain-link fence. I stand, brush off the silt and gravel, sweep my hands like new rags down my legs, rub the day back into my eyes. The metal pipes rise again into a bicycle, I pull it off the ground, remembering why we invented the wheel. I turn away, away—

—and realize the stockyards across the road are gone.

We played hide-and-seek in those arks of animals bound for slaughter. Their terror entered us, their shit got under our nails, on our knees, their doom thumped down our own narrow throats.

But the stockyards across the road are gone. Someone has taken and hidden them away from the children who come here now, Saturday afternoons, with their father.

This world, changed. This world, unrecognizable. When I turn away from the cement yard, a field spreads open before me, across the road, the gleaming body of blown grass, dandelion, milkweed. And, beyond, a bridge. And above, the unbound realm of sky.

One prayer

THE UNBOUND REALM of sky: my dream is graceful movement through immense blue spaces. If I cannot be a fish in my next life, let me be a swallow.

That is the dream. The reality is an enormous backpack waiting to be filled, and my bedroom floor hidden beneath paper, books, clothes, objects. Mid-August. Mid-August? What a cruel jester time is, juggling the fire and colour of our days so well, we scarcely notice as he swallows them down. A branch of leaflets on the mountain ash tree has turned bright yellow. The mock-orange blossoms fell weeks ago, and real oranges never grew.

Backpack, tickets, train pass, old shoes, a sheaf of postcards, a photograph, an ancient coin from Mexico, something to remember you by. Some things to remember my life by. Why is it always so difficult to decide what to take and what to pack away? It's never right in the end, anyway. What I have always intended to leave behind is what I carry beneath my skin. What I bring with me is so often discarded after I arrive at my destination. I have left a trail of clothes, books, and currencies of spirit all over the world.

Oh! I say to myself, breathless, like a child who walks alone into a grove of trees for the very first time, the word "forest" finally her own. Oh! How strange everything looks when you're leaving it behind for a year or more. *Partir est morir un peu.* What else is this, but a small dying? People don't forget the dead, but they go on living without them. I have not left yet, but my friends are already closing up the small hole my absence will make, planning their parties, their meetings, their performances, their weddings, their births. I will not be here, and really (although they protest otherwise) I will not be missed. Yet I know we love each other. I know this.

I was at the farm again. Early evening, I walked beside the horses for miles, stopping where they stopped, watching them, watching the land absorb the falling light. Cimmeron, the bay horse, hot-skinned and sleek, what did she smell like? Fields, sweat, Spain, grasses, rain, earth. Finally I left the horses in the far pasture and walked back alone, the darkness coming down in one thin veil at a time. I came upon a whitetail doe standing in a pool of water. She was unbelievably still; I slowly came to the conclusion that she was not a deer at all, but an artful arrangement of tree branches and my own longing. Only when I slid down to the water's edge, cracking twigs and disturbing rocks, did she stamp a splash out of the water and bound lightly into the trees.

As soon as she was gone, an owl called from the

eastern hillside. I began climbing up the creek bank again; a beaver slapped its tail against the pond and dove away. Is this a Walt Disney movie? I asked out loud. (Thumper, waiting in the nearby bearberry bushes, said nothing.) My eyes followed the rippling trail of the beaver until they were distracted by strange metallic points shining in the water. Phosphorescent water bugs? Fish eyes? I looked up, I looked back down, and started laughing. The strange metallic points were the reflections of stars.

Jubilant. Who needs LSD? Go for a walk in half-darkness and everywhere there are mysteries beyond number. I was warm, almost hot under my sweater, although the air on my face was like a cold mouth whispering *stone autumn snow*. I walked along the path (past the place where I met the frog) and closed the big gate to keep out the cows. A few feet later, I heard heavy steps through the grass near the top of the hay field: a huge bull elk jumped over the fence. His enormous rack of antlers was just white enough to show up against the black wall of trees. It was as if someone had lifted and shaken the fields, and all the animals were turned out of their hiding places. (Or had I been lifted and shaken? I was turned out of my hiding place, the city, and could finally see.) Before I reached the road, I saw more deer, two coyotes, a great-winged bird gliding silent above the barn (the owl whose voice I heard earlier).

Those hills around me, and the sky to the west extraordinarily blue, but falling. That blue—the blue of desert and mountain twilight. If I ever have a house, I will paint my bedroom that colour. I started to name things as I walked. "Here I am, it is almost dark, a strange bird is crying in the willows over there, here is the line of balsam poplars. There is the foaling barn, empty of foals. Inside the house in the spruce grove my mother is getting older, my niece is in bed, my sister is sleeping. Everyone is sleeping and I am awake and the creek is running like a silver horse, like a herd of silver and black horses through the willows and poplars, down the chasms of darkness and hollows of green."

What I am trying to do with all these words, with all this singing, is to say,

I love this, I love all I see

and,

Thank you

This is a prayer.

This is my one and holy prayer.

The modern fairytale

HOWEVER.

Who owns this, all I see? (All I saw, because I am, in fact, at the house on Hope Street drinking ginger ale.) Who owns the land on either side of the creek? Who owns the beaver pond? Who, for all intents and purposes, owns the beaver? Many would argue that even if someone owns the land, no one owns the wildlife, but animals, like poor people, have trouble procuring good legal representation. Surely if one has the right to hunt, kill, eat, and/or stuff wild creatures, one exercises an undeniable kind of ownership.

The land my mother and stepfather live on is a quarter-section, one hundred and sixty acres, some of the most beautiful ranchland in Alberta, in western Canada. They live on it, much like the animals in the fields and woods beyond the house they live in. They do not own the land, nor the miles of fences, nor the house, nor any of the barns and farming equipment which they tirelessly repair and maintain. Everything, including a very big luxurious house on the southwestern hill, is owned by a wealthy couple who spend most of their time at their other ranch, or at their house in the city. One of my mother's occupations is to tend the couple's house and garden. Both she and my stepfather devote hundreds of hours a week to "the land". Most fascinating of all, they earn poverty-line wages.

I will write about it, I will write a fairytale about a good woman who goes every day to a castle. For years she goes, with her mops and rags and brushes, to clean. The king and queen live in a far-off kingdom. Once a year, they come to their castle to visit and inspect the work of the good woman. The good woman is patient. She wishes they would come more often, to praise her, to make her toil worthwhile, but they are busy, their kingdom is wide, and they are not interested in making the good woman's toil worthwhile.

Like many peasants, she has a hardy constitution, strong arms, practical intelligence, and a sense of humour, dignity's preservative. She works night and day to keep the castle free of flies and vermin. She washes sheets; ghosts sleep in them. She cleans windows; ghosts peer out of them. From distant lands, the king brings tables made out of elephant feet and beautiful rugs of black and white fur. She polishes the elephant-feet tables, she shakes the zebra skins free of dust. The water buffalo and leopard and tiger skins mystify her—she has always preferred simple woven rugs—but she knows her master the king is a great hunter who has travelled the world, so she never asks where the pelts come from, or why there need be so many of them. She polishes and shines, she scrubs and waxes. Dutifully, she kills more flies, more mice, more flies, which seem to be breeding in the furnace ducts, in the very heart of the house. Some days she goes up to the castle and every window looks as though it is covered by a trembling black curtain. The flies. Realizing she can't kill them all, she opens the doors and windows and herds them out of the house like a flock of minute, airborne sheep.

When she grows bored, as she often does, she stands on the veranda smoking a cigarette, left hand on her hip, wondering how long it would take to walk straight into those mountains which rear up and buck the sky like carousel horses painted blue and gone wild. Every spring, the good woman plants and tends a garden to rival the gardens of England, but, season after season, no one sees the flowers. The king and the queen stay away from the castle in the summer, although they insist the woman plant the beautiful garden in their name. The thousand flowers, in a riot of colour and scent, grow and die without being seen. This is painful to the good woman, who knows too much about the death of beauty. She lets the deer eat them. She makes bouquets for her friends. She fills her house with them, but it's no use. No matter how many lilies and zinnias and irises she clips from the grounds, the garden itself remains hidden from other people.

One day, the queen arrives at the castle unannounced and angrily calls the woman.

WHAT DOES the queen say?

I don't know, my mother rarely tells me. She only makes jokes about being a Canadian serf. If I continued writing, I would be departing on a fictional voyage, and I don't want to go. After all, this isn't a fairytale, it's my mother's life.

And it is her life that interests me, not the lives of the kings and queens.

But there they are, the extremely wealthy, who own the land I love so much. There it is, the enormous, empty, thirty-appliance house on the hill in a country where thousands of people are homeless. There they sit, the real elephant-feet tables, which once belonged to real African elephants' legs.

All that needs to be understood.

Who can I ask?

Certainly not the elephants.

I remember a photograph in a magazine, a side shot, of a gaunt, toothless man shining a businessman's shoes. The businessman is reading a newspaper. He is sleekly plump, like a seal. *Como una foca,* they say in Spanish. Like a seal, his black hair lies flat and shining against his skull. His lower lip protrudes (in anger? disgust? disbelief?) as he reads his paper, oblivious to the man below him. The newspaper is a wall between the two of them, despite their physical contact: the poor man's hands touching the rich man's shoes. The newspaper is a wall the toothless man can neither read nor climb, yet he stares up at it with an open mouth. He is not completely toothless: two or possibly three teeth are visible above his bottom lip. He looks ten years older than the businessman, though of course he may be the same age, or even younger. He has a close-shaven head, a convict's simultaneously tough and vulnerable head, lightly scarred. Why is his mouth hanging open like that? Perhaps he has just asked the businessman what sort of polish he wants. Or has the front-page photograph caught his attention? Or is he beseeching a god who does not listen? Or is he Jesus, doggedly washing the feet of a disciple who does not even see him?

And here, delivered fresh to our door daily, like bread used to be in old countries, we have the newspaper. We must try to eat the newspaper every day, without crying, without becoming heartless on such a steady diet of pain, and without throwing up. We must try not to look away. We must see those who suffer our wealth, our impossibly good luck.

I admit it: I am a failure with the newspaper. I look away all the time. I understand nothing. I go for a walk.

Meanwhile, my mother, who wants to leave the employ of the queen, makes uncomfortable jokes about becoming a bag lady and living on Ninth Avenue.

The unbound realm of blue. Who can have it but a fish or a swallow?

Are your accounts in order?

HOW DID IT HAPPEN?

Days ago, it was summer. Even now it is summer, they say, because the leaves are still green, and the children are not back in school. But something has happened. I felt it last week, a few days after swimming in the river. During the hottest part of the afternoon, a ghost of chill entered the air. Every day this phantom has more presence, more body. At night I feel the sharp elbows of this ghost in the halls of the house. I know, despite all protestations, that the cold is coming.

I am glad. The cold makes me glad. Time leaps, surges over us, pulls us along. Our lives take us. Our lives take us so quickly we barely know what's happening. Where have I been? What have I been doing? Why didn't I read fewer books and hike more mountains? I meant to do a thousand things this summer. Already it's too late.

I am sitting on the roof again. How different the

sun feels now! The tiger has returned to India. Three in the afternoon drops a great slab of shadow over the brown-tipped lilacs. I move closer and closer to the roof's edge in my loyalty to the sun. Soon I will either fall into the front yard and break my ankle or I will crawl back in the window and get a sweater.

The wind has changed. My cousin says that when the wind changes, it's time for me to go.

This morning, sitting outside my favourite cafe, I watched an orange dog try to swallow a white butterfly. Snap gulp. The butterfly kept ambling back through the cool air, but the dog missed every time.

I have to pack soon. Are my accounts in order? Is my heart in order? My mother called to tell me they are selling Cimmeron, the bay horse. Two days ago, I lost my favourite ring, the star of Alexander. What does it mean when you lose a horse and a conquerer's sign in the same week? Sometime at the beginning of the month, I lost my watch.

All of us here are losing this season. Fewer and fewer evenings in the back yard with wine and the guitar. Yes, despite August, it's fall. When I went for a ride along the river, a shiver ran over me. The path was a cold tunnel and three of the poplar trees in Stanley Park have turned completely yellow and even as I write this, a cool wind shivers the blinds—

Is it autumn or my nearing departure that makes everything seem mysterious, untouchable, too beautiful to hold? Yet the crisp light of these mornings clarifies the vision: this is my life, the lives of my friends, the lives of these streets.

My accounts are not in order. My heart has never been in order.

By the time you receive this letter, I will already be in another world. How long will it be before someone says my name? And when they do, what will it sound like?

If you do not have a map

Caminante no hay camino
camino se hace al andar.
                    —Antonio Machado

The garlic-sellers

GYPSIES LOITER OUTSIDE the post office, selling garlic and looking at us with black and almond-coloured eyes. It is clear they know things we will never know. Every child is made of elbows and knees. Each of the men is intimately involved with a cigarette: lighting a cigarette, rolling one, flicking one away, inhaling with closed or open eyes, butting one out against the sandstone wall of the post office. The women who bring the ropes and boxes of garlic here are massive, with muscular forearms and faces like full nets.

"My heart is broken," I say, coming out of the post office, in response to the fact that I've received no mail. The Gypsy woman standing closest to me laughs, "If it's only your heart, you should give thanks to God. My whole body is crumbling like a granada." A granada is a small local cake which, as you can imagine, tends to crumble.

The Gypsies.

They are the dispossessed, the despised, the

ones who have lived and still live on what we throw away. But if you come out of the post office and are not afraid to stand close to them, you see your own face in their eyes.

The seductive generosity of butchers

BESIDE THE POST office stands the market, where I go almost every day, even if I don't need anything. There is an irresistible energy in market-places, the living force of real people grappling over real food. As soon as you walk in the double swinging doors, you know: this is what it's really all about. You are greeted by row after row of fruit, dead animals, and radiant flowers. Look: the long raw body of a lamb dangling upside down, head still attached, and more lambs, dozens of them, hung one after the other. At the next stall, stacks of plucked chickens and pheasants in full plumage, their tails fallen over the wooden edge of the cutting board. Then the great scarlet sides of cows, ribs lined with muscle and white nets of tendons and fat. Front and hind quarters swing from their own hooves. (Remember their gentle eyes and velvet noses, and so much white milk? *Moo.*)

Two things I have never encountered in Spain: an ugly waiter or an unhappy butcher. As I walk along the meat counters, staring at cow tongues (blue, gray, black, spotted purple, many of them a foot long) and pigs' feet and spongy-looking brains and endless ropes of sausage, the butchers greet me with huge grins, as though they love women who eat tofu. They ask if I need any scraps for my dog (this is a running joke; for months I've been telling them I do not own a dog). Still smiling, at least one of them tells me I'm looking very pale, or tired, would I like a free blood sausage, a free liver, a free cut of steak? Do the butchers have a bet among themselves? Do they believe their good humour will eventually induce me to eat red meat?

There are old butchers and apprentice butchers and a dozen boys wearing white blood-stained butcher-shop clothes. When you meet their eyes, they break into dazzling smiles. Even when their teeth are bad, their smiles are beautiful. Beaming, full of obvious good will, blood and animal fat smeared on their hands, they ask you how you are, where you've been, how your relatives are doing. I've watched their gleeful politeness showered upon widows, housewives, school children who come on errands for their mothers. It's enough to make me want to abandon vegetarianism, give up writing, and become a butcher.

Even when you slip into the inner rows of the market to recover among bunches of carnations and baskets of apples, the loaders still seem to cross your path, carrying huge cuts of meat on their shoulders and backs. One day I turned suddenly and walked straight into a man who carried a huge basket of piglets, little pink bundles piled on each other like a surplus of naked dolls. (Their eyes were rolled back in their heads.) When the man and I collided, a couple of the piglets tumbled off the top of the pile and, before quite realizing what they were, I executed a series of acrobatic twists to save them from falling on the floor. There is something both heart-rending and embarrassing about piglets. After stumbling out an apology in Spanish, I literally fled, but even among the strawberries and nectarines, I could hear the piglet-carrier guffawing with laughter.

Outside in the street, trucks on their rounds to the town markets leave their tall doors open: nothing but big red death inside, hanging from hooks. Roast beef! Sirloin! Life! Mooo! Visiting the butcher stalls of the market is like bodily entering the chapter on muscles in a medical textbook.

(Why do doctors and butchers wear white? Wouldn't it be easier to wear red-brown? Have the people who deal with life-giving or life-saving blood traditionally worn white? Blood on white cloth appears in its own vibrant and pure colour, proving there is no need, no desire to cover it up, to hide it. Blood can be a proof of innocence as much as, or even more, than a proof of guilt. Thus the Gypsy women describe hanging out the bloodied linen after their marriage night.)

I walk dazed past the stalls and down the rows, my head full of outlandish theories and ruminations about cows' kidneys and pigs' hearts. Ironic, and somewhat suspicious, that a vegetarian spends so much of her time at the market thinking about meat. Do you suppose it's sexual? The men behind the chopping blocks are amused at my studious expression, but today I ignore them. I stand in front of a pile of iced tidbits, trying to imagine eating bull's testicles, and the effort demands all my concentration.

The lid over Europe

EUROPE HAS A sooty pallor. One sees it in the faces of most Europeans over forty-five. History begins to appear on their skin like age spots. Strangely, this is not unattractive. Faces that wear the true age of a body and a country are, in fact, very comforting, and sometimes extraordinarily beautiful.

There seems to be a kind of lid over Europe. Not a coffin lid; maybe not a lid at all; maybe a thick, motionless haze. Europe is sealed into itself, into its own exhaustive history and proud traditions. You don't have to go to the museums and churches to find history here. History is a living animal that wraps around you when you walk down the street. (Along with certain over-affectionate men.)

What is Europe? A smug, rich old gentleman with great charm, bad teeth, and peasant relatives. (I can't help being attracted to him, though; he tells a good story.) America, as a continent, is a sexy young woman whose origins, morals, and fashion sense are questionable. (I can't help being attracted to her, either.)

Yes, I know the metaphor only goes so far, because the world is becoming less and less divisible, and we are more alike than we know. When I was five years old, I went to the zoo where I saw, among other wonderful creatures, the chimpanzees. We were separated by a wall of glass, which I could not see. One of the chimps extended its arm, stretched a hand towards me, and looked directly into my eyes. When I quickly leaned forward to touch the outstretched hand, my nose and cheek banged hard into the glass. Nosebleed, tears, awful desperation as I was led away. For weeks afterward, my mother had to explain to me that the chimpanzees were not strange furry people, but primates. Like the wall of glass, I could not see the essential difference between myself and a chimpanzee. None of the pictures of monkeys I'd seen had prepared me for their eyes. To the child I was, the eyes that looked into mine were human.

Twenty years later, I am struggling to understand a different, though related problem. Why don't people recognize each other as the same species? Spanish, Basque, Catalan, southerner, northerner, Irish-Canadian, Quebecois, Chinese, American, African. Whatever arguments we make in favour of them, these labels of division never illuminate the mystery of human existence, and they never allow us to move closer to each other. Beneath all the trappings of culture and sex, of ideology and language, we *are* the same people. I know this. Our lives begin and end with journeys made alone.

Tristeza, morning

SOMETIMES I FEEL as if I weigh a thousand tonnes with my words and my nightmares and my camera eyes and my memory. How can our minds weigh so much when our skulls are so small? My skin barely contains my life. Oskar and Jorge are downstairs drinking coffee and reading old newspapers. I stand on the terrace of their mother's old farmhouse above the hay fields of northern Vizcaya. I cry and cry as I hang up clean wet shirts and underwear.

All this exists: the old flagstone yard, yellow with flowers, its stone fence sprouting weeds, the stone houses in the fields beyond. Green hay spills from the deep lofts of those houses. Bunches of corn hang to dry on either side of the lofts. They *exist*, the folding fields of corn and grass, the orchards of apples and pears. The tough sway-backed pony pulls milk cans up from the family dairy.

Every day in the wooden wagons, men and boys bring in a harvest of alfalfa, purple thistle, small red flowers tangled in rich weeds. I hear roosters, en-thralled with the dull morning, impressed today as they were yesterday, crowing their throats awake. The uneven ringing of cow bells is unceasing, like the frogs and crickets at night. Now, on this morning of clouds and impending rain, the plaintive music of the birds is so perfectly in tune with the day that I barely hear it. On this terrace, I see stone houses, fields below me, whitish clouds smothering the faces of the hills. I smell humid grass and rain and ponies and the clothes I've just hung to dry.

Beautiful, no matter how it's described, a place so gracefully hidden that most people never see it and many wouldn't care anyway. I cry on the terrace, knowing that the details are clear to me, valuable, knowing that this land, in some secret way, is my own. Or that I belong here. Or that this place has taken me, keeps me. What is it? Why am I crying?

One phrase, over and over in my head, *My life, the gift I cannot equal.*

At first, among the roses and blue days and silver water of Sopelana, I felt overwhelmed and humble but happy to be where I was. Now it's heavy, like this salty gray mist, I cannot see the sky and why am I so alone and who brought me here and how do I get home? Could this exquisite place be home? What does one do with so much beauty? I carry it down the narrow stairs and rush into the kitchen, crying, *Look, look at this,* but Oskar turns the page of last month's *El Pais* and Jorge swears because it will rain today and we wanted to go fishing. . . .

Handfuls, mouthfuls of beauty like birds, like small, bright-winged birds. But Oskar and Jorge can't see them because they don't want them. The birds fly out the windows, right through the glass, right through the walls, they fly back into the fields. When all the beauty has disappeared, Oskar looks up from the newspaper and asks, "Why are your eyes so red?"

Out of the insane asylum

DEAR ONE, I have been walking.

I walk through wind-blown and white-edged days, the sunlight on my back heavy and salted like a canvas sail. I walk through nights so cool and wet that salamanders appear at the base of the eucalyptus trees surrounding the convent.

If I run up to the fifth floor of my apartment building and hang out the hallway window, I can see inside the convent's walls. During the days, the nuns walk, too, pacing their great garden, or pulling its weeds. So many old women shrouded in black! Who has ever touched the backs of their knees, that vulnerable, scalloped flesh? Beyond the high stone walls of the cloister, the cars roll back and forth like coloured beads. Every day at four o'clock, children who will never get old chase a brown and white dog in the park, under the plane trees. Every day they passionately yell the dog's name, "Café-Con-Leche, venga! Café-Con-Leche, no te vayas a la calle!" The nuns, walled in by stone and traffic, cannot possibly hear the children shouting for Coffee-With-Milk. The nuns are old. Some of them walk with canes. Even the young ones wear age on their faces like a veil.

I run up the stairs to see the nuns, I run down the stairs. The stairs are part of my life, the start and finish of all my walking. They are made of very old, unfinished wood. The middle of each board has warped under the weight of everyone who has ever gone up or down. The landings always smell vaguely of sawdust because woodworm is consuming the entire staircase. You can see the tiny holes and narrow tunnels in the sagging stairs, in the banister, in the creaky floorboards. It's a long slow labour, but the place is being eaten out from under us.

When I leave the woodworm palace, I cross the street and pass through the park to the *paseo* lined with plane trees. Their smooth trunks are white-washed and their limbs have been trained to grow into each other, forming a canopy over the lane. September, late summer in Spain, the leaves are still green above us. I throw my head back sometimes, walking, and pretend I'm floating down a very small tributary of the Amazon. (What does a very small tributary of the Amazon look like? Certainly there should be vines, and birds more colourful than pigeons and sparrows.)

I walk and walk. Yesterday I sat down on a bench in the park called Maria Cristina—the people here call it *el parque de los viejos,* the park of the old ones—where you receive a wide view of the Cantabrian Sea, ships sweeping the harbour, the farther Atlantic pressed against the sky like a silver mirror.

I took one of my shoes off to rub my aching foot. When I held the shoe up, trying to see why it was hurting me, I got a coin-sized view of the park railing and the far-away water. The old lady sitting on the bench beside me said, "Oh, my dear, you have a hole in your shoe."

"Yes, I've just seen it now."

"It's a very big hole."

"Yes, my foot was sore, and now—"

"—you understand why," the old lady deftly finished off my sentence. "How did it happen, are you very poor?" She folded up her *madrileño* gossip magazine and pivotted towards me, a very old, very small woman with auburn-rinsed hair. She wore a bit of lipstick and a lot of face powder. A very proper lady, with silver buckles on her shoes. She asked again, "How did you get this terrible hole in your shoe?"

"I've been walking. All over. The cliffs to Sopelana, Las Arenas. I've been walking a lot."

"Sopelana? On foot? It's eight kilometres away!"

"The cliffs are very beautiful."

She raised her eyebrows and pursed her lips as if to say, Is that any excuse? Aloud, she repeated her other question, "Are you very poor?"

"Well, no, I—I teach English. But I'm a writer, in fact."

"Oh, my poor child. Pobrecita! A writer. So young. My dear God and Jesus. I had an uncle who was a writer and my mother told me he starved to death. Until he became a civil servant."

I slipped my shoe back on, smiling.

"Are you hungry?"

I laughed. "Always. Always hungry." The look of

concern that deepened the lines of her face made me continue, "Though that has nothing to do with being a writer. I'm fine. Really, I am." (I am round, a study in spheres. How anyone could ever think I didn't have enough to eat is something of a mystery to me.)

"Why don't you come to see us for lunch next week?"

"No, that's not necessary, really, I have my own lunch."

"Sí, sí, you must come, we will have chipirones, octopus cooked in its own ink, a Basque delicacy. We would be very happy if you came. An honour."

"I am embarrassed, we are strangers."

"Don't be embarrassed. No one is a stranger in God's house. Or where I live. Please come. You must come." And now she opened her purse and brought out a very sharp pencil. When I asked her why she had a pencil and not a pen, she explained, "Because I have never gotten used to pens. They can explode and ink will stain everything. A pencil is much safer." With her very sharp pencil, she wrote her name and her address on the back of a church handbill. Each letter came slowly, with proud painstaking care. People who don't write often have such respect for the very act of forming letters; I should learn from this, I should remember. Beneath her address, she printed in clear, block letters, MIERCOLES 2 PM.

Before I continued on my walk, we exchanged names. She told me hers was Amatxi. *Amatxi* means "grandmother" in Basque.

I must buy a pair of new shoes before going to Amatxi's house for lunch next week, but for the moment I've taped a piece of cardboard into the old ones and have continued on my way, though not along the cliffs. I've been wandering around the town, sneaking down the narrowest, forgotten streets, peering over garden walls, into the crumbling mansions of the old neighbourhoods.

As though they were flowers, I gather the faces of people. The colour of the Basque people's eyes astonish me. One is taught in school that Spaniards are dark and short, but the Basques are tall, often fair-haired, with eyes a hundred shades of green and blue. I am not polite, I stare, my face is too open. Obviously I walked out of the insane asylum grounds when the gardener left the gate open.

The hands of thieves

THEY SAY FRANCO and his cohorts used to summer here, in the cool Atlantic breezes. The Fascists held grand parties among the people who hated them. (The town of Guernica is just over an hour away.) Imagine the women of Madrid in ball gowns made of rainbow silk; the slender men in tails, their black hair slicked from their faces. Evenings of lanterns and diamond earrings glittering on the marble terraces, ballrooms a sea of wine and scent and Cuban cigars, the sound of Spanish voices as open, as lulling as the tide sliding out. (During the day, Basque children were whipped if the nuns heard them speaking their strange language.) At night, I can hear the ghost of a one-hundred-piece orchestra playing in the grand hotel at the far end of the beach. After dark, I go just close enough to hear the music, no closer: it's infested by rats, bats, stray dogs, antisocial heroin addicts. At the other end of the beach stands a concert hall as big as an arena. It's boarded up now, water-stained, growing a rug of moss and lichen. Grass and small violet flowers grow out of the cracks in the stone walls.

Stone walls! If only they had eyes, these stones, eyes and mouths. Press your ear to a shell, you hear the ocean. Press your ear to a stone wall. You hear silence. You hear human hands and voices building their world out of rock. Sometimes you hear two or three guard dogs barking and growling with such ferocity that your heart gets stuck in your teeth. But even guard-dog-terror cannot undo the truth: history presides inside stone walls. They awe me.

Clamber up the ivy, feet and fingers grappling for holds. Drag yourself through the emerald moss, over the butterfly cocoons and the tails of lizards. When you reach the top ledges, you are dusty and tired. Torn vegetation shows green under your fingernails, there's sweat on your nose, your whole body is stretched and blood-filled like a muscle. Be careful not to tear your fingers on the coloured glass and nails embedded in the mortar to catch the hands of thieves.

We are thieves, then, if we want to see over the walls. The shards and nails are meant for us. A phrase comes to my mind, unbidden, from—where? the *I Ching?* "Two thieves will steal everything." Is it possible to see too much? To see what is not supposed to be seen? I will live my life mad to find out what is on the other side of the wall. This is a return to the question of hunger, the insatiable hunger of the eye.

To the lucky and the persistent, the world offers everything: its own splendid, savage self. What are we willing to see? I would be an arsonist if I were allowed to stand and watch the fire consume the mansion, red tongues of flame licking out of the shattered windows.

Instead, I set fire to my days and see them burn like illuminated parchment. Who has doused this world in oil? All I see kindles, flares, falls, rises to newness. I walk to the highest cliffs, where the sun stares the earth right in the face. The mechanics of flight seem uncomplicated. The canary flies out of its cage to sing and sing on the edge of my skull.

The slingshot child, mysterious comas,
sand dancing

SMALL CHILDREN can see. When I was looking after
the little boy, I loved him despite his parents, despite
his spoiled nature and his fixation on slingshots and
rats (a disgusting combination). I loved him because
perfection occasionally flickered in his face and
body. He shone. I loved him above all in the bathtub,
with the polish of water playing over his ribs and
belly and happy penis. He was a pale, smiling seal
in the tub. In sunlight, his hair was a shade deeper
than polished copper. The dark green eyes swallowed whatever they touched: old men's hands,
shadows on the great doors of San Ignacio, coins,
lighters, pop cans, stones in the sand, ants drowning
in rain puddles, rainbows of oil in the gutter, vines
twisting around the forgotten rake, the delightfully
long and purple gash on his shin. Only when the
television came on did his face grow unnaturally still.
Children can be so ruthless, but they are also purely
animal, the way we are before life fits us out with a

wristwatch and a brown overcoat.

Now I teach English verbs to students who are not much younger than I am. Every afternoon they break my heart by refusing to emerge from their mysterious comas. Sometimes I think I'm living in *The Invasion of the Body Snatchers*. I can't understand it. The study of English bores them. I bore them. Their lives bore them. Will someone please tell me how they got this way? Seventeen-year-olds the world over seem a dull, conservative lot. No wonder I hated being with them in school.

Were you ever so hopelessly bored? I can't remember boredom. I recall the dreadful waiting of adolescence, each real and typically adolescent state of alienation, loneliness, multilayered pain, but boredom had no place in those emotional storms. When I left home to begin travelling, I knew I was on the verge of my real life. And it began with such wildness that I could barely breathe. Now I hang back sometimes and watch it move on, almost without me: it refuses to be still.

Sometimes in the day, I have to swing my arms to keep from dancing. At night I don't care, I run down the one hundred and thirty-seven stone steps to the beach and stretch myself awake, walk on my hands into the water, incite my back to be a wave, turn walk-overs and handsprings and cartwheels. High fluid arches are the main objective, the grace and thrust of water through my limbs. I move until I don't think I'm tired, until I am so tired that my arms shake. The sand, when it slips and shifts under my hands, feels strange, like skin being pulled away.

I am afraid that I will somehow forget this. I will somehow forget myself and lose my eyes.

Pili in the market-place

AN OLD WOMAN lives in *la calle* San Francisco, in the nearby city of Bilbao. She is a Gypsy woman. Her name is Pili, short for the very traditional Spanish name Pilar. Most weekdays, she leaves Bilbao and sets up a table in this town's indoor market. One afternoon while I'm looking for a cheap pair of shoes and taking photographs, Pili waves in my direction. I imagine she is waving at someone else (in the rows of kitchen wares behind me) so I ignore her, and continue looking at the world through my camera. I'm taking pictures of a Gypsy boy playing the accordion. He is about eight years old. I've seen him before, numerous times, both here and in Bilbao. Usually he does bright, catchy tunes, but today he isn't playing very well. Perhaps the boy senses that no one is going to give him much money this morning. (It is drizzling outside, for the thousandth day in a row; drowning weather, as my roommate Maru calls it.) Indeed, the accordion case lying open at his feet looks forlorn, just worn flowered lining and a few pesetas.

After the shutter button clicks yet again, he looks up at me without enthusiasm, stops playing, and wipes his runny nose on his sweatered forearm. "You better give me some money for taking all those pictures," he says in a surprisingly deep voice.

I take the camera away from my face and smile at him. He sneers back. I keep smiling. Little rotter. "Five hundred pesetas. And I'll buy you a danish if you want."

"Bueno," he sighs, like a very small old man. But then he grins for an instant, sticks out his tongue, and continues playing in the same dejected way as before. After giving him his money, I go and buy a jelly-filled danish. "I like chocolate better," he says as I hand it to him.

When I look in the old woman's direction, she waves again. She doesn't call me, she just waves, and even the wave is discreet, inward. One of the reasons I like the Gypsy people so much is because, in comparison to the Spanish, even to the Basque, they are very quiet. I don't mean they never make noise. A Gypsy fiesta is as rip-roaringly loud and crazy as a Spanish one. I mean something else. The Gypsies carry a silence inside them, a stillness, especially around *los payos,* us, white people, non-Gypsy people. As though they have so little that they refuse to give anything else away, even their voices. (One learns, around the Gypsies, precisely how much a voice is worth.) I respect this. Their quietness forges an iron dignity. Even the accordion-playing boy has it already, that refusal to waste words on some camera-happy foreigner.

So the old woman waves me over. I say hello, how are you. She's perched on a stool behind a table of white lace curtains, all but the sample pieces packaged up in plastic. "I'm fine," she says, but it is immediately clear that she is not interested in making small talk. She eyes me, eyeballs my camera. "Do you know how to take photographs?"

The directness of this question makes me self-conscious about my Spanish, which causes me to stumble over it, excuse myself, start again. "Yes. Not the greatest photographs on earth, but well, yes. Yes, I take photographs."

Unlike many of the older Gypsy women I see in Spain, Pili is small, almost too thin. Her thick gray hair is pulled away from her face and hangs in a braid down her back. She has very pale brown-green eyes, surprising eyes for such dark skin, and pitch black eyebrows. (Her eyebrows are so black they seem dyed; I will ask, if I get the chance.) Strong chin, high cheekbones, a hawk-curved nose, all draped in loose, sun-wrinkled skin.

The Gypsy race is sometimes easy to recognize, but always difficult to describe. You look at Pili, and you say, She is *gitana*. But what is it, exactly, that makes her a Gypsy? Partly it is skin colour, a dark olive tone in the skin heavier than the typical Mediterranean colouring, if such a thing exists. Partly it is the facial features, which seem Caucasian but are not, at least not entirely: there is something distinctly Asian in Pili's face, in many Gypsy faces, but I don't know exactly what it is. Gypsies come from almost everywhere and belong nowhere. There are Gypsy settlements throughout the Middle East, eastern and western Europe. Anthropologists and historians tell us the Gypsy race originally came from the Punjab and Sind provinces of India, probably in the eleventh century.

Whenever I have mentioned to any European Gypsies that they were originally from India, they have given me a look of annoyance, amused disbelief (the amusement comes from their perception of me: a misinformed, charmingly stupid *paya* with a funny accent), or boredom. One of the garlic-sellers told me, "I don't know exactly where I was born. My mother said they were camped on the side of a road, near a pear orchard. She never told me the country. We were eleven. Eleven children, and I was in the middle. Too many! Always someone being born somewhere; how could she remember it all? We were always moving around. She's been dead for a long time, and my uncles, before they died, couldn't remember. One of them said Italy, the other said Spain. And I have an older cousin who thinks I was born just over the border, in the French Pyrenees. But no one ever said anything about India. The great India! Qué ridiculo."

But all I talk about with Pili in the market-place is my camera. She asks questions and I answer each one while fondling packages of lace curtains. In the middle of the conversation, she points to the curtains and asks, "Do you want to buy those?" I tell her, No. She resumes interrogating me.

"Was it very expensive? . . . Really? All the way from Canada! . . . Have you ever taken pictures of your mother? . . . What does your mother think, anyway, a little girl like you far away from home?"

This is what she names me, as we are speaking. *Niña*.

After asking me what I do here, she leans forward and whispers, "I've seen you here before, you know. Many times. And at the post office. And you go to the market in Bilbao, too. I've seen you."

I smile, vaguely uncomfortable but also amused. The observer, observed. A peculiar feeling.

"My son has a camera—he has two cameras!—but all his pictures are full of water." In Spanish, *llenas de agua.* Blurry. "And many times I've seen you wandering around the market, here and in Bilbao, and so often with this camera. Taking pictures of the Gypsy children . . . I know his mother." She indicates the accordion player with her chin. He is no longer playing accordion, but helping someone pack and cover up their cheese graters and carrot peelers. It is just after one; people are beginning to load up their wares or cover them with large sheets. It is almost *la hora de comer,* the typical late lunch of Spain, which rarely involves sandwiches or soup, but a full, two- or three-course sit-down meal.

Pili carefully slides off her perch. I restrain an impulse to put out my arm to steady her; I don't think she wants steadying. "I have to watch my hips, that's all. I'm not young like you, you know. I have damp bones. Madera vieja! Old wood!" She slaps her hands against her flanks and groans. Standing, she is now smaller than I am. Once again she leans over, her eyes slightly narrowed. "Why don't you ever take pictures of old Gypsy people?"

"Because I'm scared of them."

"You're scared of me? A little old lady with bad hips?" She laughs at me.

"Not like that. Not exactly. It has something to do with respect. Sometimes I do take pictures of adults; they have the best faces. But children don't have the same wall as adults. It's easier to see them. Sometimes I'm embarrassed to take pictures of adults. But sometimes I'm not. It depends."

"Would you be embarrassed to take a picture of me?" She smiles in a posed, almost grim way, head to one side, as though for a portrait.

I laugh. "No. Do you want me to take your picture?"

"I thought you would never ask. I was waiting and waiting. I didn't want to ask. I didn't want to be impolite."

So. I photograph Pili behind her table of lace curtains. I photograph her with Jorge, who sells leather shoes. I photograph her with Yolanda, and Yolanda's green-eyed, black-haired daughter Camino. (*Camino* means road, or pathway. Or, from the verb *caminar,* "I walk." A moment of realization. If I have a child, Camino will be my child's name.) I photograph Pili standing outside the doorway of the market-place, which is difficult, because many people are leaving now, crossing in between us, and Pili keeps saying goodbye to people, *hasta luego, hasta mañana.* They hurry out into the gray rain with black umbrellas bobbing over their heads. Pili smiles for the camera. She smiles in a completely heartfelt way; sometimes she even laughs, more natural than most children, or turns her head away to say something to one of the other sellers.

She is old, tiny, wearing a dark blue skirt and a brown coat. One of her upper front teeth is yellow; many of the bottom ones are missing. She wears black boots that go up to her skinny ankles, and flesh-coloured knee stockings. She has a finely proportioned, strong face. Once she was as beautiful as Yolanda's sixteen-year-old daughter. But her delight in being photographed has little to do with vanity, I think, or vanity's ghost. Pili seems to be interested merely in having fun, and in getting some unblurred photographs of herself.

She stands beside Guillermo, seller of knives. He lays one hand gently on a silver fan of blades; the other hand, around Pili's shoulders, pulls her close. Guillermo is a Gypsy man of about forty, perhaps forty-five, with slicked hair and a large, waxed moustache. He is debonair and smarmy in manner, very good-looking, dressed in well-cut trousers and a white dress-shirt. The two of them laugh and talk as I change the aperture and focus. Before I click the shutter button the second time, Guillermo turns his head and looks at Pili looking at the camera, and I snap away a couple more times, caught by the tender expression on his face. He no longer smiles at the camera, but at her, Pili, pulling her closer still, and what I see also makes me smile: he so obviously loves her. If we had the time or the inclination, or the courage, would every new human face move us or make us afraid?

We leave the knife stall and return to Pili's lace curtains. I use up the full roll of film. "It's finished. No tengo más."

"Bueno. That's a lot, isn't it? How many do you think we took?"

"Over twenty. Twenty-five. Maybe twenty-seven."

"And certainly some will be good."

"I think so."

"So how much does the roll of film cost?" She

unbuttons the breast pocket of her coat and pulls out a worn black change purse.

"Oh, no, don't give me any money. If the developing is very expensive—"

She interrupts me. "No, I will have them developed. My son knows someone in Bilbao. I would like to pay you for the cost of the film."

Somehow I think I've misunderstood. Standing behind her table once more, she begins to put the lace curtain packages into a wooden crate. Her dark hands are wrinkled but soft-looking, as though oiled. I put my own hands on my camera, which is hanging around my neck. I feel slightly possessive. "It would be easier if I just develop the film here in town, and then I'll bring you the photos."

She heaves the box of lace curtains onto a hidden shelf on the other side of the table. She says, "But I would like to keep the negatives."

She uses the word "negatives" like a professional. I laugh, still confused. "Wait a minute. These photographs . . . I took these photographs. There are seven or eight that aren't of you. I'll be happy to give you copies, but why do you want the negatives?"

"I'll be happy to give *you* copies, but I don't want my face to be out wandering in the world without me. I asked you if you took good photographs. You asked to take photographs of me. I've said I'll pay you for the film and give you some copies. And I'll give you the other pictures, the pictures of Daniel."

"Daniel?"

"The accordion boy."

"Oh." I am at a loss for words. Her lace curtains are packed away. She bends down with a padlock and disappears for a moment. But I barely have a moment to think before she bends upright again and walks out from behind the table.

She is so small, yet she looks up at me with a firm jaw, conviction set in her entire face. The whites of her eyes are slightly yellow. "Pili . . . I'm not accustomed to giving my film away."

The corners of her mouth turn down, her lips and eyebrows lift up: the facial shrug. "I'm not accustomed to giving my face away."

We stand there for a moment, staring at each other, on a small island between laughter and irritation. It is clear that offering her a danish, chocolate or jelly-filled, would be a useless manoeuvre. I take the camera in my hands and begin to rewind the film. She smiles. As I hand her the roll, I say, "Do you mind if I ask you a personal question?"

This request surprises her. She even frowns. (She's taking away my Kodak Gold film and she doesn't want to answer one small question. What a tough woman.) But she says, "All right. Ask."

"Your eyebrows are so black. Do you dye them?"

She smiles as she smiled for the camera, her face released, clear. "No! And you are tonta and maleducada for asking an old woman like me a question like that." *Tonta* and *maleducada*. Silly and rude.

The origin of gang rape

BETWEEN THE POST office and the market-place opens a wide, arched passageway, almost an alley, into the next block of shops and apartment buildings.

Almost everyone in the town walks through that passageway a few times a week. Gypsy children often sell garlic and hair ribbons there, sitting on the back steps to the market with their baggy acrylic sweaters stretched over their big knees. The best graffiti is written on the dirty concrete building that forms the south side of the corridor. Twice, early in the morning, I have found and thrown away the used needles of the heroin addicts who go there at night in search of darkness.

Some days, if the wind is right, the arched tunnel floods with the scent of fresh bread. A bakery in the next street opens at five every day. More likely than not, the passageway smells of human urine. Two bars burrow into the walls of the opposing buildings. Their bartenders resemble each other in many ways.

Both are good-looking, physically meticulous men in their late fifties or early sixties. Both wear spotless white shirts with black arm bands, white aprons, black trousers. Both ignore the filthy toilets in their bars, a fact which inspires even their most timid customers to urinate outside under the stone arches.

The bar closest to the market and post office is frequented by old men. The other bar, closer to the next street, is patronized by young men and a very few hard-looking young women.

Everyone who uses the corridor passes these places. They hurry through the invisible clouds of urine; they read the graffiti on the walls. I have watched the bartenders hose down the reeking cement and cobblestones, but they never attempt to wash away or paint over the graffiti as other shopkeepers do. The graffiti is supposed to be there. The slogans are written in Spanish and in another, more difficult language: Basque, *Euskara*, a tongue laden with x's and z's, full of long words that seem to be composed without vowels. The origins of the Basque language are unknown, as are the origins of the people who speak it. What does the Basque graffiti say? I don't know. The bright red and green graffiti in Spanish reads, *Sabes que el gobierno de España tortura a los hombres? No tienen derecho! Basta ya. No olvidar.*

Do you know that the Spanish government tortures men?

They have no right.

Enough already.

Don't forget.

Sometimes there are long lists of names with reproduced photographs pasted over the dirty walls, rows and rows of small faces. If you read the fine print, you discover that the men and women in the poster have fled illegally to France or have been imprisoned for sympathizing or possibly working with ETA, the Basque separatist organization. ETA actively uses terrorist tactics to further its cause. To quell those tactics, the Spanish government and national police force actively use or have used torture, detention without arrest, and arrest without due process in cases involving ETA members or sympathizers. Many of the people who go to the young people's bar on one side of the passageway are known supporters of ETA, or at least vocal Basque nationalists. Many of the old men who go to the bar on the other side fought against Franco in the Spanish Civil War, or lived in exile in France until he died. Like many of their younger townspeople, they are opposed, in some way, to Spanish Socialist rule.

Although the old men are thinner and quieter than the young men, they seem more solid, as if their years have given them physical density. The old men are slower, darker in their long overcoats and black berets. Their dignity is impossible to ignore, even when they are frail and walk with canes. The young men, whose dominant characteristics are anger and an enormous, confused energy, do not have such dignity. Until I came here and saw nineteen-year-olds scream about the massacre at Guernica and what happened to their parents and grandparents during the civil war, I did not really understand what history means to most of the world. When I listen to the young men talk about the president, about the strikes, about the Guardía Civil, even about the bastard who lives upstairs, I feel afraid. As they stoke up their own and each other's emotions and bravado, I often think, Ah, here it is, the origin of gang rape. At these times, the tension in the air always has something violently sexual in it. In the name of Basque nationalism, they demonstrate repeatedly and unconsciously the terrifying power of the pack. I wonder if ETA is made up of similar people, whose fury must be directed not only at their government, but at this *time,* our own era of failure and violent upheaval.

The rope, yanked

I PREFER TALKING to the old men, who, angry and disappointed as they may be, seem kinder. Together with their unsatisfactory compromises, the old men have made their peace. What they want more than anything—even revenge—is to tell their stories. So I listen to them. History books line the shelves of their bones. Like babies' eyes, their irises are often an indistinguishable colour. They are the old sons of Euskadi's green and tumbling stone-gray hills, its mountain *caserios,* its cold white and blue Cantabrian waters. I've tried to imagine how they looked thirty, forty, fifty years ago, but it's impossible to peel the decades away and find the careless lips, the thick hair, the smooth faces.

I see them often in the passageway that is almost an alley, a tunnel scented by piss and fresh bread, decorated with graffiti and the sunflower-seed shells of the Gypsy children. After leaving the post office today, I pass Señor Aracama, who is quitting the bar and going home for lunch. He nods to me and asks how I am.

Muy bien, I reply, and ask him about his garden on the outskirts of town. Tucking his loaf of bread under his arm, he begins to gesticulate with his hands, describing how a neighbour's horse recently ran through one of his fences. A face will lose decades for a brief moment when it begins to move and speak, but the hands stay old. Señor Aracama has lived through a world war, a civil war, the deaths of a loved wife and a son. His hands are thick with scars. Time is like a wet rope that has burned his palms and knuckles, cut the insides of his fingers.

Every moment is a length of that rope, yanked again. We can do nothing with time but hold on tighter, feel it more, let it pull us where it may.

Old men and Maru

WHAT IS SO heart-rending about very old men?

My roommate Maru says, in her feisty, matter-of-fact way, that the last people who should move me to tears in this world are old men—they were all young men once, *cabrones!*—but the fact remains that their fragility sometimes makes me wince. Old women, no matter how frail-looking, always seem tougher, at least here in the Basque country. When I pass old women in the street, they meet my eyes squarely, and smile or not, but their physical bearing says, "I know, I understand this, my crumbling, beautiful body. Be happy you're young, but don't be smug. And get that look of pity off your face before I hit you with my umbrella." Whereas the old men seem bewildered by and even afraid of what time has done to their bodies. Some of them shuffle and cane through the streets like timid children with white hair.

Speaking of hair, Maru has cut off her gorgeous

dark blonde locks and dyed the spiky remains flaming red. Her sculpture teacher swore at her when he saw it. Señora Echevarria, the woman who rents us the apartment and lives next door, asks me every day in her high, uncomprehending voice, "¿Porqué tenía que hacer eso? ¿Porque? ¿Porque? Las chicas formales no tienen pelo rojo. Porqué lo hacía?" Nice girls don't have red hair.

I came home and the whole place reeked of chemicals. I thought Maru was mixing paints or cleaning brushes, but when I went into her studio, there she was, almost bald, looking as though she'd just stuck her head into a can of blood. All she said by way of explanation was, "I have to wait half an hour, and I'm starving. Could you run down to Maritxa's and get me a croissant with ham and cheese? There is nothing to eat in this house but tofu and carrots!"

We're going to San Sebastian for the weekend to visit her parents. I have no idea what they will say. In the end, it will somehow come back to me—the foreign influence, the *señorita* whose earrings never match, the one with the accent. Maru's parents are good, traditional Basques. They like me, but they're not entirely sure if their daughter and I should be living together, sharing a bathroom, drinking from the same glasses.

A shrunken human head

MARU IS THE perfect roommate. We both disappear into our respective rooms and work for hours. She paints on one side of this big apartment, I write on the other side. Overtired, full of unpredictable, nervous energy, we reconvene in the kitchen to create masterpiece soups and curries. Most other meals tend to be some combination of canned tuna, apples, wine, cheese, and/or bread. And the walnuts and raisins Maru's aunt Charo sends from Irun. Maru is the perfect roommate because she is even more frugal than I am. Last month we competed to see how little money we could spend on food. She won by a thousand pesetas so I had to buy her a bottle of wine.

It's chilly these days, often colder in our apartment than it is outside. We walk around the house wrapped in sweaters and robes, wool socks and caps. Today, during our coffee-break, we sit and admire the grease stains on the wall above the gas stove.

Maru says, "Da Vinci drew inspiration from the water stains on his ceiling."

"He did, did he? I hope you're not telling me to write a poem about our greasy wall."

"Of course not. I think you should write an ode to that lettuce we forgot in the bottom of the fridge."

"That's not a lettuce! That's a shrunken human head! Our landlady's."

"That explains why we haven't heard her for so long."

Our landlady and her husband try to scream each other to death at least once a week. Those furious voices vibrating through the wall scare both of us, so we joke about them.

Maru sticks her fingers in her water glass, flicks water at me, and crosses herself.

I wipe the water spots off my glasses with the edge of my cotton scarf. "What did you do that for?"

"I blessed your soul," she explains, with only a hint of a smile on her mouth. I love her.

La niña gitana

I AM NOT telling you everything. You're getting my good side, almost all the time. A lover once sent me a postcard that read, "I am whiny, moody, difficult, opinionated, stubborn, sarcastic. I'm warning you." I never saw him again.

If I tell you the truth, will you stop reading? What about the stories I leave out, the omissions, the acts I edit from my own life? Here is one, and years from now—I know this—a certain slant of light or a child's brown forehead or an ochre shade of fabric will make me remember, and feel ashamed.

We have the light of deep afternoon, the light photographers love, and we have an unexpected wave of heat from North Africa. Summer once more, for days at a time, although we know the winter rains will come again, accompanied by those ice-haunted, humid mornings. But not now. Today we are at Aitor's little bar in the *paseo,* Albero is hauling out the white patio chairs, Oskar is asking where his guitar pick is, he's learned another Elvis Presley song. (And, for a Basque man, he does a great imitation of the King.) Albero turns and kisses Julia on the cheek as he hands a package of cigarettes across the table. Lourdes with her blonde-highlighted hair and her coal-black eyebrows is to my left, her head thrown back in the sun. These lovely ones, these women, these men. I receive the weightless green scent of Estebelith's cologne and then, in a wave, the smell of bachelors, their aftershaves as intense as their glances. But I adore them because they know how to laugh.

The slenderness of wrists and wineglass stems fills the afternoon. We eat olives and drink La Rioja, now we are eating calamari and drinking beer, now we will order some *tortilla de patata* and a pitcher of sangria. In the summer, I went swimming with these ones, I went to the Lake Elosu with them and fell in love with a singer and a sleek yellow dog. Now, almost every weekend, I eat and drink with at least one of them. They have found me, or I have had the luck to find them. They give my days shape and leave me with nothing more than a few new words and the reassuring warmth of their voices, which I need more than anything else. Now we sit around the white table, pulling sweaters and jackets over our shoulders because the sun has dropped away behind the buildings. Instead of calming us, the gathering cold makes us talk more, compels Aitor to turn up the music, pushes us to remember jokes and stories we've never told. We try desperately to believe in the illusion of summer.

Oskar claps in a Flamenco rhythm when a small group of Gypsies comes around the corner of the *paseo*. They appear like a theatre troupe, carrying two guitars and a mandolin. The women, with their coloured skirts and shawls, are the true madonnas of summer. The band approaches the small plaza where we are sitting, just off the main thoroughfare of the *paseo*. Either they are traditional people *del camino,* who dress up whenever they're in town, or they are sedentary Gypsies in from Bilbao for a party, because they are decked out in fine fashion. The women are wearing red, black, dark purple skirts, crinolines, decorated black scarves over their heads, snakes and clasps and braids of silver and gold jewellery. The men are in dark suits. They all wear hats. Children come running ahead of them, three boys and a very small girl, only ten or eleven, a miniature version of her mother, wearing a layered ochre skirt, a black cotton blouse, a scarf over her head.

The boys run ahead, down the *paseo*, but the girl turns in at the long stone-lined flower bed, and walks toward our table. We are still laughing and talking, but we become quieter as she approaches and touches each of us with her eyes. This is the first moment I feel something, but I ignore it and sit up to pour out the rest of the sangria. (If we had the time or the inclination, or the courage, would every new human face move us or make us afraid?) There is nothing unanticipated in her walk, no discernible sign in her body or her face. We know this is another *niña gitana* come to ask us for money.

With this realization, the lull in the conversation fills. The little girl, with her exotic clothes and steady stone-black eyes, ceases to command our attention. She becomes part of the summer illusion again. (This is how quickly we deny people their humanity. Children transform into scenery in half a breath, and disappear.) *La niña gitana* comes to the table without saying anything. We expect her to speak in a dramatic, breathy child's voice. "Señora, por favor, por Díos, que me ayudes un poquito—" But even when she stands in front of us—her narrow-chinned face level with Jorge's shoulder, because he's sitting closest to her—this hooded child says nothing.

Her parents and older relatives stop walking. They are on the other side of the *paseo,* in front of the stationery shop, waiting for her. Quietly. This motionlessness is a detail we scarcely notice, though it must bother us unconsciously, because Gypsies rarely stand so still, so silent, waiting for their children. They don't even speak among themselves; they don't even smoke. The Basque people who promenade up and down the *paseo* arc carefully around the Gypsies, staring as they pass, glancing over the flowers to our table, where the daughter begs for money.

Her hands form the shape of an almond, pale heels of the palms close, fingertips together, as though she's caught a small frog. She comes to each of us in turn, opening her hands to show what she has inside.

Are there still lepers in Spain? I don't know. I don't think so. Is this what leprosy looks like? No, no, not at all, not really. But that's what we're thinking. We're thinking *plague.* We glance at her hands and look at each other and shake our heads in her face. Her palms and fingers are covered in large boils, with dark red skin around the edges. She opens her palms like an oyster shell, making a blistered pink bowl for any money we might want to give her. We see that the boils continue up her wrists, under the cotton shirt sleeves. Are they burns? No. Blisters the size of silver dollars, the size of halved limes bubble up between her fingers, onto the tops of her hands. What affliction is this? All I know is that none of my friends will give her money. They are afraid of accidentally touching her, being infected. The thought passes in and out of my head like smoke, You could just drop the coins into her hands, you wouldn't have to touch her. Like any moment of judgement, this one is over in seconds. Oskar, Albero, Julia, Jorge. They don't give her anything. She passes me. I don't give her anything. She moves around the table opening and closing her hands. Rotten butterfly wings. Lourdes grimaces and says, "Qué te vayas de aqui." Go away from here. After half-circling the table, and receiving nothing, not even a telltale reach for a wallet or pocket, the girl turns her back on us.

We lose our appetite for talk. The sun, disappeared behind the buildings, has left us in a flood of shadow. The girl walks back the way she came. When she reaches the group of waiting adults, her mother bends and kisses the scarfed head—

I look away when Aitor comes out of the bar, rubbing his hands, asking us to think about bringing the chairs back into the bar, it's too cold to sit outside.

As the Gypsies continue walking in silence, in such uncommon solemnity, I realize that they've been to a funeral. *Slap,* heel of the hand to the forehead. Obviously. That is why they're so solemn, why they're dressed up. How stupid of me, of us all. They are even walking back from the direction of the cemetery.

What would it have meant to them if we had given the girl some money? Would it have been a good omen, a sign? What kind of evil wish do we cast upon the beggar when we offer nothing at all? What wish do we cast upon ourselves?

Latin lovers

PERHAPS I WILL write a book with this title and my politically correct Canadian friends will never speak or write to me again. I have a friend who says that the term "Latin lovers" is discriminatory. All right. A disclaimer: not all Latin men are like the ones I keep meeting. When I meet a substantial number of these other men, I will write about them. But now, I will write about Latin lovers in general.

They are men who assume I will sleep with them, providing they want me to. Conversely, if *I* want *them* to sleep with *me,* they suggest I be more subtle, lest I acquire the reputation of an over-aggressive slut.

I've told Spanish men that it's classless to assume that foreign women fuck on demand, but they just grin and give each other knowing looks.

Why do so many men here think they are so desirable?

Why do they all want to marry virgins?

Where does it come from, this idea that I (or any

other foreign woman) want to take them home and into bed?

The Basques could choke a horse with their arguments about why they are different, distinct from the Spanish race, but when it comes to sexuality, they *do* fit all the Latin clichés, with one difference. The northern, noble, somewhat reserved Basques fit them more quietly. They are not big whistlers.

Latin lovers. I must be exaggerating. Surely it's my fault. Isn't it always? I must be going to the wrong bars, the wrong beaches, the wrong movie theatres, the wrong parties. I must be walking down the wrong streets, buying bread from the wrong bakers.

Latin lovers belong to movies that none of us directed. I'll have to remember that when I become entranced, wet with longing for those miles of Mediterranean skin, those amber eyes. If a woman's body were juice, they would suck it up through a straw. Slurp: she would disappear. This is the life, say the tourist brochures, but there's a hidden price to pay for the warm loaves of bread and the pure dark chocolate.

Okay, I admit it: leather riding boots turn me on, and I adore the almost genetic ability these men have to play guitars and sing in tune and stand around looking as though they're good in bed. I love their *maleness* even when I see through it, recognize it as bravado, machismo, noise. Sometimes I don't think of it as bravado at all; I think of it as sexy.

But most of the time, I catch myself thinking, If only they wouldn't speak. If only I didn't know Spanish, how genuinely attractive I would find many of them. But they do speak, a lot. And—more disheartening—I understand what they say. When men try to get a woman into bed here, it is almost always a game played with affection, camaraderie, and a humorous foreknowledge that they will probably lose. Sometimes it's fun. Very rarely is it threatening. Male strangers here, for all their come-ons, are less genuinely aggressive than male strangers at home. But they are a thousand times more persistent and tiresome. (So, in the end, despite the humour and the salacious grins, isn't their aggression simply *different?*)

I've seen them in their homes, too, married with 2.3 kids and a nice car. Latin lovers never know where anything is! I refer to pots, pans, towels, children's clothes. Their elegant wives polish shoes and carry coffee trays and spread their legs, first for the men, then for the children who come after. Sometimes those tasks seem identical: they begin one night and end fifty years later, when the body has stretched like a leather sack and begins to tear at the seams. Days after male friends fuck several different tourists in Barcelona, they talk about the great culture of the Mediterranean and assure me that I come from a race of barbarians.

What would it be like to have a real lover here? (Instead of the ethereal ones I send home before they fall asleep? *Pon-te las botas y a la puerta!*) To live with a man who resides on the inside of a male-dominated culture is to live that man's story. This applies especially, I think, to foreign women, who are doubly removed from cultural power: I am not male, I am not even native female. The men are the main characters here. Women have supporting roles. (Is this true or is this how I perceive things from the outside? Yet many women here agree with me.)

I wonder what would happen to me if I stayed here for two, three, ten, fifteen years. I would change. I have already changed. I listen smilingly, I accept their bullshit, I give in sometimes and, out of lust or loneliness, take them home. But forget about my lust and pay attention to the *giving in*. A woman who has sex with a man is giving in. It's never verbalized, it's never mentioned, but there it is the morning: the sense that something has been taken away from me, I've been had, literally and figuratively, they've *won*. As men add notches to their belts, women shrink. Am I shorter now than I was when I arrived in Spain? Is it like this in Canada? Am I just forgetting? I have to doubt myself; I always have to wonder. What I know absolutely is that this culture (every culture) is bigger than I am. I can push against it as hard as I want, but even my resistance moulds me in ways that I am powerless to control.

Tristeza, evening

I CAN BARELY find the energy to walk but I know if I don't walk, I will cry. In the worn light just before darkness, I leave the house in shoes not meant for cliffs. Out of the town and up, up, onto the open fields that in turn plunge down to the ocean. It's dark now, windy. If I walked over the edge, how long would it take for my body to wash up? And what about the rest of me? No, no, of course I'm not contemplating suicide, but it's a curious question. When we're dead our bodies disintegrate, disappear, but where do *we* go?

I walk for a long time, this will be an all-nighter. I push my heart into my feet and keep it there. If you walk on your heart long enough, it goes numb. The cliff paths lead me up and down, along the savage edge of the Atlantic. Hundreds of feet below me, the waves crash in like black witches liquified and furious, rushing though the night with their white hair blowing back. The wind shakes my shoulders, knots my hair. The wind is the ocean without water, storming. If I had a moon, I would be able to see the paleness of the raw cliffs, the strata of rock and earth banded one above the other. But it's so dark I trip on the pathway stones and stumble into thistles. A rat and I scare each other senseless, jump backwards, and continue on our nocturnal haunts.

When I get past the old gunner bunkers, I stop, climb a small hill, and close my eyes. I stand in the folding dark in my own darkness for a long time. When I finally open my eyes, I am surprised because the stars are there now, out above the ocean, suddenly luminous.

It's dark on this edge of the earth, but look at the stars. Tonight the sky is brighter than the little Basque town will ever be, held as it is between the fog of the sea and the white mist of mountains. This sky, deeper than any ocean. I stare until my neck is sore. To the humans beneath them, stars have always intimated other lives. Depending on the culture, these other lives take any number of imagined forms. For reasons I don't fully understand, I believe the stars themselves are people, the infinite lives of all time, past, present, future.

What of the present? Today was a broken day. I went out this morning and found a cat dead in the *paseo*, the greenish foam of poison around its mouth. And then the two women in the market-place, screaming at each other. In the newspaper, another policeman shot, uselessly, by ETA. When I was six years old, my sister predicted that I would live in Spain, but she is not alive now to receive my letters.

Again, I lift my head up to the sky. Science has its own vocabulary, its own explanations. I have my truth. The stars I see are alive.

This story has an epigraph

THERE ARE STORIES we like to tell and stories we tell reluctantly, in low voices. There are stories we never tell, because we barely know them ourselves. Then there are the stories we are breathing, our lives, which make so little sense in the moment.

I am beginning, finally, to learn a hard lesson. We can never know the truth of our days. The truth is always behind us, already accomplished, already there, but we have eyes for the horizon only. Years later we turn around and find the truth following us like a patient stray dog. Years later we see it: the clear vision of our lives now, what we truly need, who we really are.

From *The Five Nations,* a dusty book I discovered in the basement of my childhood. I was eleven years old. Only now do I understand. It was the book where everything began:

Who holds the rein upon you?
The latest gale let free.
What meat is in your mangers?
The glut of all the sea . . .

Who come they for your calling?
No wit of man may save.
They hear the loosed white horses
above their father's grave . . .

'Twixt tide and tides returning
Great store of newly dead
The bones of those that faced us
The hearts of those that fled . . .

—from "The White Horses"
by Rudyard Kipling

If you do not have a map   a story

A WOMAN CAME to this place once, and disappeared.

How easy it is to get lost in the streets of these foreign cities. You can go missing if you arrive in the dark during a thunderstorm.

If you fall out of the train exhausted by hunger.

If you do not have a map.

And she did not have a map, my sister. The geometry of directions, even of simple left and right, was difficult for her. It doesn't surprise me that these streets of dark buildings and black-mouthed churches swallowed her whole.

Northern Spain, the Basque country. *Las siete calles de Galea.* The seven streets of the city intersect seven other streets, and those streets spawn cramped passageways and damp paths that run along the convent walls, around *la plaza mayor,* over the brown river, into *el barrio* called Lobero, where some of the lost people may be encountered, if not found. The streets spread like a spider's web spun in shadow, endlessly linked, half-invisible, a marvellous, dangerous architecture.

Her last postcard, dated the sixteenth of June, says nothing of danger:

> How to name the colour of light on the sea? Not silver, not gold, not green. How does the wind feel on my shoulders at night, after screwing on the beach? (Then we fell asleep in the sand—have you ever fallen asleep in the sand? You wake cold and heavy, like a stone with eyes.)
>
> Julie, it's so beautiful here, almost obscene—that it could be this way—I don't understand it. Can you own what you don't understand?
>
> I've seen white horses running on the cliffs above the ocean. Really, I have.
>
> I love you. Please don't be angry—could you send me some money? Even $100. Please.
>
> Eva

What did you do with the money? It wasn't enough to buy a white horse, or to pay a month's rent, or even to indulge in a decadent weekend, pleasure nights with friends, bottles of wine and the best seafood on the Cantabrian coast. But you could have bought a map. Several maps, an atlas, a compass for your journeys against the dark. I sent you two hundred dollars, poste restante, an international money order with calligraphy in twelve languages around its border. I remember the envelope, I remember the stamp, I remember the bracelet I wore on my wrist that day.

This is what love comes to, Eva.

It comes at midnight to a city of labyrinths, years later, still crying your name.

A BLACK STRAY and its smaller yellow companion cross the plaza at a slow, purposeful trot. Clearly they know where they're going, in this silence of late afternoon siesta. Their long nails click and lift off the cobblestones. No wind. Beggars curl like sleeping snails in the cathedral archway, filthy jackets pulled over their heads. Even the resonant bronze clang of the church bell fails to rouse them. The chimes ring out above the buildings, waking the bells of other churches in other streets, until all of them are tolling, lifting and shaking the hot silence. The bells are inescapable here. They sound the quarter-hour, the half-hour, the many, many hours late at night, an echo of God's ghost stumbling over the city.

I've been here long enough to know my way, like the dogs, who don't even look up at me as our paths intersect in the centre of the plaza. Across the main thoroughfare, under the high green arches of plane trees, across the bridge—don't look at the filthy water—up the narrow street on the north side, not quite in the Lobero quarter but beside it, close enough to smell it. Pass through invisible clouds of vapour: boiled cauliflower, cat spray, crackling olive oil, dog excrement, and, under a constricted stone archway, human urine. I breathe through my mouth until the end of the street, where I turn left, sharply—and a police officer coming from the op-posite direction startles a gasp out of me. He inclines his head but doesn't speak or smile. Located halfway down this new, wider dead-end lane are the Guardia Civil offices.

THE INSPECTOR HAS the photographs. The vital statistics. Such distastefully clinical words, but how perfect they are in their irony. From the Latin, *vita,* for life, the Spanish *vida.* Of course the French, *c'est la vie.* They are so vital, these statistics, the colour of the eyes, the hair, the irreplaceable contour of the chin, the height and the weight.

I brought the dental records, too, those frightening x-rays of the lower skull. Without flesh, our jaws are frozen in perpetual, macabre laughter. I brought at least two dozen papers in three dull brown file folders. I had to explain and argue to get these documents, as if anyone else cared about the life they recorded. The inspector has buried all this evidence in his own brown file folders. The only thing I refused to give him were the postcards: one from London, one from Amsterdam, two from Paris, the last one from this place.

Imagine, Inspector Hernandez. She was not always invisible. Her feet left footprints when she walked on wet earth, even when she weighed less than one hundred pounds. Something to know her by: the white scars on the backs of her thighs, like the score-marks on uncooked loaves of bread. She was taller than I am. She measured five feet, six and three-quarter inches. *Centimetros? No lo sé.* Long dark hair, with auburn brightness, naturally curly; brown eyes; pale complexion, a scar through her left eyebrow. A childhood accident? On a bicycle, or was it the stairs, or was it a slamming door?

I hear the questions you don't ask, Inspector. Your eyes are the questions, each angle of your motionless face has the bony, immovable weight of a question. Yet you never ask with words. I told you, "She was never well, she was never happy," and you nodded. But I hear what you must be thinking. It's what I think myself.

Six years. Why did you leave it so long?

Surely you see that I am fairly young; I was at school. I didn't have much money.

But six years. Your parents, what about your mother, your father?

You won't understand, Inspector Hernandez. My whole life, I've never understood. They washed their hands of her like you wash your hands after gutting a fish, a grimace on your face.

Six years. Do you know how long that is?

I told you the truth, I was busy. A scholarship at a university on the other side of the country, in Montreal. Then a fellowship, so I stayed on, continued studying. I was far enough away. You can't imagine how big Canada is, Quebec is almost a different country. The Quebecois are like the Basques.

But there are no political terrorists in Canada, are there?

No. No political terrorists. The Quebecois simply want to separate from the rest of the dominion. That's what I love about Quebec; that's why I went there. Eva fled to Europe; I went to McGill.

Canada is a beautiful country, isn't it?

Yes, Inspector, very beautiful, but don't be fooled. You might think it's mountains and forests and rivers named by noble savages but the savages who live there now wear business suits and look so clean, so clean you know it can't be real. Europe may be dirty, but in North America we're just good at hiding our garbage. We have more room.

How easy it is to get lost in the streets of these foreign cities. How much easier, though, to lose yourself in the beige maze of a suburb. You can't imagine them, Inspector, the houses gulping down the earth, gulping down the hills, swallowing ground squirrels, young trees, children.

Don't you miss your home?

Oh, I love that sky blue and tall as mountains, I love those mountains wider and stronger than all the hands of men, but I've never lived in the sky. I've never lived on a mountain.

Six years. Didn't you think of her? Six years.

Yes, I thought of her. I waited for her. I wrote letters telling her to come home. And I thought she would. I waited for her to appear carrying a suitcase and a grocery bag full of apples and bread. I'm still waiting, Inspector. Here I am.

WHEN I ENTER the office, he's already lifted his eyes from the papers on the black desk. He looks exactly as he looked the first time I came here, and the second, and the third. He never changes. Cool despite the heat of the second floor, dark, clean-shaven, very still. His hands clasped on top of the desk. He is a spare man with hazel eyes set in a wide, bony face. Despite his leanness, he looks heavy; iron fills the centre of his bones. Not only his eyes, but also his shoulders and chest and torso seem to stare, gauging my movements by their motionlessness. A framed photograph faces him, its image hidden from view. A marble pen-holder sits to the right of the photo. Aside from these items, and the papers associated with me, his desk is bare except for a package of cigarettes and an empty espresso cup.

Today, Inspector Hernandez has nothing for me. Last week there was a possibility: an unidentified body found four years ago in a construction site outside Barcelona. But the dental records did not match up. We know now that not one of the unidentified female bodies found in Spain in the last six years was my sister. Three days before that there was a woman in a church-funded insane asylum not far from Bilbao. She fit Eva's description perfectly, but at fifteen she'd lost all her teeth to a gum disease. Eva's teeth didn't start falling out until just before she left Canada. Ten days ago, he found another woman in another insane asylum: but she didn't have Eva's identifying marks.

What do I learn from this late search among the ruins?

That we will be known by our scars.

That the ruins are wide.

The ruins are deep, buried all around us, like the remains of a great and savage empire. Kick the earth and you will find a bone. My sister was not the only one who entered without a map.

"MAY I SEE THE postcard again, the one she sent from here?"

I take the card out of my handbag and pass it over the desk. He doesn't look at the writing—he has a copy of that. He looks at the front of it, the reproduction of the black-haired Flamenco dancer in a red dress, fan in hand, the Spanish cliché. "She must have bought this at the border. Or in the interior. The Basques won't sell this sort of thing. Flamenco dancers, bull fights. Images like that piss them off. They hate those images because they can't understand them."

I stare over his polished black desk, trying not to look stunned. He normally offers nothing extra, not a single wasted word or gesture. Unlike the other people, the women at the market and the postman and the old lady who runs the pension where I'm staying, he doesn't inquire if the weather is too warm for me, if I have eaten octopus, if it is cold in Canada. His speech until now has been like his body—lean, tight, every muscle fastened to the correct bone. Now he is speaking. I am shocked. He has used the words "piss off".

"You know this already, no? We are in the Basque country, but the Basques are not Spanish." The impatience in his voice is like anger. Or is it anger? "Just as the people of Catalonia are not Spanish, but *catalan,* and the Galicians are *gallegos,* and the people of Castilla are *castellanos.* Yet of course we are all Spanish. But you know the Basques are most resistant, don't you? You know ETA, the terrorist group, they want the Basque country to separate from Spain, and so they blow up cars, murder innocent people and—"

He cuts himself off. "I am sorry. You have not read the newspaper today?"

"My Spanish is not very good."

"Of course. How stupid of me. Excuse me. Our politics have nothing to do with you, do they?

Excuse me." He passes the postcard back and clasps his hands together again. "One of our officers was shot last night, off-duty, in the old port. A friend. He had just had a drink with his brother." Inspector Hernandez turns his head toward the open window beside his desk, where nets of light sink over the tenements and shops of Lobero. This same light slants into the office, illuminating the man's face and the green threads in his irises. A vein in his forehead throbs.

"It's very strange to say these things in English. It makes them seem less true. As if I am telling a story. A friend of mine is dead. Un amigo mio está muerto." He shakes his head and looks at me again, smiling his tight smile. Knowing I am astonished by so many words, he continues, "I apologize. My profession deforms me. This place deforms me. All of us." He pulls his hand over his mouth, smoothing something sharp from his voice. "None of us is from here. We are sent here; it's like being sent to hell. The people in the Basque country hate the Guardia Civil so much that my friend's death is nothing to them. An item in the newspaper. Some bastard shot him in the back of the head." His voice has risen again. I expect him to stand up. I expect him to throw something— the espresso cup, the paperweight—out the open window, or at the wall. But his hands hold each other down. "Jesus." He yells this word in a voice that deflates to a whisper, "He worked with *young* people. His job had nothing to do with ETA."

What do they say, in Spain? "I'm sorry." He stares out the window. I blink repeatedly, trying to do the same. My eyes have become small mouths swallowing their own tears. The ruins are deep. Kick the earth and you will find a bone. Walk down any street in any city on earth and you will pass a terrorist without knowing it. But we are disciplined, the inspector and I. Our separate griefs allow us to stare hard out the window, watching the gold and red light bind every rooftop and brick wall.

Of all the animals, they say we are the only ones with an articulated language, a word for everything. Why, then, is it so difficult to speak? I would like to comfort him. He has been helping me voluntarily, he is not obliged. I would like to comfort him because I believe he is a good man, but I can only feel the hardness of the chair's edge against the backs of my thighs. The air in here is too warm, it's hard to breathe. With the whole concentrated eye of his physical being, the inspector stares out the window.

"Should I come back another day?"

"Could you?" He glances at me. "Sometime next week. There is a new investigation going on now, because of my friend's death." He spits out a laugh. "There is always a new investigation after one of us is shot. It keeps us busy. I don't even have the records from Madrid that I expected to have for you, but there was no time to call and cancel our appointment. I'm sorry you've come into the city for nothing."

I rise from my chair, putting the postcard back in my bag. "Wait. I will return your sketches. I made several copies." He reaches behind his desk and passes me the large black folder.

As I leave, quietly closing the door, I see him behind his desk, turned to the window again, motionless under the red net of dusk.

EVA, TELL ME:

Where did you buy the last postcard?

Where are the cliffs?

Did you really see those white horses?

As soon as I learned the Spanish words, I asked the old lady who rents a room to me, "Dónde estan los acantilados, los cabellos?"

She looked at me as though I were mad. "Acantilados? Cabellos?" She put a fluttery hand to her violet coiffure. "Cabellos? Cabellos de quien?"

Days later, thumbing through the dictionary, I understood my mistake. Horse in Spanish is *caballo. Cabello* means hair. This would make you laugh.

The last time we spoke, you said, "My Spanish is finally improving. It's the language of desperation, I should know how to speak it." And you laughed. Did you call before or after you sent the postcard? I can't remember. Why can't I remember details that seem important? Surely the phone call was important. Why did it seem unreal? Your voice, disembodied, belonged to no one. Is that why I've forgotten what you said, what you wanted? The last postcard, that loose blue lettering, is stronger evidence of your life. Once, you fell asleep in the sand. You saw horses running on the cliffs above the Atlantic. Were you dreaming those horses? You were probably strung out when you wrote that. You could have seen anything. You often did. But even if the words are not true, they are still real. You wrote them down, you signed your name. Where are your hands now?

So many of the little towns scattered on either side of the capital city are coastal. I stay in one of them. I have visited most of them, looking for you. I have been in bars and community clinics and all the small police stations with a photograph and photocopies and my pathetic Spanish, doing what people in movies do. Those movies about missing persons, there are so many of them, it's annoying.

I get off the local train and walk toward the ocean. June in the Basque country. June, the month you wrote on your last postcard. Sometimes it's raining; I open an umbrella. My feet get wet. Walking through the fog, I become one of those shadow-backed travellers who have come a long way and still have forever to go. Sometimes it's blankets of sunlight and blown grass, the wind warm on my face. When I get to the water's edge, I am breathless, agitated. The waves become a tide of voices. I pray you will appear. In a secret crevice of my mind, I believe you will appear, I believe it. We will laugh and hug and say to each other, "Ah, you came through, you're all right. Here you are." Later, people who listen to our story will say, "A miracle." For six years, I have envisioned this meeting, this forgiveness: that you would laugh and have arms strong enough to hug me.

Eva, so much has happened during your absence. I've read a thousand books. I've gotten my degree and completed my thesis and I've been offered jobs that are offered only to sane, well-adjusted women. Six years. The texture of my skin has changed. Six years of lovers leaving, returning, leaving, like migratory birds. Two years ago, I cut my hand at the cutting board. Eight stitches. We will be known by our scars. Every spring I plant my own herbs and a bunch of tomatoes in my tiny front garden. And they grow like children. Six years of nights and breakfast plates, new telephone books, this postcard stuck in the frame of my bedroom mirror. Six years, and I still have it, the dream of you crying below me in a place like a well, no windows and cold walls.

At last I have made this journey toward your voice. I walk to the edge of the ocean again and again. What do I find on the dark sand?

Fish eyes, fish bones. Too many condoms for a Catholic country. Bottles without messages. Shoes without feet. A rotting gull.

When will I meet your shadow? When will I find a bit of your hair or skin?

WHEN I GET home—to the pension where I stay—I sit down on the soft bed and open the folder of sketches. They were made with good ink and have not faded much.

A woman stands, sits, turns her head and shoulders to the wall. The rib-cage is visible through the flesh of her back, two warped ladders, two ladders left out in a storm. She lies coiled in a foetal position on a bed with flowered sheets. Her hair is like a horse's tail after elaborate plaits have been undone: twisted gleam to the small of her back, around her shoulders, spiralling across her face. Big, black-rimmed eyes, though these eyes are often closed.

In most of the fifteen sketches, she is naked, often drawn at a three-quarter angle from the back, clutching her knees with her arms. Daddy-long-legs' arms, too thin, impossibly thin for big, fat North America. The elbows are disproportionately large mallets of bone. The spine is a starving snake, every vertebrae knotted, stretched tight under tight skin. Thighs press against shrunken but strangely girlish breasts.

The carved face strikes the eye. Once she was beautiful but in the sketches she is no longer quite human. She is mythic, she has become everything at once: a child, the young woman she is, a shrivelled crone. I see her, Eva, but I also see the other lives lost inside her. Her features are frightening but terribly familiar. Certainly Inspector Hernandez has seen them before. They are all over Spain, in the churches and sanctuaries of the smallest villages, in the hospitals and cramped streets and bars of every city. Eva has the ignited black eyes and keen cheekbones of a Christ, of a martyred saint, of one more heroin addict after the feast. When she hugs her knees, her shoulderblades protrude from her back like sprouting wings.

HIS VOICE ECHOES in the stairwell. A man's voice like a fist banging down the walls above the stairs. I hold on tightly to the banister, caught in this voice, unable to lift my feet, unable to move. But I cannot cry here.

It's Inspector Hernandez, on the telephone, yelling. He speaks too quickly for me to understand anything but I recognize anger, frustration, disgust. His office is at the top of the stairs; if I go up, he will see me immediately. I pause on the landing between floors, running my hand up and down the wooden banister, wondering if I should go back down and wait in the lower office. I still understand almost nothing, but the words beat around my head, on my back. I start to step quietly down the stairs.

"Miss Camden? Are you there?" The inspector's voice.

Did he see me? How could he have seen me? I haven't made a sound.

"Miss Camden?" My hand runs up and down the banister.

"Are you there? If you're there, please come up. I'm almost finished here."

By the time I reach the top of the stairs, he's hung up the telephone. "Please sit down. I'm sorry, did I scare you just now? You're very pale."

"How did you know I was here?"

"Your habit is to come on time, even two minutes early." He looks at his watch. "It is seven minutes past five. You heard me talking and so you did not want to come up. Did you stand on the stairs for a long time?"

"I'm sorry, I wasn't listening, I couldn't understand any—"

"No apologies, please. _I_ am sorry. It's bad form, shouting on the phone. I told you last week about my friend's death. For six more weeks I will argue with the chief of the Basque police force about the priority of the investigation." He inhales quickly, as though pulling words in his mouth back down his throat. "But none of that concerns you." The smooth hands tighten around each other. "I have the photographs for you from Barcelona and Madrid. Before you look at them, I should tell you that I also spoke to Itxiar Madariaga, the woman who runs the needle program in the city. The program is new—barely a year old—but Pili was a nurse at the public clinic here in Lobero. She knows the community very well. I showed her Eva's photographs and your sketches.

She will post them and get in touch with me if she hears anything. I gave her the number of the pension where you stay; I hope that's all right?"

"Of course."

"She'll send copies of the photograph and sketches to associated clinics in Barcelona, Madrid, and Sevilla. Here is her name and number, if you want to call her yourself." The inspector passes me a sheet of yellow paper. When I take it from his hand, he looks at me for a long moment, his expression open, tentative. He wants to say something else.

But he stands up, lightly taps the end of a cigarette on his desk. His hands look as though they might have stage make-up on them, they are so flawlessly smooth, every nail filed, shiny. Strong, muscular hands, but I would never have guessed that he was a policeman. "I'll leave you to look through these photographs. It's unlikely we'll find anything there, but we can try. There is no Camden in any of the records, but when foreigners have no papers, they are sometimes imprisoned under assumed names. It's happened before. If you find anything, just come down the hall. I'm in the office on the left."

The inspector puts a large square book on the desk in front of me. Over four hundred photographs of foreign women who have been or are in Spanish prisons. I stare down one row, another, another. Six photographs in each line, each page six lines deep, covered in plastic. The odd page taped at the edges, as if someone has paused, unsure, and picked meditatively at the lamination: is that her, or isn't it? Do I recognize that face?

I stare at each woman. Each woman, trapped in

the tiny cell of her black and white photograph, stares through me. No, not her. No. No. No. No. Ugly and attractive women, with sharp faces, with faces half-entombed by fat, with hair chopped across their foreheads or pulled back, bound up. You, and you, and you: What did you do? What did they do to you?

My eyes run over the rows, down the pages. I see the women but the women stare through me, into a territory far behind. Even those with the hardest expressions look stunned, hollowed out, full of echoes. Whose daughters are these?

I sit on the other side of the inspector's desk, leaning on my elbows, head bent over their heads. Outside in Lobero, old church bells chime and chime a new hour. Every woman is my sister but none of them has her particular roundness of cheek, nor her eyes, set slightly too far apart, with a child's long, curved eyelashes. She always looked younger than I did.

When I reach the end of the book, I close my eyes. Rows of mostly indistinct faces float in front of me, though a few of them have entered and insisted on a real place in my memory. I see their anonymous faces in detail. Why do we remember some faces and forget others?

The truth is that I barely remember Eva now. All I have left are the photographs, the sketches, a few disjointed memories from before, when we both lived at home, the first lifetime. The other images are blurred, those last two meetings, the coffee in Vancouver when we went for a walk on the beach and it started to rain. We both cried then, could not look at each other. Bad weather for distinct memories.

The last, cold time in Calgary, she was buried under wool, wouldn't take off her hat, her scarf. Almost refused to take off her gloves.

I stand up now in the inspector's sparse office and walk to the open window beside the desk. Once again, brick-coloured light falls into the room, over *el barrio* Lobero, the narrow spidering streets and those filthy bars crammed with men and women who look like spiders, thin limbs and starving black eyes. I spend evenings in those places, a photograph in one hand, a dictionary in the other, Spanish caught between my teeth. If she lived here at all, she probably lived in Lobero, in one of the looming gray tenement buildings, where the people hang their laundry to dry over the thickest traffic jams in northern Spain.

I turn around, leaning my lower back against the window sill: the inspector's desk from a different angle, his angle. What I see immediately, because I have been curious, is the photograph. A dark-haired woman and a small girl stand in the thick of summer, green grass around and sun-struck water behind. The girl's lips are stretched over her teeth, a posed grin. The woman hugs the child to her side with one arm and holds something in her other hand. Two slender ropes, or pieces of leather? They stretch away from her. I step forward, staring at the picture.

Reins. She holds a horse's reins, but the horse is outside the photograph. The woman smiles, too, but more naturally than the child. Her head is crooked a little to the left. She has a delicate, almost narrow chin, and brown eyes set a little too far apart.

They look alike, the inspector's wife and my sister. More alike than any of the women under plastic. Many Spanish women resemble Eva, if only because their hair is long and dark, and their bodies small. Superficial similarities. The inspector's wife truly looks like my sister, but her cheekbones are different, and her lips are fuller. This coincidence is eerie but unsurprising. Now I understand my first visit here, when he said there was very little he could do for me. He wanted me to talk to someone down the hall, but I pushed Eva's photograph across his desk, determined not to be sent away. After seeing her, he asked me for the other papers, the records, more pictures.

When he appears now at the door to his own office, I am not taken aback. His unblinking stares and motionless face won't make me nervous anymore. I have understood something, some secret rule he must have, a superstition about life like my own.

"You didn't find anything?" He looks at the heavy book on the desk, at the back of the picture frame, at me. "You didn't find anything?"

"No." He remains standing in his own doorway, almost awkwardly, while I stand beside his desk.

"On American television, I never see policemen drinking with the people who come to see them, but here it is common. Perhaps because we have so many bars. Or because so many of us are alcoholics." He smiles his small smile. "Can I invite you to a glass of wine?"

I nod. He takes his jacket off the coat stand and waits for me to pass through the door before turning off the light.

WE LEAVE THE police station and drive to a nicer part of the city. Businessmen and women gather here to drink and talk after work. Everyone drinks, eats olives and *pinchos,* or smokes cigarettes. Spanish wine on an empty stomach dissolves the invisible black desk. Now the inspector and I have a round slice of cool marble between us, an ashtray, small glasses. Smoke and mirrors glimmer all the way up to the high, stamped-tin ceiling. Beautiful people sit here, there, the next table over—why are they all so beautiful?—speaking, murmuring, their voices a music made without instruments.

"Can I ask you about my sister or would you rather talk about something else?"

"I didn't think we would make polite conversation. The weather is fine, I do not play golf, you are not here on vacation. What else do we have to talk about?"

"We could talk about other things—"

"But you would like to ask something about Eva." He is afraid to talk about other things, but that is what he wants to do. Other words shift and flex behind the words he speaks; other words coil up inside his throat. That's why he closes his mouth tighter and rarely shows his teeth. That's why he never uses my first name; he rarely uses my name at all. We remain separate and safe from each other even though we are spared the silence of strangers.

"We could talk about something else. If you'd like."

He smiles. The inspector often smiles, but the

look of his face has no connection to happiness. He smiles sadly, ironically, apologetically, bitterly. His smile now is one of polite disgust. "I am a poor conversationalist. I know about antique cars and my job, that is all." He looks at me and laughs an almost genuine laugh. "Don't look so sad! I won't force you to listen to me talk about either!"

"No, no. I'm curious. Not about antique cars. Can I ask you why you became a policeman?" This question is out of my mouth before I knew it was in my head.

"My father was a policeman. He wanted me to be a doctor; he sent me to school in England for three years, hoping to get the idea of being a policeman out of my head. But I was young and stubborn. I wanted to be like him. It was what I wanted from the time I was small."

"And now?"

"Now I am no longer small."

"You're not happy?"

He lights a cigarette and frowns at me. "What a strange question. Happy. What is happy? Happy is a word we use when we talk about other people. Happy. Feliz." He tastes the word in his mouth. "No lo soy. I'm not happy. But I don't trust the word."

"Why not?"

"Because the last time I felt truly happy, I was carrying a dead man's head in my hand. By the hair." He grasps the air with his elegant fingers. "Over a year ago. An ETA member. He was killed while trying to plant a bomb in a policeman's car. Of course I was happy, even happier that he was mutilated. I had to cross the street to pick up his head, and this was funny to me. I was laughing." He rubs out his cigarette, glances from the ashtray to my eyes. "Your face loses colour so easily. You look afraid."

"No. I mean, I'm not afraid of you. I'm sad. Or shocked. Or afraid of what we can become." We. The confessional no longer works. Priests and holy men can't absolve us any more. If and when we want absolution, we want it from sinners like ourselves.

"What I *have* become. I know I have said to you, My profession deforms me. So often I say this to myself. It's the same in Spanish, me deforma. To de-form, to take apart. To stop evolution and go backwards." He stares intently at the ashtray. "The first time I showered to wash a man's blood off my body, I cried and cried, standing there under the water. The next time, I cried less. Now I do not cry. Now, as I said, the deaths of certain men fill me with joy. And the deaths of my friends—I do not feel so much sadness anymore. Me siento solamente rabia. Only rage." Again he looks up, a smile covering his face. He stands up slowly, he does not want to appear abrupt. "Excuse me for a moment. I have to go to the toilet." Then he walks deftly around the small tables with their beautiful people and disappears into a hallway off the bar.

One says too much when one knows too much, it's a mathematical equation involving the brain and the mouth. At the mere threat of torture we'd tell everything, wouldn't we, Inspector? We might even like to be tortured, just to heave the facts out of us, just to be free of the truth. It almost makes you long for suffering, for being turned inside out, for *telling*.

Can pain justify this knowledge?

No.

Is cruelty what you need?

No. No, of course not.

But it's an attractive possibility, isn't it? If nothing else, agony makes you feel alive.

WHEN THE INSPECTOR returns from the toilet, he is apologetic. He has also washed his hands very well; the scent of flowery pink soap cuts through the bouquet of wine and smoke. "I rarely talk about my work, you know. Not even to my friends. It is not a heartwarming topic, is it?"

"I asked."

"I am sorry to be so personal. But it interests me."

"What, exactly?"

"How to do my job and remain a human being."

I can say nothing for a moment. I feel—ill. Ill with sadness. "You have been very human with me. Thank you."

"De nada." He smiles almost imperceptibly; possibly this is his first real smile to me. "It is not so difficult with you. You are searching for someone you've lost. There is nothing deformed there; you are trying to put something back together. A life. History. It is right to want to do this. A human act."

I drink the last of the last of the wine. "Do you want a coffee?" he asks. After ordering coffee, he leans back in his chair. "I have done all the talking now. Is there nothing you want to ask me about your sister?"

"There is something. I've been wondering about this for a while, though I don't know exactly why. I mean, it might not be important. But—the horses she wrote about in the postcard, the one sent from here? Were they real?"

"Why do you think they might not have been real?"

"Because she saw things that weren't there. She told me that it was like dreaming while being awake. Anything could happen—I mean, she saw impossible things—she hallucinated. But the hallucinations always made sense to her."

"They say it's like dreaming. You understand without knowing how."

"Even when the hallucinations terrified her, she understood them. She said she recognized them."

"It makes sense that she recognized them. They came out of her." I wait for a question, I wait for him to poke at this, try to squeeze more out of me. But he only says, "I think she saw the horses. Certainly she could have seen them; they exist. An old man owns a farm at Azkorri, the last town on the local train line." Inspector Hernandez's voice has changed, now that he's not talking about himself. It's become softer, rounder, like the bones of his face in this light.

"I don't know the old man's last name; my wife calls him Luis. His land borders the cliffs. When the spring rains come, he stables his horses. When the rains stop, he lets them out. Because they've been stabled for days, they often gallop out across the fields. A few of them are half wild." He is no longer a police inspector staring watchfully over his desk, but a man talking about white horses. While speaking, he inadvertently smoothes and unsmoothes the nap of his dark green corduroy trousers, just above the left knee. Such an unconscious and sensual movement could not exist in his office. "The old stallion he has was one of the town's famous racehorses. People sometimes go out to Azkorri just to

171

watch the old man let his horses go. They're all Spanish mounts or Arabs, very beautiful. Both the horses and the Azkorri cliffs."

"You've seen them."

"Yes. There's a proper riding stable up there on the other side of the highway, and all the people who ride know the old man. He's a local character. My wife's brother keeps a horse; she rides. She often comes home telling stories about el viejo."

"Are they really only white horses?"

"White, dappled gray, gray-white. They say he's been like that for fifteen years. Once he's bought or bred a white horse, he hates to sell it. He sells the dark ones, but people have to make very good offers for the white ones, and even then, it's like getting blood out of a stone. He says the white horses are his children."

A waiter brings us two *cafés con leche*. The inspector tears open one of the small envelopes of sugar. "The coffee in Canada isn't like this coffee, is it?"

"Well, it's not so bad. We're beginning to understand the importance of good coffee."

"Progress."

"Yes." We sit quietly for a moment, stirring. The spoons chime against the insides of our cups.

"Could I—do you think I could go and see them?"

"The white horses?"

"Yes."

"I think so. If you go on a day after it rains you might even see them on the cliffs. But if not, just go to Azkorri and ask where the old man's place is, and they'll tell you. I am sure he would love a young woman to visit him." Here the inspector smiles fully, authentically, and adds, "Just don't go into the stables with him. My wife says he's a true Casanova."

I TAKE THE train to Azkorri. I do not have a map; I have to ask the way. I say "Perdoname" to the woman in a loose dress who is sweeping her front patio. "Estoy perdida," I explain to the wrinkled man who burns weeds by the road. They listen to my question about Luis and *caballos,* then they point, talk too rapidly, gesticulate. They explain where I have to go, then they explain again, because I forget *la izquierda* and *la derecha* in Spanish. But eventually the words fit into my mind like a key; I understand the directions. Or perhaps that's a lie; perhaps I understand as I walk, the path presents itself, there are not many choices in such a small village balanced above the Cantabrian. I take the right streets to get to the wide *avenida* lined with plane trees. I walk beyond the two churches and the bar called *Plenzia.* When a narrow road bisects the *avenida,* I cross it and emerge from the cluster of small apartments and houses. Then I walk down the big hill. At the bottom begins a clay path. The people have told me I must go to the top of this path.

I walk up, and up, almost climbing, bent over, trying not to slip on the wet earth. My nose begins to sweat now; my wrists fill with blood. Grass and purple thistle spread away from the path. On the crest of the hill, I look down into the small valley where Luis has built his farm and planted orchards. Beyond it, the lush fields disappear abruptly, drop away into blue sky and water. How to name the colour of light on the sea? Not silver, not gold, not green.

The wind on top of the rise rears up suddenly and knocks the breath out of me. I close my eyes for a moment. Sun on my skin. Current of saltwater wind. When I open my eyes, I see everything, I understand. The green land rolls out like a wave to the white farmhouse and stables, to the cliffs of Azkorri. The old man is down there, letting go his children. And I know beauty now, I hear her name, the blue crash of the Cantabrian and a sound like thunder rising in my ears.

The eighth dwarf and two white horses

THE EARTH HAS shifted away from the sun. After blowing all night, an icy wind left its ghost sleeping in the stairwell. It slides down the banister as I run down the stairs. I swing around the corners, careful of the place on the second landing where the floorboards are warped enough to break ankles. Despite the diamonds and silver beads on the dew-soaked grass, it is undeniably cold. The *avenida* is altered by its emptiness, a lovely, silent promise of itself. Saturday morning in Spain, only fishermen and farmers are up at eight o'clock.

And ancient Andalusian horse-breeders. Luis, the old man from my story, exists. He exists impatiently, sitting hunched over in his ancient white Fiat, half-submerged in dirty wool and a dirtier navy blue jacket that is filled, he proudly tells me every weekend, with real goose down from Andalucia. Between the top of his blue cap and the collar of his blue jacket is his crooked, narrow-eyed, deeply wrinkled face. Luis is the eighth dwarf; the other seven kicked him out at an early age for gambling away grocery money on the horse races and trying to get Snow White alone in the barn. A smelly cigarette sticks out of his mouth. When I open up the car door and bend down with my habitual "Buenos días, ¿qué tal?" he growls, "Where have you been, for God's sake? You know there's no heater in this car, I'm freezing my balls off in here." A piece of raw tobacco is stuck on his lower lip, left of the cigarette.

"Why didn't you wait for me in the cafe?" I have learned to argue with Luis. Because he is so tiny and old, I used to think that I had to be nice to him. Then he tried to get me alone once—behind the barn, actually, not inside it—and I realized what a little shit he is.

"The cafe's closed, cabra. And I haven't even had my coffee this morning."

Tell me, is there a Spanish equivalent for *Someone got up on the wrong side of the bed this morning?* I only say, "Calm yourself." Behind us, Lucia, the proprietress of the cafe, pushes open her door to shake out a small rug. She watches us with amused, sleepy eyes. "Come on. She just opened. I'll buy you a coffee, viejo."

AFTER OUR COFFEE, Luis charges through the empty streets of the town and roars out to the nameless hamlet where he has a ramshackle farm. The town merges into the countryside by degrees here. Apartment buildings shrink, grow older, less sure of themselves. The evolution of architecture goes backwards. Soon the only structures on the road are small country houses with green and red crossbeams and shutters. Olive oil tins full of geraniums and winter flowers sit on the patios. The sharp edges of the town falter, fail, and finally give way to the healthy untidiness of farmyards and nondescript country bars and shops.

When we get to Luis' place, I jump out of the car before he's even turned off the engine. Green despite the cold, the wet earth smells of tree bark, grass, dead and living leaves, cows, old tomato plants, wood smoke, cow shit, horses, soil, sea wind. I swear I was a golden retriever in my last life. My phantom tail wags uncontrollably. I want to bark, leap, run along the filthy creek with my nose in the weeds and mud.

Luis has harvested his garden, picked most of his orchards, but the pear and fig trees are still ripening. Even the wet grass we walk through on our way up to the stable is like a tempting fruit. To Luis, I say, "I'd love to eat it."

"What?"

"The grass. It looks delicious."

Luis, contemptuous of such enthusiasm so early in the morning, says, "Madre mía! La loca niña canadiense." The crazy little Canadian girl. He winks at me and gives a lopsided, rotten-tooth grin. "When we stop in Sopelana for lunch, I'm having a steak. You can eat the goddamn grass." He tramps on ahead of me, cursing under his breath whenever he slips on the muddy path. I love him. He is almost seventy years old, shorter than I am, at least thirty pounds lighter, as tough and quick as a weasel. A friend told me he needed someone to help him exercise his horses. After coming out here for almost two months, I am beginning to understand what he says. His southern accent is so strong that sometimes I think he's speaking Arabic mixed with Portuguese.

Morning fog folds around the hills like sheets slipping from a green bed. It makes me think we are the only ones awake in all of Vizcaya. But no, the shots start to echo and ring down the valley as we saddle the horses. Men are hunting birds near Berango. The horse I ride most often is Ubidea, "stream of swift water" in the Basque language. She is silver-white but for the fine spray of inky hairs through her coat. Luis rides a stallion as lean and nervous as Ubidea, but wilder, gray-white in colour. His name is Barbaro. Both of them are jumpy, fine-boned, overbred Arabians, the kind of horses Alberta ranchers laugh at.

Before we leave, Luis makes Barbaro prance in high steps with an arched neck and tail like a court mount or a Lippizan. They show off together for the benefit of Ubidea and myself. Then the old man gallops out ahead of me, reining Barbaro in like a jockey. Was Luis a jockey once? I've never asked, but seeing him now, so wiry-small, his arthritic knees high on the stallion's sides, I can imagine him thirty years ago, slicked up in racing silks and track mud.

We ride up the hill toward the stand of oaks and down the path into the first valley, near the village of Berango. Centaurs existed once, didn't they? If you're not afraid of a horse, you grow into its body, mesmerized by the waltz that shifts your shoulders and hips, unhinges your skeleton, hooks your joints together in a new way. From a horse's back, the landscape is transformed because your medium for moving through it is different, but nothing like a car or a motorcycle. Your medium is another animal, like yourself, with its own fear and power. A good rider slowly learns to see with two sets of eyes, her own and the horse's. The ground is far below, the trees close by in a new way; even the wind, higher up, has a new scent.

Ride a horse and you begin to see music. Guitar-curves roll out of the road. Drums swell in the distant pastures, pounded by wind. Crescendoes rise and fall under four human legs. By noon, the flies waken, buzzing and dipping around Ubidea's chest and head, searching out the heat under her mane. They flatten against her and gradually swell deep ginger-red with blood. Drinking music. Horses remind us that the first and crucial rhythm originates beneath the skin.

These days of ice-licked air and blue sky inspire the impossible, a desire to remember whole hours perfectly. I write in my mind as I ride, narrating details even as the horse carries me through and beyond them. How much do I forget, even as I tell you this? I used to believe that what we lost was simply what we didn't need, but now I'm not so sure.

Keep this, then, for me. The feel of Ubidea, the magnitude of muscle and dance beneath me, the mingling salts of horse, rider, hidden sea. Remember the sight of live sparks jumping from Barbaro's horse-shoes when we canter over the gravel road. See the dried brown fern on either side of the trail burn when the sun rises into the trees; we ride between hedges of gold. Now the sound of hooves on the village roads, the steady beat ricocheting off the farmhouses, mixed with the wild barking of dogs.

Remember the tabby cat and her black kitten,

curled on the top hay bales of an old wagon. The mother closes her eyes to the morning sun but the kitten sits up, tense, staring, stunned as the horses trot by, an arm's length from the tiny feline skull. Two yellow eyes open wide, uncomprehending. The kitten cocks its ebony head back and forth, trying to grasp the enormity of horses and riders, eight hooves striking the ground. Watching the kitten watch us, I am struck by the expression on its face, the evident struggle to understand. I recognize this expression. It stays with me all the way down the green-shadowed road, back onto the hunters' trails, into the forest.

I love you, I want you
(or, Why women don't run the world)

LAST NIGHT, OVER a glass of wine with friends from the language academy, I had a well-educated, polite fellow patiently explain to me that women were obviously less intelligent than men because they didn't run the world. (He should read the newspaper, which serves as a sublime commentary on the intelligence of men running the world.) Women were made to have children, he said. Why do you think they were given wombs? It is very difficult and possibly pointless to argue with such men because I never know where to begin. "You're an asshole" is a stupid way to begin a debate.

Lately, I've been so sick of the leers and adolescent come-ons and insulting presumptions. Is it PMS or the male Latin race? I keep getting into circular arguments. Like many men who belong to societies that dominate women, the men here tell me, "But our women have power in their homes," as if that's going to make up for the fact that they have less power everywhere else. Even their initial assurance about the matriarchal force of women at home makes me suspicious. When women do not have independent economic and political power, what *is* power at home? What does that *mean?* Are they allowed to cook whatever they want and choose the pattern of the new wallpaper? Tell their husbands that they have headaches? For women who live with violent men, the question presents itself: Is being beaten in your home better than being beaten in an alley? If I lived with a Basque or a Spanish man, I would forfeit an incalculable amount of freedom and power.

That is a large part of their definition of love, as far as I've been able to understand it: love equals a woman's submission, love is taking the woman, possessing the woman more fully than anyone has ever possessed her before, even herself. Does that explain this mediaeval fuss about the ever-diminishing supply of virgins? The verb "to love" in modern Spanish is *querer. Querer* also means "to want". This fascinates me. When you say, *Te quiero,* you are saying one or the other or both: I love you, I want you. The notion of possession—I want you, I want to have you—is inseparable from the notion of love—I love you. It's *embedded* in the language. Excuse the pun.

Love as submission, though not as one might imagine it taking place in Spain, with all the attendant clichés. There are no dark-haired maidens in loose-laced bodices and long skirts being whisked off the ground by handsome brutes on horseback, etc., etc. This may be a bit of a backwater town, but the people I know here aren't peasants. They read books and go to movies and university. The women are doctors, lawyers, journalists, artists, students. A surprising number of them are virgins, or have had very little sexual experience. Losing their virginity is a serious event. They reluctantly acknowledge that they may not marry the man they first have sex with—however much they would like to—but he still has to be extremely "important". When I was growing up, I was like most of my Canadian girl-friends. We wanted to get rid of it. Our virginity, that is. It was like a bad cold, a sliver, an unfashionable dress. Take it away!

As a North American woman, I find myself in a strange land, though not so strange that I don't recognize it: the land of the male conqueror and the conquered female. The whole game of seduction is different here, bigger, older, full of symbols I prob-ably don't even see because I haven't learned them. In North America, there is less game and more talk about the last HIV test. After establishing we're safe and the condoms are relatively new, and hopefully lubricated, we leap into bed. Sometimes awkwardly, sometimes with embarrassment, fear, romance, pure lust, whatever. Even if we leap right back out again, we still leap in.

It's not quite so straightforward here, at least for many of the Basque Spanish women I speak to. A woman isn't supposed to give in. She should hold out as long as possible. There's more waiting, some-times delicious and painful, sometimes just painful. Religion, family, who might find out, what might be said in the bar down the road: all these concerns play a much bigger part in a single woman's decision to have sex with a single man. And I am talking about women in their middle and late twenties—not six-teen- and eighteen-year-olds.

How do you have an orgasm?

FOR THE LONGEST time, one of my woman students wanted to go out for a coffee with me, but our schedules kept conflicting. Finally, we sat down on a rainy afternoon over *café con leche* in a quiet bar with comfortable plush chairs and sofas. After the usual half-hour of pleasantries, I could feel she was finally warming up to her real topic of discussion. We switched from coffee to red wine. At last, after talking about her boyfriend for fifteen minutes, she asked, in a flustered, almost loud whisper, "We've been trying so hard, but it never works! *How* do you have an orgasm?"

This woman, twenty-nine years old, grew up in the town. She was too embarrassed to buy a book, too ashamed to ask her friends. She couldn't even think of asking her mother. I smiled and smiled as I spoke. In my peculiar Spanish, with a lot of panto-mime, and a bad diagram on a serviette, I did my best to explain. "Practise," I kept saying. "A lot of practise."

I can also play the violin

TONIGHT I LEFT my window open and woke with rain on my face. 2 a.m. Now I leap out of my narrow bed, restless, grinning like an idiot, the sea beating in my ears. Foghorns sound beyond the harbour. In two or three hours, after making these notes and working on the violinist story, I will fall asleep and dream more bizarre dreams. Beautiful ones, nightmares, more blood and violence than I will remember.

Insomnia and insane dreams. What have I been eating?

On the weekend, I spent a few hours talking to the Gypsies at the market in Bilbao. They told me that if you have bad dreams, you need to travel. One of the men immediately invited me to accompany him on an upcoming journey to France. We all started laughing at his proposition, but he got quite offended and told me he was serious.

Shall I go travelling with a Gypsy who carries a knife and supplies cheap goods to street markets? His name is Paco. He will be in France for six months. He roared on and on about the spring *fiesta de los gitanos* in St. Maries de la Mer, describing the way he lives on the road in his little caravan, visiting the relatives and friends who are scattered hospitably through southern France and northern Italy. He was a thin, leathery man with an Indian face and long, nicotine-stained fingers. I let him talk, and bought him a coffee while he sat at his stall (sweaters, scarves, and patent leather shoes). When it was time for lunch I said I had to catch the train out of Bilbao. He looked hurt. Will you come with me to France? he asked. I smiled, said No. His face wrinkled up like a child's, but then he gave me a rust-coloured scarf with gold threads, for which he staunchly refused payment. I wrapped it around my neck and buttoned up my coat. We exchanged polite, Spanish, cheek-to-cheek kisses. As I left the market stalls and walked out into the street, he called after me, ever hopeful, I can also play the violin!

Smiling, I wove through the Saturday crowds in the gray, Gothic streets of Bilbao. As I approached the train station, I started to laugh. A violinist stood at the bottom of the train station steps, his music almost completely drowned out by traffic and a departing train. It was necessary to stand close by to hear the sound. I noted the extraordinary colour of his hair, gave him one hundred pesetas, and caught my train home.

Now I'm awake, it's past 2:30 a.m., it's still raining, and what I'd really like to do is go for a walk, but I'll resist, because I should use this nocturnal energy for writing. I am writing a tale about a girl and a violinist. Tomorrow I might go back to the market in Bilbao and tell Paco I'm packing my bags for Paris.

The Violinist   a tale

IN THE SPRING, a strange thing happened to Jurdana Ramos. She took to the cliffs with Sebastian the spaniel and walked there for hours. She marched off the paths and scratched tiny cross-hatched designs on her naked ankles. The bushes were sharp with spiny yellow blooms; Sebastian, after these jaunts, returned home spotted in flowers.

These long treks were attempts to walk the growing pains out of her lengthening arms and legs. Even her hair grew too quickly. Her mother looked at her sideways and asked, "What have you been eating?" Jurdana swore she was not drinking the cream or buying sausage *bocadillos* after school. At night, alone in her room, she held her teeming head in her hands and prayed for peace.

In April, the girl no longer wanted to sleep or eat or study. She closed herself in the music room and punished the piano for the new difficulties in her life, playing scales the way a woman runs up and down a staircase when pursued by love or hornets. Her confusion fired up inside her belly, making it difficult to sit still in class or eat garlic or take coffee to Señora Milena, the widow who lived two floors below her family's apartment. Jurdana could not tolerate the lavender-haired old woman retelling the horror stories of Franco's reign. In the midst of her own civil war, she had no patience for the past.

Late one night, Jurdana pounded at the piano until her mother drove her from the music room with threats. "Jurdana, you will go deaf! You will wear off the ends of your fingers. Stop!" The girl slammed into the bathroom, locked the door, and stared in the mirror. Why do I look so healthy? she wondered, stretching her eyelids up off her white eyeballs and turtle-gray irises. Her mouth opened, revealing a dark pink tongue in perfect form. She knelt down and rested her head against the cool sink. In an inaudible voice, she whispered, "What's wrong with me?"

Her mother rattled the door. "Hija mía, what's wrong with you?"

This privacy-invading echo enraged her. "Nada. Absolutemente nada. Leave me alone!"

SO HER FAMILY left her alone; they loved her. They tolerated her mood swings, erratic diet, solitary walks with the dog. Her father secretly feared a gene of insanity last found in his great uncle, who had died proclaiming he was St. Francis of Assisi. Even her brothers tried not to tease her. But no one could do a thing about the young men from the university who whistled and clapped when she passed their cafés. A few of them had taken to asking her the time even though their watches were strapped to their wrists and functioning perfectly.

The girl had never felt pretty before. She felt she was too serious to be pretty, and her mother never let her wear jewellery. But nothing could conceal her hair, or the new way her body moved, one roundness sliding on top of another like gold ball-bearings. The alterations in her life delighted and horrified her simultaneously; this unreasonable combination of emotions disoriented her even more. In the end, she became angry with the violinist, because the root of all her problems began with him.

HE FIRST APPEARED very early in March. Odd-looking, probably a Slav, travelling around like a tramp, incapable of speaking Spanish. He appeared in the *paseo* one day with a velvet-lined old case open at his feet. Jurdana barely saw him as she strode past, books clamped tightly to her chest. She thought street performers gauche. Four days in a row he played there, so tall and blond that people believed he was from somewhere else. He had the battered look of a serious wanderer. From one day to the next, he did not change his clothes.

Then he disappeared. On the fifth day, Jurdana walked home from school down the *paseo* and knew he was gone even before she rounded the corner. She couldn't hear his music. The absence of this sound left the street colourless. She realized that, every day, before seeing him, she had walked slowly up the *paseo,* listening to the arpeggios and crescendoes from a distance, trying to determine the key he played in. Now all she heard were children's shouts, a radio, a broom beating a rug over a balcony.

She walked very quickly past the place where he played. Two boys were throwing a ball against the wall where his jacket, leather bag, and sheet music used to lie in a disorderly pile. Jurdana's eyes did not search for a sign the violinist might have left behind. She ignored the spot completely.

But she dreamt about him. And she dreamt about him again, and again. In these dreams, she was never allowed to speak to him; he was always at a distance, walking down a narrow street, away, or crossing a bridge, or watching her as the train he sat in pulled away. He appeared in her dreams with such regularity that during the day, when she walked by the place he had played, she began to miss him. Her chest ached. She wished she hadn't been so cold. Why hadn't she stopped to watch him play? What made her so stubborn?

DAYS AFTER THE violinist disappeared, Jurdana paused in her walk along the beach to watch Sebastian jump open-mouthed into the waves. An impulse strong as an electric current swept through her. Strip naked and go swimming right here and now, she thought, shocked as the thought revealed itself. It was still early spring, when the water of the Cantabrian Sea is as cold as a high mountain pool. Her jacket and shoes and socks dropped into the cool sand. When she turned to twist off her skirt, though, she saw Padre Luis appear at the other end of the beach, looking no less holy in jogging pants. The sight of his yellow gauntness brought the image of a giant praying mantis to her mind. Jurdana whistled for Sebastian, picked up her belongings, and ran along the water's icy edge, away from Padre Luis.

The new season had arrived and lit down in full force on the town of Azkorri, bringing southern winds from Africa and the smell of new grapes. This time, spring caught Jurdana physically. Everything she saw impressed her to the point of exhaustion. Each day at dusk, when she took the dog for a walk, the sky lit up and roared like an inferno. Wherever the girl found herself at sunset, on the end of the pier, in the *paseo*, on the cliffs close to the sky, she stood wrapped in a fire that did not burn her.

OF COURSE SHE could not concentrate on her studies. After a particularly atrocious day at school—she was so bored she wanted to pull out her eyebrows hair by hair—Jurdana walked slowly up the *paseo,* pulling a stick along Señor Aracama's iron fence and enjoying the heavy wave of sadness washing around her. The clatter-song of stick against fence drowned out the sounds of the violin. When Jurdana rounded the corner and saw the violinist, she lost her breath.

He was tuning. He still hadn't begun. But as she leaned against the fence to watch, Jurdana understood that simply tightening the bow was entrance into a dance. A white veil of resin dusted the bridge of the violin; though the girl was too far away, she imagined the clean pine scent of it. His fingers turned into waltzing spiders. She watched him begin, turn inward, and fall away, caught in the web of his own music.

What music! Jurdana wanted to tell the mothers returning from the shops and the children playing in the plaza to stop, to listen to the sound swelling from the hollow heart of the violin. He played without looking at the people. His eyes skimmed over the music sheets on the small stand in front of him, or on his fingers, or on his reflection in the café window directly across from him. Jurdana entered this café and sat for two hours with a single tiny cup of espresso, stirring it around and around, trying to stare at him without being too obvious. She closed her eyes and dropped her whole mind into his music, where it dove and leapt like a fish.

She breathed deeply and held on tight to the sides of her table, wishing she recognized the music he played. It slid and trembled and rang all up and down the *avenida,* calling people out onto their balconies. Dogs stopped barking and cocked their heads to one side, whining on the high notes.

THE VIOLINIST WAS in the *paseo* the next day, and the next. Jurdana hurried from school and went into the candy shop beside the café where she lingered over the red ju-jubes and stared at the jawbreakers with enormous concentration. For the following two days, she returned to the café, where she could sit and watch him, or close her eyes and then open them to make sure he existed. Four afternoons in a row, she noticed that his case was lined with coins and small bills. This continued for almost a full week, until the people grew accustomed to his music, as they had grown accustomed to flowers and starlight. They began to walk by without paying attention or coins.

The first time Jurdana gave him money, she worked up the courage to look deeply into his violin case, which glimmered worn crimson velvet and hundreds of pesetas. The second time, she looked fearlessly at his black shoes. They were unpolished, scuffed leather, cracking across the toes. The laces were frayed. The worst surprise was his socks. One was black and one was purple. Purple! She did not know that purple socks were made, let alone worn by anyone. She tossed coins down into his case a little absent-mindedly, as if she were throwing away old sunflower seeds. At this moment, when she gave him money, the knowledge that she could never speak to him brought back her exterior coldness. After the money clinked down, she strode off in the direction of the church, pretending to be in a rush. At the first side-street, however, she doubled back to stand on the opposite side of the cafe, her back to the wall and her face to the sun. Across the street and beyond a small park with blue benches, the cliffs slid down to the sea in a tumble of gray stone and green shrubs. In one breath, Jurdana inhaled sea, pure light, and music.

IN THIS POSITION—on tip-toes, eyes closed, mouth tilted upwards, drinking sun—she finally came face-to-face with the violinist. When he saw her, he laughed and said, "Are you going to fly?" She opened her eyes. The glare of the sun and the shocking presence of the blond man made her yelp. She turned the sound into a cough. The violinist, oblivious, was already sitting down against the wall. He took a sandwich out of his music bag and devoured it in seconds. After brushing the crumbs off his pants, he reached in to the bottom of the bag and produced a large yellow apple. Opening his mouth to take a bite, he suddenly shot a bright blue look at the girl who stood still against the wall, staring at him. Jurdana was stunned, not only by the violinist and his voice, but by the overpowering, delicious smell of ham and cheese. The man asked, "Is there something wrong?"

How could she answer that? Could she say, "Yes, I love you?" It was the season of conceivable miracles. Apple and lemon trees were in blossom already, roses twisted up and around the iron gates like pink hands. And the lovers appeared, too. Jurdana saw them every day at dusk, quick and desperate as mice in search of darkness. At first only their knuckles brushed each other's legs as they walked, but eventually they were unable to contain themselves. They embraced passionately under streetlights or in the shadows of trees and doorways. When walking alone with her dog, the girl took great care to detour a wide margin around them.

Yet she could not mention any of this to the stranger beside her, even though he played his violin the same way she played the piano. Both of them were inside the same circle, and the lovers were there, too, vibrating like guitars. Some people were instruments themselves, with music flying around inside them, trying to escape. They needed to be played.

But she would never say these things to the violinist. She would never say them to anyone.

Instead, when he asked her, "What's wrong with you?" she answered, "I'm quite hungry." He tossed her his apple. "Why don't you sit down?" he said.

Jurdana needed an hour to nibble the yellow fruit to the core. She took tiny bites, chewed for a long time, and felt her eyes get wider and wider as the violinist told her stories.

With one yellow apple and a thousand words, she was full to brimming all afternoon. The violinist waltzed her through tales of Italy and Portugal and the festival in Avignon where he made enough money every year to take a holiday. She half-turned her head to watch him talk, to memorize his cheek-bones, sharp as ivory blades, the shape of his skull under the close-cropped blond hair. She felt her fingers grow longer as he spoke, and thought, The notes I missed before I will catch easily now, perfectly.

The sun was rolling down the hill beyond the harbour, rolling down the slope of Portugalette like an enormous orange. Jurdana's back, pressed against the stone wall, was cold. She shifted, wriggled, but refused to stand up. She did not want to move away from the violinist. Several times now, his knee or ankle had accidentally touched hers. The echo of these touches still sounded in her skin.

"It's getting late, isn't it?" he said.

"Oh, no, it's not so late," she lied. This very moment, at home, her mother glanced at the wall clock, shook her head, and frowned. Jurdana knew this as though she had been in the room, watching. She was supposed to be at home doing her lessons, eating her habitual *merienda* of digestive cookies and yogourt. But how could she go, how could she go *now*, when his knee had brushed her thigh and she could feel heat radiating off his elbow into her arm? She decided, As long as I live, I will never eat another digestive cookie.

Without warning, the violinist slapped his hands against his thighs. "My backside's like a rock," he said, laughing, and hopped up and away from her.

Now here was a strange thing. He stood over her, looking down, still laughing, and she felt so weak that she couldn't stand up. She wanted to touch his legs.

The violinist turned now to face the sea, and began to talk about the sunset. Jurdana tried to think. Useless. She could only feel. She shook her head in an attempt to rattle her brain back to order. "Oh," she thought. "Santa Maria." Some neighbourhood children appeared below, in the park with the blue benches, walking a puppy. "Café-con-Leche!" she heard them calling, and shrank down against the wall, praying they wouldn't look up, recognize her, and go straight to her mother.

The orange fell out of the sky now. The children went away, dragging the puppy out to the *paseo*. The violinist appeared to be surveying countries hidden across the water.

Jurdana stood up, slowly, unsure of what to do with her arms and legs. The violinist turned to her. "We should have clapped."

"I beg your pardon?"

"I said, we should have clapped. When the sun went down. It was quite a show." He smiled at her. She smiled back. "Shall we go to the beach, mademoiselle?" he bowed with a flourish, taking off an invisible hat. Together, wordless, they walked down two hundred stone steps to the sea. "I would like," he said, "to walk to the lighthouse." He pointed to the end of the pier, almost a mile away, where a tall, narrow structure swung a blue-green beam out across the water. When he took Jurdana's hand, everything in the middle part of her body leapt upwards. They walked over the solid wet sand, pressed together by the slow crash of waves a few steps away.

Jurdana whispered, "Soon it will be warm enough to swim."

The violinist smiled with very straight, white teeth. "You could swim now, you know. If the sun were still out."

A shocking thing happened after they climbed the steps onto the pier. It would have embarrassed Jurdana even more if the growing darkness hadn't shadowed her face. The violinist began to sing. He sang a song about a fair and a far-away girl. He finished and sang something different, then something else. Some songs he sang in Italian; these Jurdana only half-understood, which made the lyrics sound like secrets. He sang something in French; Jurdana understood nothing but the word "amour".

The violinist's voice carried them all the way to the lighthouse. The fishermen leaning against the rails smiled and turned to watch the two figures pass. Even when the violinist did not sing in Spanish, the old men hummed anyway, sliding into a depth of memories and other music. Light from the town shone down in the black water, trembling around the port's edge like shreds of old lace.

On the cliffside, rising up the steep path, Jurdana and the violinist stopped to catch their breath and lost it completely. It is difficult to know how these things begin because they occur in darkness and whispers, even in silence. Jurdana had gone to church every Sunday in her life (except during the flu and chicken pox). She felt obliged to protest, "I cannot kiss you."

The violinist smiled. He closed his eyes to inhale the close warmth of her face. "Why not?" he asked.

Jurdana frowned. Dizziness swayed her when she glanced down at the glittering water. To balance herself, she pressed her forehead against the violinist's chest. It smelled of salt and skin and, very faintly, of soap. Or was that resin from the violin? "I can't kiss you because . . . I wear glasses. They are very unromantic." She was serious.

But the man looking down at her threw back his head and laughed so loud that a dog somewhere above them began to bark. "Take them off!"

Looking down caused hair to fall over her face. For a moment the glasses got tangled in loose strands. But as soon as she blinked up at him, he kissed her, out of focus. She felt almost nothing. His lips were so dry and soft, just a current of hot air. She was disappointed. Only when he touched her face with his fingers did she realize exactly what was happening. She opened her eyes then, wanting to see whatever she could. Warmth rose and dove through her; her ankles began to sweat. She felt water running up and down inside her body.

The violinist leaned against the stone face of the cliff. He and the girl were lost to each other's skin. No one knows how long they kissed. It could have been five minutes or one hundred, but Jurdana was freed within seconds. Padre Luis could have come by singing a hymn with his collar on and Jurdana wouldn't have stopped kissing. She was convinced that she could stand in the plaza in broad daylight and kiss this man with ill-matched socks. She did not care.

They kissed until the wind off the sea blew cold, pushing them reluctantly up the stone steps. The *paseo* in front of the cafe where they said goodbye was hushed and empty. Light as a moth, the violinist brushed Jurdana's eyelids with his lips. "We will smile while we walk away," he whispered, then turned to go.

EARLY THE NEXT morning, the violinist left on a train for a city in France, where a girl slightly older than Jurdana lay sleepless in her bed, thinking of his arrival and the blue dress she would wear to meet him. Jurdana herself woke just after sunrise, knowing he was gone. She wanted to play the piano, but it was too early: she would wake up everyone in the apartment, and her parents were already angry because she had come in so late, flushed and humming some foreign song. For a moment she lay quietly under the sheets, listening to the doves pining in the garden. From the next yard came the chatter of sparrows. Jurdana slid out of bed and pulled on the wrinkled clothes from the night before. She thought her blouse smelled like the violinist. The sensation of his fingers still played over her shoulder-blades. With shoes and towel in hand, she whistled low for Sebastian, shutting the door very gently when he was at her heels. Then two steps at a time, she ran down, singing, to swim in the sea.

Jamais Avignon

"He who has not seen Avignon
under the Popes has seen nothing."
—Alphonse Daudet

On ne danse jamais sur le pont d'Avignon

IT'S POSSIBLE that I will write only postcards from this place, because the image on the card will show you that at least the exterior is beautiful. *Sur le pont d'Avignon, on y danse, on y danse.*

The truth is, they never danced *on* the bridge called Saint Bénézet. In the Middle Ages, the people danced underneath it, on a little patch of land known as Île de la Barthelasse. And now? No one dances on the bridge of Avignon today, or below it. No one has opened a disco nearby, either. The Avignonnaise are not enthusiastic dancers.

Once the tourists pay their twelve francs and set their feet on that broken bridge, they are determined to be awed, or deeply interested, or at least respectful. *Ils dansent pas.* One has the sense in France that if one does not solemnly respect all these relics and historical sites and staggering monuments, one will be taken out and flogged behind the barn (or castle or museum). I watch tourists walk on the bridge. They let their feet tread gently; they peer down at the stones they walk on. (After all, they paid twelve francs; they should be seeing something that they cannot see from the road.) Without fail, they walk to the end of the bridge, which only stretches across half the river, and stare down, where they may or may not see the bird's nest half hidden on a stone ledge. (I've seen the nest and its large dark water bird from the other side of the river. I refuse to pay twelve francs to walk on a bridge that doesn't take me to the other side of something.) What the tourists see without fail when they lean over the end of Saint Bénézet is the brown, languid water of the Rhône. There is something unmistakably French about the Rhône. It has a reputation for being beautiful, and everyone agrees it's beautiful, and the guidebooks all say it's beautiful, and the Avignonnaise say, Oh, isn't it beautiful? as though they were speaking of their child.

And I look at the dirty brown water and smile.

The palace, the prostitute, the poet

WHATEVER HAPPENS TO me here takes on the surreal quality of certain kinds of memory; I experience momentary lucidity and unbridgeable distance at the same time. Everything I lived this early evening—coffee alone in La Place de l'Horlage, the walk alone down Avignon's stone-cold main street, my salutation to Isabelle, who nodded back, then quickly walked away—those events feel as though they took place fifteen years ago. As soon as they happened, they felt that way, charged with unspoken meaning, weighted, and finished. Now I sit here at my luxuriously large desk, writing a letter to you. If I stood up and went to look in the bathroom mirror, would I be forty-five years old? Fifty?

I've been in Avignon for a few weeks but I feel I have lived here, against my will, since birth. And it seems as though my birth took place a long, long time ago.

Why is it this way? Because I am lonely? Because

the fierce mistral wind of Provence drives people mad, as the legend says? Isabelle has her own theory. She says that the Palace of the Popes, the monstrous gray fortress standing guard over the city, exercises power over everyone who lives here. A line of poetry: "the stones of the palace were trained to terrify . . ." A few days ago, we walked to the end of Rue de la République, through La Place de l'Horlage. Two small women stood in a field of flagstones, staring up at a mammoth of stone. I cannot describe the enormity of Le Palais des Papes. The men who conceived and constructed the palace wanted it to be beyond my grasp, and it is.

Isabelle sneered and stuck her tongue out at the Virgin Mary, who stands on top of the bell tower between the court gardens and the fortress. "When you saw *le palais* for the first time, what did you think of? God? Who thinks of God when they see Le Palais des Papes? No one but a fucked-up priest. It looks exactly like a prison, and its walls go all around the city, and we live inside them." Isabelle's own words, though they sound like lines from a book. That's something about Avignon. Even among prostitutes and assassins, you find committed poets.

I wonder if Isabelle is right. I wonder if some places are like those people who have sorrow inside of them, a cistern that never runs dry. If you live in a place of sadness and drink its water and breathe its air and become one of its people, even for a while, what happens to you? What's happening to me? I don't know yet. Avignon is a beautiful city, but it's been decaying for centuries. If you walk up to the palace on a windy, sun-struck day, you can see chalky white powder blow off the massive stone walls. If you are close enough to see the light shine through the dust, you are close enough to breathe it in. When the mistral blows hard, I've watched small sections of stone fall off the top ramparts of the towers. A rough whitish wedge of rock sits in front of me, on my desk, the size of a broken wine cork. A piece of the palace.

Where is the torture chamber?

IN 1309, POPE Clement V moved to Avignon, which was still a city belonging to the vassals of the Italian popes. Clement V left Rome to come here because he was worried that some rival was going to poison him. Thus the papal court was re-established in unexciting Avignon. A later pope, Benoit XII, began building the simple, austere palace-fortress in 1334. Almost ten years later, Pope Clement VI added a new structure, complete with ingenious architectural flourishes and secret passageways and hidden chambers. Clement VI was flamboyant. He wanted more bell towers, large and small chapels, grandiose embellishment. I imagine trap doors and sliding wall panels and secret messages in the frescoes, too.

Like many religiously inspired mediaeval buildings, the enormity of the palace makes you feel like a lump of wet clay, small, uselessly soft. I haven't gone inside yet. It's winter; the place isn't open to the public because they're restoring several of the halls. The truth is, I'm not tremendously keen to go inside. Even the palace's exterior exhausts me. The interior will bring me to my knees, as it was intended to do. When I see the palace, I know I am in the presence of enormous power, but not the refined, stained glass and gold-leaf power of cathedrals and monastery libraries. It is more savage than that. When I first saw the palace, I immediately wondered where the torture chamber was.

But maybe there is no torture chamber now; maybe there never was. In mediaeval times, Avignon was an open city, whereas many other cities in France, including Paris, were closed. Closed to ex-convicts, lepers, vagabonds, poor people. When the Popes were here, Avignon became known as a city of refuge for the poor and homeless, *la ville ouverte.* Over five hundred years later, the Popes are nicely resettled in Rome, but they left the beggars behind. Isabelle says that the vagabonds and raggedy men come here for the summer theatre festival and simply never leave. That's how she got here herself.

An enormous cockroach

SILENCE, REVEALED NIGHTLY like a wound that will not heal. Evening wraps its tail around and around the city walls. I live outside the ramparts, in the ghetto neighbourhood of Montclar, just on the edge of the Gypsy and Arab quartier. I rent a room from a small, tough woman with steel-wool hair and a twangy Provençal accent. Lucette is her name, which, for some reason, strikes me as hilarious. Lucette, of the high morals and pinched francs. A couple of weeks ago, when she went to Paris, she left me without any heat in the house. Temperatures dropped to historic lows in Avignon; I spent most of my time in cafes, writing, slowly drinking expensive coffee, dreading the time when hunger would send me home to make supper in the icebox kitchen. Winters in Provence, said the back of a book, and I had illusions of Mediterranean heat and people with bronzed faces.

But it is cold here. It is cold as I walk through the quartier, on my way into the city to watch a movie.

The mistral blows knives through my coat. Everyone's shutters are closed. If something were to happen to me here, on this very street, Rue de la Valfenière, if I were to scream "Aidez-moi!" at the top of my lungs, I believe that the shutters would remain closed. It's a whisper I always hear, walking past these houses and apartments at night: *they will not help you.*

For its population, Avignon has one of the highest crime rates in France. (I did not know that until I arrived.) I have been followed here, persistently, by men in cars, on foot, on seemingly innocent bicycles. On one occasion, lost in the rain, I hid on the second level of a fire escape while the man drove around the same buildings for almost an hour, trying to find me. That was, quite simply, terror. Worse than terror is what I learn daily here. I learn to straitjacket my joy because if they see it, if they see me as I really am, they think—What do they think? That I will get into their cars? That I will happily perform fellatio in a parking lot? That I will love them?

Along with my French verbs, I study the constricted gaits of the women. They do not swing their arms wide unless they are out with men. Passing strangers do not meet each other's eyes if they can help it. It goes against my nature, not to look into people's faces, but I try, I try to close up, in the way of these men and women, like a fist. I simply *must* be careful and not look at men. The impact that eye contact has here is physical, like an intimate caress in public. A woman accidentally catches a man's eye and he turns his car around or changes café tables. And there is no humour in these actions, no sense of play. There is either hungry seriousness or bald desperation.

Sometimes, when I wake to the incessant cooing of the pigeons on the window ledges and rooftops, I sense with dismay the unfamiliar rigidity of my own skin. I get out of bed and peer into the bathroom mirror. Is that a hardening shellac I see or just the metallic light bouncing off my skin? Living here requires a sort of exoskeleton; I think I'm turning into a beetle. One day, K.C. woke up and discovered, without surprise, that she was an enormous cockroach . . .

La ville ouverte

IN ONE OF LUCETTE'S old and completely unused encyclopedias, I read that Avignon suffered regular bouts of the plague in the Middle Ages. The plague *liked* to come to Avignon, as did the mercenary soldiers who used to descend upon the city when they were between jobs. *Les routiers:* good, old-fashioned, bloodthirsty highwaymen. They would leave only after receiving large amounts of money and a papal blessing. How ironic. They came, raped, pillaged, and wouldn't go away until the Pope essentially thanked them for visiting and gave them their allowance. (The French mediaeval version of the Gulf War.)

La ville ouverte. Yes, Avignon was a city of refuge, but apparently it didn't just harbour beggars and lepers and pickpockets. It harboured notorious criminals, heretics, prostitutes, pleasure houses, filthy taverns. In the midst of this wonderful debauchery, we also have *les penitents noirs,* a famous fourteenth-century order of hooded flagellants who marched barefoot through the streets.

Imagine walking in a black cloak through the teeming, crowded lanes, denying yourself every loathsome sin afforded by women, wine, and song. For most of the year, your feet are numb with cold, infected with small wounds, bound in callouses. In procession you pass over the dirty cobblestones, gaunt, pale, oblivious to both rats and cleavage, on your way back to your tiny damp cell where you get out your whip and lash your naked back. And there's no cheating; you really make it hurt. Then you fast and pray before sleeping for three cold hours. You will wake in darkness to the first cock's crow. Then, for love, for salvation, you will begin to pray again.

Petrarch, the great poet who lived just down the way in Île de Sorgue, did not like Avignon. He wrote all kinds of spurious things about my adopted city. The one I like the most is this simple, direct affirmation, "Avignon is a sewer where all the muck of the universe collects."

Oh dear.

Here I am.

Rain and bread

SHEEPDOG WEATHER of gray clouds, warm wind bounding through rain, sudden leaps of sunshine. The world, washed, shaken out, becomes soft again. I love the beginning of the rain because it quickens the people on the streets all at once, like a conductor rousing an entire orchestra. They seem to wake from slowness and move suddenly, gracefully, within a plan. Their eyes get wider, darker, brighter, their faces become light. This unexpected grace in strangers' faces allows me to imagine they are gentle. Children out of school run down the main street, their jackets open, their book bags thumping against their backs. I walk my slowest now, watching the easy miracle of moving people, feeling the urgency of their last-minute errands, their rush to get home. Every second person carries a loaf of crusty bread. I know that without bread, many people would lose faith in life and die quiet deaths.

When I enter the little *boulangerie* close to

Montclar, I realize I've come too late. All the racks are empty, sold out. I am disappointed. The shopkeeper smiles and pulls a loaf from under the counter. "I always save this for my husband and myself, but we never eat the whole thing." She breaks a large portion from the loaf, almost half, wraps it in a sheet of paper, and hands it to me. I am saying thank you when the little old lady who often serves me comes out of the back room and exclaims, "Ah, la petite canadienne, comment vas-tu?" The unexpected *tu* instead of *vous* is so friendly, combined with the half-loaf of bread, that I can hardly bear it. I almost cry with gratitude. Bread is such elemental food, a food of promise. The woman refuses to let me give her any money. "It's not even half the loaf. Stop! Put away your change purse."

I leave the shop smiling, smiling, with bread in my hands, a gift, the body of France.

This is a man

EVERY DAY I watch the man's swollen eye rot closer to blindness. I wonder why none of us, the passing pedestrians, does anything about it. He sprawls outside the city gates near the post office. Or he stands dazed in front of the antiquities museum, or dozes on a bench in the little park. The bruised eye is huge, purple and black, raw-looking, like a peeled plum. It is not easy to look at. People hurry past him, pretend not to notice. When I saw him for the first time, I thought he was a new street person, a recent arrival to Avignon, but now I'm not so sure. Did I fail to see him before because he was unobtrusive, just another raggedy man with a cup and a dirty roll of blankets? Now, slightly mutilated, he is more visible.

His eyelid, swollen shut, is easily as big as a plum, and puffs larger and darker each day. But this is not rotting fruit, despite the purplish colour, the dark red split through the eyebrow, the swelling. When I enter the city walls and pass him, I give him

217

money. I think of curing him, but I don't have the touch.

Where are you now, the saints and holy men of the city of Popes? A question from my childhood of Bible study, "Who sinned, this man or his father, that he was made blind?"

Who sinned? How did this happen to him? Was it a fight in the underpass near the bridge? Over wine, or cigarettes, or an old army coat, heavy with the stench of human dirt? He didn't fall down, or walk into a lamp post. He was beaten. Witness the smaller bruises and cuts on his chin, his cheek, his lip. Some other person or persons beat him this way. Now one of his very blue eyes is sealed under his eyelid like a crushed robin's egg.

During the week, his eyelid changes colour by degrees, burgundy in the centre, and yellow and green around the edges. The swelling does not go down. The gash through the brow, still unhealed, is now infected as badly as the eyelid itself.

One day, I stop as I'm giving him a coin. Standing before him, I speak. He looks over his shoulder, the old gag, to see if I am talking to someone behind him. "No, no, I wanted to tell you—I wanted to say, about your eye—" this in awkward and faltering French, because I don't know how to address him, this beaten-up old man, this misplaced grandfather with a doormat beard—"I only wanted to say your eye looks like it might be—maybe you should go to the clinic. The hospital." He doesn't reply at first. People walking by look at me, astonished, as if I were trying out human speech on a bear.

He peers down at me with his good eye, sizing me up. He was a big man once, quite tall, but now he hunches over. He makes himself smaller, his life has made him small, beggars are supposed to be small people. We don't want big strapping beggars, do we? He stinks; every layer of his clothing is unsalvageable gray, permeated with the reek of his body. Look there, face that, the open wound festering in his ruined eye. In my mind, I say, This is a man. This is a man. What separates us?

"I don't need to go to the clinic, ma belle fille. Seulement un peu des sous, un peu de vin, un peu de pain." A little change, a little wine, a little bread. His face bends, the lips beneath the moustache crack into an exhausted grin. And so I realize that he doesn't know what he looks like. He doesn't know what he looks like in comparison to the rest of the world, because the rest of the world means nothing to him. He has surrendered it like a war. This is a man who lives without mirrors.

La Poésie dans un Jardin

THE SIGN SAYS *Librairie et Centre des Rencontres.* Poetry books are displayed in the window; I go inside. How civilized, I think, a bookstore and a meeting place for Avignonnaise writers and artists. A large storefront room with high ceilings, La Poésie dans un Jardin is lined with bookshelves, scattered with mismatched tables, ashtrays, papers. Water stains darken the ceiling and cracks spider over the walls. A sign hanging on the hook of a small door reads "The toilet is out of order." Beneath it, someone has scribbled *again* in a different hand. I am, I think, the only customer in the store.

At the far end of the long room, two men and a woman sit around a card table, arguing vehemently. I crane my neck. James Joyce. They are arguing about James Joyce. A pile of books sits on the table. They talk at the same time, almost yelling, gesticulating in the precise, indignant way of the French, rolling their eyes, pouting their lips. The French always seem so astonished, so indignant that other people's opinions differ from their own. As the woman's cheeks flush with exertion, her eyes get bluer, her opinion louder. Curvaceously plump, strong-looking, she speaks with a cigarette voice. The two men are opposites. One is small and chubby, pale, with a bald spot pinking through his dark, almost greasy hair. He reminds me of uncooked pastry. The other man is a tall, thin, coffee-skinned Arab, with a wiry mess of black and gray-streaked hair pulled away from his face.

The Arab's voice is deep as a subterranean cave. The most indignant of all, he makes his own echoes. His black eyes spark and widen with outrage. He wears a long black scarf, the end of which he sometimes lashes against the table top for emphasis. I can't understand what he says, but he looks great. I haven't been here long enough to eavesdrop on passionate, three-way arguments, but I do the best I can, navigating closer one bookshelf at a time. I am dizzy by the time the pale man puts his hands in his corduroy lap and interrupts in a quiet voice, "Wait, wait. Are we going to have a coffee or not? I had the impression we came in here for a coffee."

The woman immediately gets up from the small card table. "But yes, of course, Arthur, I completely forgot." She disappears behind a curtain. The Arabic man asks after her, "Do you have anything to drink?" Arthur looks at me inquisitively for the third or fourth time. I stand in front of the closest bookshelf, holding a poetry collection by René Char. When the pale man speaks again, I have my back to him, but I know he's talking to me. "Would you like a coffee, too?"

I turn around, smiling. How much gratitude shows on my face?

Too much. Entirely too much.

Show me something beautiful

AFTER THE COFFEE, Shaquil, the Arab, leans toward me and asks, "Do you think we should, ahh, go for a walk through the streets of Avignon?"

I am here, as easily, as miraculously as breathing in. I could be anywhere else on earth but I am here, and now I have found three people, we are speaking, I am no longer alone. A man with pitch black eyes leans forward (I can smell cigarettes and sweat, his African skin) and asks me to go for a walk with him. I stand up and thank Marie for the coffee and shake Arthur's deboned white hand. Wind hammers at the windows. Shaquil holds the door open as I button up my coat and wrap a scarf around my head.

A walk through Avignon like a waltz, with the streetlights flickering on and the wind in our throats as we speak. I stumble over French and flagstones. Shaquil walks too quickly, which I like, because we're half-running, warm, breathless, pulling each other up the palace stairs and around the tight street corners.

The squares and courtyards are empty, but warm yellow light reaches out from restaurant windows.

The labyrinth of streets around the palace have names like songs and we sing ourselves through them. From Rue Banasterie to Rue des Trois Colombes, onto Carnot, past the flower shop, around again, almost in a circle, to Rue Ste. Catherine. Rue Peyrollerie. Roll the syllables from the throat, and remember this: the Street of the Three Falcons. Shaquil takes me to see the famous carved door of a cathedral and shows me the shop of ancient books. "They had a three-hundred-year-old Bible once, and an even older Koran two years ago. You wouldn't believe how rich some of the people around here are. This house, see the cross beams, the narrow doors, those windows. It was built in the sixteenth century. Full of antiques. One curtain cost more than my car. No! I've never been inside but I used to go out with one of the maids. C'est vrai. She used to steal wine for me." The great clanging palace bells strike the hour, but I lose count. Is it nine or ten? Or eleven?

The later it gets, the hungrier and happier I become. Light-headed, laughing, I say, "I feel drunk."

Shaquil hits me lightly with his scarf. "That's because you're breathing more than your share of the air. Leave some for me! I'm an old man." I look at him from the corner of my eye. Thirty-five? With a lot of gray and white hair. We stop walking at the same time and stand in the unlit street. I hold my breath. On either side are very tall, old houses. The highest window of one of them is unshuttered. A woman in the attic is singing. "What language is that?"

"Polish?"

"Hungarian?"

We listen for a couple of minutes, our hearts beating slow. Our heads lean far back. We wish she would appear at the window. She doesn't. We walk on.

So I enter Avignon with a raven of a man whose loose black coat sleeves flap as he talks. His hands fly up to point out gargoyles and stone reliefs above doorways. We walk around the back of the palace, where one of its unfinished rock walls rises like the face of a mountain. Opposite, on the wall of another building, painted figures loom out of painted windows. They are eerily out of place, these jovial men and women grinning at the palace, at each other. "It's for the festival, the summer theatre festival, the only time this place isn't a graveyard. You're staying until the summer, aren't you? Then you'll understand why anyone lives here. It becomes a French Venice during the summer, full of foreigners and artists and acrobats."

We walk back into the maze of streets. In a square I don't recognize, Shaquil tells me to close my eyes.

"Why?"

"What kind of a question is that, why? Because I want to surprise you." We stop walking and turn to each other. He makes a face. "Don't you trust me?"

"Yes, but why do you want me to close my eyes?" Closing my eyes in Avignon strikes me as a dangerous act.

"Merde, c'est incroyable. Tu es vraiment dure. Une dure canadienne."

"This has nothing to do with being Canadian, Shaquil."

"You don't trust me?"

"I don't know."

"Merde, don't be so serious. I want to show you something beautiful. Let me blindfold you." He unwraps the long black scarf from around his neck.

A couple walks by us just now, past a darkened storefront. Both the woman and the man shoot me a disapproving look. Not a concerned look, not a look that says, "You silly foreign girl, don't you realize this is the town rapist?" No, their expressions bother me because they so easily and quickly convey disgust. Disgust and anger. They don't look at Shaquil, only at me.

I am confused. Shaquil swears under his breath, but I don't understand. "What is it?"

"Ma piel," he says in an angry voice, then, in the next moment, smiles broadly and flicks the end of his black scarf toward the couple, who is already far down the street. "Votre problème."

When I see his face now, after seeing theirs, I remember. He is Algerian, a very dark Algerian. And I am quite white, especially in the dark. The contrast is the source of their disgust and their anger. The clarity of this delayed realization makes me furious. They don't approve of the mixture here, they don't like it. The colour combination offends their fashion sensibilities: we don't *match*.

"All right," I return Shaquil's smile and open my arms. "Blindfold me. Show me something beautiful."

He wraps the scarf around my eyes twice, enveloping me in darkness. The scarf smells like Shaquil: sweat, cigarettes, skin, cold night air, something vaguely minty. And then the smell of the street, settled car exhaust, night-dampened stone . . . paint? Could someone have been painting here today? My feet

225

consciously remember what I've already come to take for granted: the treacherous nature of cobblestones. I smell the faint but growing scent of food. He walks me forward, down, up—it can't be very far but it feels far because I'm blind, half-floating, unsure of where the ground is, convinced we are walking past trees and one of the lower branches will hit me. Now I feel buildings rise up on either side. The wind doesn't blow here. The sound of his voice has a new solidity to it.

I hold Shaquil's arm, but not too tightly. Once over the initial lack of balance and the weird shiftiness of the unseen world, I enjoy the intense blend of fear and excitement. Braid upon braid of delicious scents loosen in the air as we move forward. My mouth waters. What food is this? A steamed smell like rice, but it's not rice, is it? The smell of vegetables, some tender meat turned and simmered in a garden of spices, herbs, seasonings I don't recognize, except by colour: ochre and saffron, burgundy, heavy crimson, olive-oiled gold.

"Now we have to go up—" we step up a curb "—and down. Another one. One more." I'm sniffing the air. Shaquil laughs. "Comme un chien. T'as faim, eh? Moi aussi. Now just stand there a moment while I open the door. Because it's heavy."

"Can I take off the blindfold?"

"Absolument pas!"

When he opens the door, I hear music for the first time. Indian music? North African? Cretan? After passing through one door, then another, we are inside both the music and the intoxicating smell of the food, buoyed on a quiet sea of human voices.

"I'm taking off the blindfold now, I can't stand it any more."

"Wait. I'll do it." He stands behind me and undoes the unwieldy woollen knot. Unwrap, unwrap—

—and I open my eyes, squinting, dazzled. Where are we? In a tent in Morocco. In the Algerian desert. In a Bedouin camp on the edge of an oasis. Rugs hang above and spread below us, fabrics woven with gold and bronze threads, low tables and embroidered cushions crowd the shadowed corners. Oil lamps burn on the walls. Men in long gowns carry platters of fragrant food past us. One of them greets Shaquil, hugs him, and grins at me in a greasy, sexual way. (Am I the twelfth foreign woman that Shaquil has blindfolded and brought here? Have I just played a part in the theatre of Shaquil?) The grinner and Shaquil speak Arabic together for a couple of minutes, then the grinner leads us to a table inlaid with silver. We take off our shoes before we sit down on the cushions. One of the men—who are so solemnly graceful that I hesitate to call them waiters—places an ornate silver bowl beneath our hands, then pours warm water over them.

"Now," Shaquil says, "our hands are clean. We are going to eat a feast."

The south of France
(or, A tiny piece of the big yes)

HARIRA SOUP. Charred and peeled peppers garnished with fresh green cilantro. *B'stilla* of cinnamon and ginger. The most expensive Medoc on the menu. Fine gold phyllo stuffed with shrimp. The aroma of paprika and fresh flat bread. More Medoc. Phyllo stuffed with spinach. Lemon wedges and a blue bowl of Moroccan olives. Medoc once more. Sole tagine with the spicy *elhout m'chermel*. Lamb couscous. The last of the second bottle of Medoc. Mint tea, poured from a silver pot and an impressive height. Strawberries and almonds, soaked in sweet syrup.

But no sex.

He is very civil about it. "Je veux pas le grand Oui tout entier," he explains to me in his car, an expression of persuasive logic on his face. "Je veux seulment un petit morceau de le grand Oui." I don't want the entire big Yes. I just want a tiny piece of it.

I cough. "I have to go in. It's late."

"Dure. Une dure canadienne."

"Oui, c'est moi. Comme la pierre." I knock my forehead with my knuckles.

He looks out the window at the looming concrete apartment blocks of my neighbourhood. "You really live here? This is the worst part of Montclar. Even I wouldn't walk here alone at night."

"Yes, I really live here. It's not so bad."

"Do you carry a knife?"

"Are you kidding? Of course not."

After saying goodnight, I leap out of the car before he can give me more than a grasping embrace. When I reach the door of my building, he blows me a kiss and drives away.

But the building isn't mine.

The building looks just like mine—a prison block—but the number is different. I walk to the next concrete barricade, turning my face away from the icy wind. None of those buildings is mine, either. Shaquil's car is long gone, though I walk out of the complex of apartment buildings and peer down the road, praying he will be persistent in his desire for a tiny piece of the big yes.

But he doesn't come back.

Across the street, I see a long row of scorched, windowless buildings, a heap of bricks and refuse in a vacant lot, a burned-out car half a block down the road. Do you carry a knife?

I haven't the faintest idea where I am. When Shaquil drove me here, it all looked vaguely familiar, in a drowsy, drunken sort of way. In Avignon, I never ride in cars; streets seen from inside a car always look slightly different.

All right. If I don't know where I am, I must at least pretend that I know where I am. Turning in circles and wandering from one building to the next is sure to attract thieves and assassins. As I walk up the street I think we drove down to get here, my teeth start chattering. I pull my collar up around my ears, push my hands deep into my coat pockets, clench my teeth but the chatter seems to travel into my shoulders, shaking them as I walk. Whenever I see a man walking toward me, I turn down a side street to avoid passing him. This brings utter disorientation and a profound sense of doom. I can't ask any of those men for directions because if I speak, they'll hear my accent, and all those warped synapses in their brains will connect and spark like lightning. What's a nice foreign girl like you doing in a ghetto like this at three in the morning?

The wind demon-howls down the street. My feet are as cold as the concrete beneath them. But it's the cold that keeps me safe; few people venture out in such icy wind.

Wait. Could it be? There, in the distance, is my little *boulangerie*. And farther down the street is the corner of the old house with the ceramic snail on the roof. I am, by some miracle or merciful accident, finding my way home. I am too tired to run to the entrance way, but there it is, my own complex of ugly apartment buildings. Lucette and two hundred pigeons are sleeping up there, on the third floor. I'm so happy I want to hug the entire building, but instead I find my keys and fumble at the lock with stiff fingers.

Beautiful island

"WINTER IN PROVENCE always makes me sad," Isabelle sighs. She smiles and looks down into her espresso cup. "It's much nicer in Paris. Grayer, yes, but warmer. More friendly." In Isabelle's very small, white hands, an espresso cup almost seems like a normal size. "The mistral makes my varicose veins get worse." She stretches her leg out from the table and squints down at her black-sheathed calves. "Merde! Just like worms! I only have a couple, but they are the ugliest things . . ." We are sitting in the dubiously named Bar Americain, on Avignon's main street.

When I tell her about my misadventure in Montclar a few nights ago, she immediately says, "But Shaquil should have known better than to drop you off in the Arab quartier! Stupid man."

"You know him?"

"Of course I know him. He owes me money. He owes everyone money. Has he asked to borrow from you yet?"

"Uh, no."

"Ha! But you only met him a few days ago, isn't that true?"

When I don't reply, she raises one thin eyebrow. "What? What's this? You don't *like* him, do you?" When I say nothing, she starts to choke. The red-nailed fingers clutch at her throat.

"We only had supper together."

"I hope! But supper can lead to death. Any Catholic knows that. Shaquil is crazy."

"I think he's beautiful."

"And I *know* he is crazy. Brilliant but cracked." With her small hands she expertly mimes cracking an egg on the edge of the cafe table. Then she laughs. "Don't give me such a disapproving look. I won't say another word . . . well, maybe just one or two. But you will see. Just wait. Lucky girl." She tosses the invisible eggshells over her shoulders.

Isabelle! Her name means "beautiful island". She was raised in a *banlieue* of Paris, and worked in the city until she was twenty-four, but to me she is pure Avignon. I asked her out for coffee after a movie because she was the only other woman there alone, and the only other one who laughed at the funny parts.

Isabelle is a prostitute. She's the happiest person I know here. Not to say she is always happy. "The tragedy of cold weather is that we are all obliged to wear too many clothes." Every time I see her, she is wearing black lace-up boots with wedge heels. "Winter apparel," she explains. Boots of the latest fashion or boots that are eighty years old? Impossible to tell with Isabelle. She also wears a black Mohair coat that hugs her waist and drops smoothly off her hips; a garment from another age, especially when combined with her little black pillbox hat. She commands the eye, above all the first time you see her, across the street or coming out of a shop, when you don't know the softer angles of her face. There is nothing coarse or cheap about Isabelle; don't imagine her the wrong way. She is like a blonde movie star (elegant French, not brash American) on the rain-slick street, her black outfit striking against the white stones of the museum. She coils her hair up on her head like a gold rope, lets it go wispy at the back of her neck and around her oval face. A very young, beautiful woman's face (though she is no longer very young), with a small, full mouth. She always wears the same shade of red lipstick. (She applies it, leaves it on for a few seconds, then wipes most of it off, leaving only the dye on her lips. When I asked her why she did this, she glared at me, pretending to be insulted. "What do you think I am? Eh? A whore?" We laughed until we couldn't breathe.)

When she walks by, we hear the *clickclack click-clack* of her boots around the puddles. *Clickclack clickclack,* then a pause when she stops at the shop windows, as she often does, because she loves clothes. Black fish-net stockings are high fashion this year, a fact that amuses her. "They'll never lose their power to seduce," she said. "Traditional *putain* attire secretly appeals to everyone. Fish-net stockings, for example." She shimmied her shoulders. "And now housewives and economics students are wearing them. Bravo! Who said progress was an illusion?"

One afternoon Marie, from La Poésie dans un Jardin, watched her pass in front of the window and whispered to me, "Bizarre that one of the most beautiful women in Provence chooses to sell her beauty."

I am beginning to wonder if it is bizarre.

Isabelle, after all, has a sharp sense of humour laced with humane irony, excellent business savvy, and good tables in all the best restaurants of Avignon and Aix-en-Provence. Once, I ventured to ask her if she was happy.

Vaguely surprised, she answered me with her own question, "Wouldn't you be?"

When we go for coffee, she rarely talks about her work. She talks about the latest "release" of wine like a publisher talks about new books. Isabelle studies wines for a hobby; she has an entire oak bookshelf devoted to the wine-making regions of France, Italy, Portugal, and Spain. She talks about her brother who lives in Montpellier, and his daughter, who recently turned four years old and has started cello lessons. She talks about the new CDs she's bought, and makes me listen numerous times to her favourite songs or classical pieces.

Today she keeps sliding back to the topic of Shaquil. "He told you how he grew up in Algeria?"

"A little." I try to sound uninterested.

"His father was a double agent for the Algerian and French governments."

"A spy? Really?"

"Yes. It's quite true. The family was often in danger. Shaquil will tell you when he gets drunk. Those are his worst and best memories: the whole family terrified, crossing the desert with a single flashlight and the clothes on their backs."

"When did he come to France?"

"As a young man, for university. How many of them came here when Algeria was still under French rule! After learning our language in Africa and loving our literature and believing that they were more French than Algerian. Shaquil studied at the Sorbonne. He has memorized more French poetry than I have ever read. But still this country is not his home."

"But why do you say he is crazy?"

"After university, he married a Parisienne, someone he had studied with. They had two children. When they came to Avignon—"

"Why did they come here?"

"Because Shaquil was offered a job teaching Arabic literature at the university. But his wife was never happy here. Who knows? Maybe she was never happy in Paris, either. These are secrets." The *peck-peck-peck* rhythm of gossip is gone from Isabelle's voice. Stretching her leg out from under the table again, she plucks a long blonde hair from the black gauze of her nylons. "She committed suicide. Four, maybe five years ago. With the children in the apartment next door. Shaquil has never been the same. Last year, her parents took him to court and won custody of the children. He was unfit to be a father, they said." She puts one leg over the other and slides them back under the table. "Probably they were right. Poor bastard."

Othello

THERE HE IS. Shaquil the Arab, walking down Rue de la République like a king, his white teeth gleaming like gems in his head, and his eyes, black gems. You would fall in love with him, too, if you could see him. Shakespeare knew something about the tantalizing bones of the Arab face. Othellos are everywhere in France, the handsomest, loneliest men on earth. Shaquil flips his black scarf around his neck, smiles at his own reflection, tips his hat to small, tight-mouthed white ladies. A rose between his teeth would not be out of place. In fact, I have seen him with a rose between his teeth more than once. The black hat is set at a jaunty angle, like his shoulders, like the line of his right eyebrow. You can see the thick strands of white in his hair, the perfect cut of his trousers. In the pockets of the long black coat, you will find a twig of pine, some green, sharp-scented sprig. He gives me a small pine branch every time he comes to meet me.

In a kitchen full of dried herbs covered with dust,

he made mint tea in a silver pot. "This taste is the desert where I was born." He recited Baudelaire and St. John Perse. He's painted poetry in classical Arabic calligraphy on the white and blue walls of his apartment. After lighting the candles on the table, on the bookshelves, on the thickly carpeted floor, Shaquil read the walls to me.

After the first bottle of wine, he began to talk quietly. I leaned closer to hear him. He whispered because he was telling secrets. Every one of his secrets became a question. What happened to his wife? Where are his children now? How to make sense of two empty hands? His eyes were very black. I smelled wax and all the cigarettes he'd smoked since his thirteenth year. He seemed to be trembling.

I was afraid of the immediate closeness, the rock-slide of words. I was afraid that if we embraced, we would knock over a candle and set the apartment on fire. He had conspired to get me into his apartment to achieve a smooth seduction. But instead, he moved, without lust, into my arms, where he began to cry.

He moulded his bony length into my arms, my stomach, my hips, my legs. I held his angular shoulders and his head of thick hair. The candles burned down as he wept.

Single portions

I WALK FROM Armelle's house to the post office thinking of Pablo Neruda, who said that the literature of Europe exists in its rooms, never outside, under the real sky. But it's more than the literature. Armelle lives her life in two tiny, joined rooms. I think of all the people I know in this town who reside in strange, cramped little apartments, attic flats with sloped roofs, the back bedrooms of family houses, rented, makeshift lodgings. Rooms inhabited by cats—always, always by cats—and dust and an overwhelming atmosphere of decay, of aging, of loss. To ward off emptiness, the people who live in these spaces fill, clutter, and pack them to bursting, until freedom to move is the only thing they don't have. Cats, old books, an empty fish tank, shelves crammed with five thousand accumulated objects, two dozen pilfered espresso cups, antique tables, a guitar no one can play. And draped over it all like another old silk scarf, the smell of cloying perfume, cat piss, the faint reek of a strong cheese.

Above the sink of dirty coffee cups and saucers, a narrow shelf is lined with single-portion cans of peas and tuna. Ah, Mediterranean fare. So many people, like Armelle, like myself, open these little cans, empty them into bowls of silence, and eat alone. In this apartment, the step from eating alone to dying alone looks very small indeed.

Armelle's cat has had another litter of kittens. Her fridge is broken, but milk in a bottle still sits inside, turning green. She says she has no time to clean up the other room in the apartment, though it's a grand, high-ceilinged chamber with French windows. (French windows. Of course. Every window in this country is French.) This excellent room is piled high, crammed full of her ex-husband's boxes. Ugh! Her ex-husband, who left her six years ago for another woman. And she still lets him have the most beautiful room in her house!

Friday. An impossible day. Depressing morning coffee at Armelle's. For breakfast, she fed me a distant relative of porridge; it tasted of stable dust. I imagine I have the rancid perfume of cat piss on my skin. Cat hair clings to my black trousers. Stupid clothes! I want to cash a cheque today and buy a skirt. Damn. The post office has closed early. What do you mean the post office has closed early? I can't mail my bushel of letters. The chain of words in my universe now dangles in space, touching nothing. The shops are packed full of elbows and obnoxious clerks. I back out of the shops. I take my cheque to the bank.

Unfortunately, it's not quite as international as I hoped. The sharp-nosed clerk glances up at me from behind her large glasses. A tight little voice escapes her lips, "I can't cash this."

"Are you sure? They told me it was international."

Bank clerk snorts her annoyance, "C'est impossible."

Slight desperation sets in. "Could you please talk to the supervisor about it?"

Turning on heel, the bank clerk hammers away in her heavy shoes. She returns triumphant, a malicious grin on her face. "I was right. It is impossible to cash this cheque."

Fine, fine, maybe she's being a bitch because she hates my black trousers. Everyone does. Even I do.

Hoping to salvage something from this ruined transaction, I attempt humour. I raise my eyebrows and say, "I guess I'll starve to death this month." She doesn't even smile.

I leave the bank dejected. Then I remember: Marie has said on numerous occasions that she would lend me money if I ever had banking problems. I begin to think, All will be well, when I see a bad omen striding toward me. A murderer. Obviously a murderer, that man, why isn't he carrying an axe? He's one of those lean, muscular men with colourless hair that can't remember being washed, a jean jacket whose sleeves are too short, gnawed-looking wrists, arms that do not swing but hang down by his sides (the hands grip invisible blunt objects). Blue, staring eyes betray a savage interior landscape. Wild boars lives in that man's skull.

But who knows, really? He's probably nicer than the bank clerk. He mutters something at me as we pass each other, but I can't decipher it.

I decide not to go to the park beside the palace. I start walking back down Rue de la République. No energy. There will be lonely men in the park, there always are. Lonely men who stare and stare, at the women, at the girls, at the little girls who feed the swans. Too depressing. Thieves and assassins. And bank clerks. And rooms full of cats. Letters I cannot send. Money I cannot get.

On my way home, when I pass the house that has a ceramic snail on its roof, I start to cry. That snail! What a joke. The concrete makes me cry; there is so much of it. There is no grass. Did I tell you, spring is coming? It's never winter forever, but do you know what the people here do? They build walls around their gardens. And if they can't build walls, they erect chainlink fences, then cover the fences in netting. No one out in the street can see inside. The people hide their gardens.

I take it personally. It seems as if they have walls simply to prevent me from being close to the earth, close to colour, close to growing things. But I manage it anyway. I peer through the chinks and crevices and unintentional openings. No one can keep me from the vision of spring inside. Trees are budding now. Even the little vegetable plots are spiked with shoots. Lilac bushes, flowers I can't name, plants, ivy greening on the walls, slow unfurling of leaves.

I howl walking home, inconsolable, defeated by fences. Cloistered gardens. Earth suffocating beneath cement.

Liaison dangereuse

"YOU MADE LOVE with me once, and now you're telling me you won't make love with me again?"

Pause of embarrassed hesitation. "Yes." Shaquil and I are sitting in his car. My fingers rest on the door handle.

"Then why did you sleep with me in the first place?"

Just how stupid will my reason sound? "Because I thought it would help you." Oh, God, *very* stupid.

"You slept with me out of pity?"

"No, of course not."

"Then why won't you sleep with me again?"

"Can we talk about this when we haven't drunk so much wine?"

"No! Moi, je comprends rien. Dis-moi. Qu'est-ce que tu me fais?" He bangs the steering wheel with his fist and the whole apparatus rattles. His face is so altered in anger that I would not recognize him if I passed him on the street. He has become ugly.

"I don't *want* to come home with you."

His lips curl up, revealing purplish gums and tobacco-stained teeth. He is snarling at me. "J'ai peur de toi," I tell him.

"You're afraid of me! I'm the one who should be afraid of you, crazy woman, for fucking with my head." As the swearing picks up momentum, I really do feel afraid. I don't even understand some of the things he calls me, but he is screaming. A violent word is a violent act. I push open the car door and almost fall into the street, so anxious am I to get out. He reaches for me as I scramble away. He would pull me back in if he could, but I'm out now, walking quickly toward my beloved prison block. I ignore Shaquil's shouts. He remains in his car but through the open window he continues yelling questions and obscenities.

I open the door, press the timer-light, run up the four flights of stairs to my door. His voice is just barely audible from here; the apartment is on the far side of the building, away from the street. Lucette says hello. She sticks her head out the kitchen door. "What's wrong with you?"

I hang up my sweater to gain a moment's respite from the inevitable questions. Then, mumbling something about being tired, I take off my shoes. But Lucette can see fear in my face, in the movements of my arms and legs. She can probably smell fear. "What happened to you?"

"Ce n'est pas grave. I just had an argument with Shaquil."

"Ah, he's a bad type, that one. You won't see him again, eh?"

"No. No, I don't think I'll see him again."

"Better for you. These Arabs, they're so—"

"Lucette, it has nothing to do with him being an Arab—"

We are interrupted by an unmistakable voice. Four floors below. Beneath my bedroom window. "Karenne! Karenne! C'est pas juste, ce que tu me fais maintenant. Tu es trop pragmatique! Tu es froide parce que tu viens de Canada!"

"Mon Dieu," says Lucette, clutching the collar of her blouse together, as if Shaquil's voice alone has the power to rip off her clothes. "Il est fou. I will call the police! They will come and take him away, filthy man."

"Lucette, there's no need to call the police. I'll just. . . ." What? What will I do? "I'll just go into my bedroom and talk to him."

"You'll talk to him from your bedroom window? We're four floors up!"

"I don't want to go down."

"But all the neighbours . . ."

"The neighbours will enjoy it, Lucette. It's better than television."

I open up my long French windows and lean over the small balcony. "Shaquil!"

"Tu es froide et dure."

"Oui, t'as raison. I am cold and hard. Thank you. No one has ever told me that before."

"What? I can't hear you."

I repeat myself in a louder voice.

"It's not a compliment!" He swears at me. Again. And some more. Lights go on in the adjacent apartment. Lucette stands behind me, at my bedroom door, summoning God and the Holy Mother. I am suddenly overwhelmed by a desire to laugh. It is all I can do to keep from howling with laughter as Shaquil calls me a bitch, a cunt, a liar.

None of this is funny. But it's so melodramatic. And the neighbours really are listening. Curtains across the street open slightly, like squinting eyes. An old woman's face peers out. Melodrama embarrasses me. When I am embarrassed, I usually laugh. There is nothing amusing about Shaquil's violent tendencies and his fierce struggle with himself and the world. But this, the balcony soap-opera rendition, the stupidity of it, my own and his, the gorgeous angry man in a hat standing below my window, yelling my name, pissing off my hard-faced neighbours, *this* is funny, in a pitiable, wearing sort of way. Like a Woody Allen movie interrupted by Fellini, or the other way around.

We shout back and forth for a while. Shaquil's neck must be getting sore from looking up. Finally, Lucette comes to the balcony and, raising a fist, yells threats about the police. An outraged Provençal accent is truly frightening: Shaquil leaves. I apologize to Lucette, profusely, and promise that it will never happen again. "This is your own fault, Karenne. I told you before I even met him that he was a bad type. Zoot! Madame Farnoux, across the way, will talk about this for two months. Drunken Arabs! No more! It will be the last time this happens or you will find yourself another place to live!"

I take a shower. Then I make myself a cup of tea and collapse into bed. I feel like I've just done an intensive course at a famous university. "Liaisons Dangereuses 406," or "La Deconstruction d'Alcoolisme 302," or "Les Politiques Sexuelles 601." Or all of them in the same semester, while reading Sartre's translation of *Wuthering Heights*.

The Gypsies of Montclar

YESTERDAY THE CLOUDS built up like battalions, thousands of muscular gray soldiers. Rain fell warm, whispering, *Spring*. In the spirit of the season, I decided to do something new.

I walked into the heart of Montclar, the Arab and Gypsy quartier where I live. But no, not really. I live two streets over, with the working-class stiffs and the lower bourgeoisie. With the white people, that is. The nice white French people.

But yesterday, I turned left, followed the street away from the city walls, past the *boulangerie* on the corner, where I crossed a frontier and entered a separate universe. A run-down universe. Graffiti in Arabic. (I remembered the poetry on Shaquil's walls.) Uglier than my part of the neighbourhood. More concrete, if that's possible. A few spindly, bald trees sticking up out of little grates. Rusted-out cars. Piles of garbage. Malnourished stray dogs. The Arabs live down there, in the huge prison-like apartment buildings that span a few city blocks, street upon street of gray jailhouses, much like the one I live in but older, unkempt, dirtier. That cold winter night, Shaquil dropped me off in one of those streets, and my own fear led me even farther away from home.

I could describe Montclar in negative terms, as though it doesn't exist. No green space. No park for the children. No community centre. No comfortable cafés. I passed abandoned and partially abandoned buildings, offices and houses with boarded-up windows and bricked-in doors.

My shoulders and neck grew stiff with nervousness as I walked to some of the farther apartment buildings. I tried to carry my umbrella lightly; it is demoralizing to see people who carry umbrellas as though they were spears. Montclar is dangerous, a well-known site of muggings, assaults, thefts. All ugly places are dangerous. I walked through the gray air, around the dog shit, around the piles of garbage. Instead of feeling afraid, I felt like an out-of-place intruder. Arab women with traditional head-coverings passed me without meeting my eyes. Boys on bicycles shouted a few unintelligible phrases as they rode by. Lone men said bonjour. One of them asked me if I want to go for coffee, but I have learned, finally, to say nothing, to never reply, to not speak.

I crossed the street and returned down the other side. The Gypsies do not live in apartment buildings that rise off the ground. They live in small semi-attached houses that face each other. The backyard enclosures face other backyard enclosures; the people, coming in and out of their houses, see one another. I wandered into the Gypsy streets trying to look nonchalant, but within five minutes I was surrounded by at least fifteen children and long-haired young girls. They crowded around me, talking, and almost pushed me into the wall of an abandoned house.

"What are doing here?" "Are you a reporter?" "Look at her camera." "Take our picture!" "Your accent is not Provençal." "Where are you from?" "Don't push her like that, she'll call the police." "No, she said she wants to talk to us." "What, what do you wanna know? I'll tell you my life story." "Carmen's getting married, take her picture!"

I was intimidated by so many voices and faces, so much movement, the hands that fluttered and darted in, close to me. How unFrench! Noisy and raucous for a few seconds, they were serious the next, then laughing uproariously when one of them made a joke. They spoke French to me, but to each other they sometimes spoke a different language. I asked what it was.

"Catalan," one girl answered.

It sounded nothing like the Catalan I had heard in Spain.

There were too many of them, too many moving faces and hands. One of the girls yelled, "Leave her alone, you pests, you're squishing her. Give her some space." She then looked at me over the cluster of black and dark brown heads, and shrugged. "They don't listen to me." I stood swaying in the centre of a half-friendly, half-mocking mob. They were fully aware that my presence on their territory gave them a right to interrogate, laugh, joke. Play with me. How strange it was to be that close to so many people at once, to be at the *centre* of so many people. Especially the Gypsy people, who are normally bound by societal mores to stay away, to stay back, to not touch anything associated with a *paille.* Yet now, given the chance, in the safety of their own neighbourhood, they were so hungry to be physically close, so curious, and so full of delight at making me claustrophobic. Resist the obvious conclusion, the traveller's fear; they were not the least bit interested in robbing me. They just want to *touch.*

Dizzy, worn-out by the barrage of questions and bodies, I was gathering myself to push through the wall of children when a voice beyond us broke into a yell. We all looked up. A Gypsy woman of about fifty, with short hennaed hair, marched toward us. I couldn't understand a word she was saying, but she was angry. Her march was angry, her face was angry, her voice was furious. I thought, Shit. I prefer these curious, slightly savage children to Athena, goddess of war. I was literally praying she was not angry at *me.* Had I done something very wrong? Was I trespassing?

As she crossed the road between the Gypsy houses and strode over to us, the children leapt away from me as though I had the plague. By the time her eyes looked at my face, I had it all rehearsed, my apology, the explanation that I was just going for a walk, I didn't mean to do anything I wasn't supposed to do, honestly, I was just—

"I am so sorry. Je suis vraiment desolée. They can be such little beasts when they get excited. You know children. But these ones especially. So much energy. C'est le printemps, tu vois? It's spring, the blood is flowing. I hope they weren't too bad."

I was stunned and relieved in equal portions.

She turned to the children. They stood in a loose group about five feet away, hanging off a lone square of chainlink fence or sharpening the toes of their shoes in the dirt, watching. Obviously for my benefit, she spoke to them in French, "You should be ashamed of yourselves, attacking this girl like animals. Mon Dieu. Janine, what would your mother say?"

Janine made a noncommittal gesture with her head, as if she had no idea what her mother would say.

My one defender, Carmen, remained standing close by. She spoke up, "I told them not to bother her."

A brief argument flared up between the older girls about who was doing what, whose fault it was, why they didn't invite me home for coffee.

"Enough! The next time you see her here, or any other stranger, don't be beasts. Now say hello properly and go play."

They all said "Hello." Despite the verbal remonstrance, most of them were already grinning and giggling. One of them even curtsied, quipped, "Hello. How do you do?" and ran away squealing with laughter.

Athena and I smiled. She put out her hand to me. "My name is Nanette. You are all right, aren't you?"

"Of course. They didn't hurt me. They were just so curious. All of them at the same time."

"Ahh, they weren't just curious. They had you, like a cat has a mouse. I was watching from my kitchen. But they don't even know, really, what they do. They don't understand. They're not bad, you know."

"No, no, I didn't think they were bad. Not at all."

She looked back toward the houses, then looked at me again. "Would you like to come in for a coffee?"

Coffee at Nanette's

NANETTE BROUGHT ME around to the front of the house, waving and chatting briefly with neighbours before she took me inside. Inside. A living-room with an old-fashioned chesterfield and two matching chairs; a dining room; the kitchen in the corner, half-hidden by a wall. Photographs and crucifixes. Ornaments: a dancing lady in a white wig, a cat, a glass bell. Landscape paintings like the ones you see in hotels, but this was a house, a family's home; witnesses to real lives and real days, paintings are transformed. The back door was open. An entourage of children came in to look at me and grab something to eat out of the fridge or the fruit bowl on the kitchen table. Nanette went into the kitchen to make coffee. The front door opened and slammed shut, spilling people in and out. Nanette's twenty-year-old son strode in; he blushed when our eyes met. What are you doing in our living-room? his face asked. I turned red in reply, equally embarrassed. He was naked to the waist like a model for Guess jeans, except that he wore cheap jogging pants splattered with oil stains. He introduced himself as Louis, then apologized for not being able to shake my hand; his were too dirty. To his mother, he said in a loud voice, "I can't fix it."

Nanette replied from the kitchen, "Wait until Papa comes home and he'll help you." Louis said goodbye but left without looking at me. The light screen door slammed behind him. A bawling little girl came in the back door. Nanette immediately abandoned the coffee production and picked the child up. She brought her into the living-room, cooed for a few minutes, kissed the scraped knee better, and sent her on her way again with a candy. Then the phone rang.

While Nanette was on the phone, two neighbour women dropped by and introduced themselves. Moussa was about thirty, with black hair loosely folded on top of her head, lots of gold jewellery, and a long, fashionable peasant skirt. Attractive, plump, made-up, she was very sure of herself, very at ease with me. She went into the kitchen to finish making the coffee. Nina was older than Moussa, clearly of a different generation, although not as old as Nanette. Her graying hair was pulled away from her face and tied up in a tight little bun. She wore a baggy print dress on her heavy body, smoked a cigarette on the sly, and became reticent, almost suspicious, when Moussa left us. She asked *me* questions, not the other way around. I was in the midst of answering them when another horde of children roared in the back door; I recognized four or five of them from the street. Were any of these small children Nanette's? At least one of them was Moussa's, who slipped out of the kitchen, skirt swaying. She pointed to the noisy throng and explained, "My daughter." Then she happily yelled at the entire group in Catalan; they waved at me, turned around, and marched back out the door.

In two more minutes, the four of us sat down together in the living-room with coffee cups in our hands.

"Is it always like this?"

"Like what?"

"So busy."

Moussa said, "So noisy."

Nina said, "So full of people."

Nanette replied, "Always. Except late at night. Even then, sometimes, it is like this." She grinned as she spoke, exuberantly proud. Yesterday, it happened: I met a vital person here. In fact, each of the women had that spark, the human flame I so rarely meet in Avignon. Through the openness of Nanette's face, in the delicious scent of the coffee that Nina carried in, with the plate of biscuits Moussa placed on the table, I knew they would speak, they would say things I would never hear at a gallery opening. I sipped some of the very strong coffee. Nanette, Moussa, Nina and I began to talk about the world, this world, our lives.

Nanette

"TO BE GITAN you must love this way of life, you must love being gitan. You must love these people all around you who can see into your kitchen and who know all your business. You must love them. Il faut! Myself, I see the difference between the two societies —les gitans et les pailles. With us, the family is still very important, very strong. We don't let our old people die in ugly buildings alone. We take care of them, we take them with us wherever we go. We live together, our doors are always open. We are still a tribe. That's what I tell the children. We are a tribe. How else can we survive as a people? The French want us to be just like them. Bah! I don't want it, I don't want their society. Even though we are sedentary Gypsies, we still have our freedom. La liberté est quelque chose dans le ventre. Freedom is something in the gut. La liberté."

Nina

"WE DON'T LIKE schedules, having to be at certain places at certain times. Tu vois, we could never be French, not really, and that's why the French don't like us. Sometimes they hate us. Just because we are half an hour late. What is half an hour? Good God! And if we get up in the morning and wash the kids and get them ready for school, we're content to take them there in our bathrobes and curlers. The French are too strict for us, too rigid. So what if we make a lot of noise in the supermarket! We are warm people. When I see someone I know, I go to them, we embrace, we laugh. I don't care if it's in the supermarket. The tomatoes are never embarrassed! Good God! I don't care if my hair is blown to the four winds and my sweater has a little tear in the shoulder. Is that any reason to call me a dirty Gypsy? And if the kids have chocolate all over their faces while we're pushing around the shopping carts, are the French going to die from it? No! At least the kids aren't howling and screaming. J'en ai marre, j'en ai marre d'habiter ici. I am sick of living here, sick of it. But this is my country. Where am I supposed to go? Where am I supposed to raise my children? They don't want us to live in the old way any more, they don't want us to live in caravans, on the roads. That's how I grew up. But now that way is dying. The pailles have finished le voyage. And this is what they offer us instead. Montclar. They treat us like dogs and wonder why we're unhappy."

Moussa

"IT'S HARD. YOU'VE seen Montclar, haven't you? And before, it was worse. The place they made for us to live was worse. They're all boarded up now, those houses, because none of us could live in them. Rooms without windows, rooms for fleas. A long time ago, when I was growing up, we used to live inside the city walls, near the palace, but then they wanted all that for the tourists, for new apartments. The city council wanted to clean it up. That's what they said, like we were dirt or something. And so they built us dog-houses and wanted us to live in those. You see why Nanette says we have to love it, this way of living, we have to love each other. Because there's nothing else for us to do."

This is not the desert

AVIGNON IS A SMALL city. It's hard not to run into Shaquil. Especially when he follows me around. "I hope you're not writing about all of this," he growled yesterday as I was leaving the little card shop down one of the those cramped and narrow side streets near St. Bénézet.

"Writing about all what?"

"About me. I haven't given you permission." He seemed genuinely angry.

"I don't need permission," I said. "I'll change your name."

"Don't you dare change my name!" He swore at me as I walked away.

Last week the phone rang at two in the morning. I leapt up to answer it, heart pounding. He hung up in my ear. Of course it was him. Marie, from Poésie dans un Jardin, told me that Shaquil believes he's coming back to Canada with me. "He is ahh, a little . . . ahh . . . obsessed. Peut-être. He thinks you'll come to see how much he loves you. He says he is going to stop drinking." She looked up from the papers on her desk and smiled wearily. "That part, about the drinking. That is a sad lie." Shaquil has thrown a chair at Marie, split her lip, and ran up a phone bill of calls to Africa that nearly ruined her business. "I've put up with more from Shaquil than I've put up with from any man in my life. But what to do? This is Avignon. C'est trop triste. He's the only person I can have a fascinating conversation with. When you get through all the shit, his mind is made of gold." She frowned, then peered at me over her reading glasses, the bright blue eyes shot with veins. "But be careful. Shaquil is just a friend. He's never been in love with me. The last person he was in love with, before you, was his wife. Just remember what happened to her." The phone rang, she turned away to answer it. When she turned back to me, the moment was gone. We started to talk about something else.

Arthur, the pale, small man who was with Shaquil the day I met him, claims he is very dangerous. "Shaquil carries a gun, you know. Il faut faire attention. C'est vrai. He imagines he is living alone in the desert like a Bedouin. But as we all know, this is not the desert. This is Avignon."

Unlike Marie, Arthur said it with such pride, This is Avignon. Of course I couldn't say, I think the desert would be fine right about now, I could really go for a little bit of desert.

"You can trust me," Arthur said, too reassuringly. "I wouldn't lie about Shaquil. Il est louche." Oh, louche, that loveliest of French words, denoting sly, untrustworthy, possibly dangerous. Louche. A word I learn and relearn in Avignon.

Arthur kept going, "Are you busy tonight? I was wondering if you'd like to go out to eat, or perhaps to a movie? Or we could just take a walk up by the palace."

Light rain with breast of cow

I GO TO THE Gypsy quartier a couple of times a week now, to talk to Nanette, the other women, the children. It's more difficult to approach the men. In conversation, they never let me past the wall of their humour and bravado. They are almost always in groups outside in the street, discussing the news and events of the day. Inside, in the cramped kitchens and living-rooms, women are more generous with their words.

When I leave the quartier, Nanette often walks me through the neighbourhood, toward my own street. "The more the people see you with me, the warmer they will be the next time you come. You will not be such a stranger."

Today we walk out the back door into a very light rain. The streets with the Gypsy houses are variously peopled, mostly with children, but also with old women who sit on chairs in their backyards, or cluster together on stools by the roadside. The most shrivelled, ancient-looking among them smokes a big wooden pipe. Her eyes are closed. Loose groups of young men stare as Nanette and I approach. After she introduces me to the ones I haven't met, I receive three generous offers of marriage. I promise I'll think about it and come back next week.

I expect the people to disappear because of the rain, but none of them goes inside. They are content to sit under the sky, getting damp, enjoying the slowness of the late afternoon. Children play in the rainy streets, all of them released from school now. Groups of older men talk among themselves quietly, leaning against cars and smoking their cigarettes with the air of tired *mafiosos*. One of them cleans the dirt out from under his nails with a pocket-knife. Some of these men smile, some scowl as Nanette and I pass on our way toward a dust and gravel compound between the houses. The scent of burning wood spices the air.

A large group of women and children are gathered around a barbecue. The barbecue itself consists of a large oil-can split in half, set on a rough wooden stand with a grate of chainlink fence thrown overtop. "What are they cooking?"

Nanette squints. "I think, mammelle de vache."

Mamelle, mamelle . . . What is *mamelle?*

Seeing I am unsure of this word, Nanette explains, "You know, the big breast of the cow."

Ahh. Cow's udder. Right.

Nanette introduces me to the women and children who stand around the fire. I will not remember these names, but I shake hands and smile and say hello. They ask me what I'm doing here in the quartier and would I like a piece of *mamelle de vache?*

I *am* a vegetarian. Most of the time. But in the interest of culture, I will eat anything. The short, fat woman who turns the meat on the grill begins to stare at me. I meet her eyes. We look at each other quite intently for a long moment. I can't read her emotion. Is she angry that I'm here, or annoyed, or just extremely curious? The noise of the children flaps around; Nanette, leaning over, talks to one of them; the wood embers crackle and flare. Light gray smoke and the smell of cooking meat rise between the cook and myself. She has a hard face, with a crooked nose, a dull gold incisor, narrow lips. And—I cannot help but notice—enormous breasts fill her brown sweater. I look down at the grill. With a quick, bare hand, she flips over the round pockets of flesh, teats still attached. She flips over the flatter white strips. Fat drippings sizzle and flare in the fire beneath.

"Have you ever had mamelle de vache before?"

"No, never."

"It's very good for you. Better than a mother's milk. It will make you stronger." She winks at me, half-mocking but friendly. Still she does not smile. (Again, that silence, even a silence in the body, in the gestures. She is kind, this woman; her voice has told me that. But also reserved, almost cold. I admire this quality because I lack it.)

No one seems to notice the light rain except for me; I don't open my umbrella. The fire coals are hot enough to withstand the damp and most of the strips of meat are done, branded with the diamond imprints of the chainlink grill. The cook begins to hand out pieces of *mamelle de vache.* A lanky boy of thirteen or fourteen who's been helping with the fire turns away now and walks over to the thin tree on the edge of

263

the compound. Coats, sweaters and a pale cloth bag hang from the tree's stunted branches. The boy takes the bag down and pulls out a heavy loaf of bread, which he begins to tear up, gently, with his charcoaly hands. He doles shares out to the children who've been playing near the barbecue, but awkwardly avoids my eyes as he hands a portion to the girl beside me. Nanette says, "Donne-la un peu du pain."

Now he glances up. Two large, black eyes. A wide, gold-brown face with full lips beneath a small, slightly turned-up nose. Strong cheek and jaw bones. An Indian face. Longish, uncombed hair. That wild look of energy around the mouth and eyes, an expression poised like a panther to leap into another place. He is so beautiful and so young that, for an instant, he resembles a woman more than a boy, especially when he drops his eyes. (The black eyelashes curtain out my face.) After tearing off a sizeable soft hunk of bread, he hands it to me with ash-covered fingers. "C'est pour toi, Mademoiselle," he explains, almost whispering, while the cook reaches across the barbecue to hand me a piece of whitish meat.

Cow's udder is very, very chewy. And greasy. I imagine, probably incorrectly, that whale blubber and cow's udder have something in common. That elasticity, that serious exercise for the jaw. With oily fingers, we stand and eat *mamelle de vache* in the rain, our bread fingerprinted with charcoal.

Nanette walks me to the street that leads out of the quartier, then kisses me goodbye. A few of the older girls walk on either side of me. They make jokes at my expense, particularly about my accent, my height, and my hair colour. They would prefer North American women to be extremely tall and extremely blonde; I am neither. When I cross the road that physically divides the Gypsy and Arab blocks from the French ones, the Gypsy girls stand at the edge of it, waving. As though they're on an island. As though the road I walk on now is a gray boat bearing me away from them, back to another country.

Lucette, la femme ou j'habite

"MAIS BIEN SÛR it's like another country, of course. What did you expect? They don't live the way we live and they probably never will. Did you see the conditions, did you? Dirty. Dirty people. Oh, really? You saw one clean house and you think that means they're all clean? That's probably the house they keep clean for the government officials to see, the welfare agents. You are so naïve, ma petite, you believe everything. So they gave you food, did they? I can imagine what kind of meat it was. A thousand times I offer you perfectly good beef and mutton, and not once, not once do you ever eat it, then you go to those dirty gitans and eat God-knows-what off a grill in the street. What was it, exactly? You don't know? What do you mean, you don't know? How could you eat something if you didn't know what it was? That's *insane*. Absolument fou. Tu es incroyable. Vraiment. Je comprends rien, moi, rien du tout. Mais écoute-moi. Listen to me. When I'm out, when I go to Arles for the weekend, when I go to Paris again next month, you must promise me: no gitans in the house. Absolutely not one. You mustn't invite any of them over, never. Don't say anything! Remember what happened with that other one, your Arab Casanova? Remember that? Wasn't that enough for you? Zoot! The neighbours are still complaining."

Gata, for her eyes

CARMEN, THE YOUNG Gypsy woman who is engaged, reminds me of Camino, the young Gypsy woman I met at the market in the Basque country. The world is made of these echoes. They both have green eyes and black hair, they're both beautiful sixteen-year-olds, and, within a year, they will both be married.

"Will you quit school?"

"Oh, I'm quitting school this year. I'm sixteen, I'm allowed."

"You don't like it?"

"No."

"Why not?"

"Because they don't like us there. All my friends are already out. So I don't have anyone. I could even quit now, if I wanted to. I turned sixteen two months ago."

"Then why don't you quit?"

"Ah, my mother says I should stay until this year's over. It's almost over. I can hardly wait."

"And you don't want to go to university?"

"Bah! No. It's too hard. Maybe secretary school or something. We'll see. And I don't know. When the babies come . . ."

"Babies?"

"Well, we will want children, you know."

"You're going to have them right away?"

"I don't think so. But that depends on my husband."

"What do you mean?"

"Well, if he wants kids as soon as we're married, then we'll start. It's important for the men to have children."

"Why?"

"Because that's what men *do*."

"What?"

She rolls her eyes. Canadian women can be so stupid. She blushes, squirms, whispers, "You know."

"Oh, that." Pause. "What if you don't want to have kids right away?"

Carmen considers this possibility. "I don't think of that." She plays with the charm bracelet on her wrist. "We'll see. That's what my mother always says, On verra."

Here, as always, words fail me, because the real voices go unheard. If history speaks through us, we are often deaf. Do we recognize that we are not only the products, but also the instruments of our own societies? It's easy for me to ask this question about Carmen, who will be married soon, who will be a mother soon, living as her mother lives, in the Gypsy ghetto of Avignon. But there are other ghettos.

The ghetto of flight and suitcase. The Vancouver condo ghetto. The intelligentsia ghetto. The bad relationship ghetto. The ghetto of the obese bank account and the bulimic soul. The ghetto of assholes. As luck would have it, we can inhabit more than one ghetto at a time.

Carmen's nickname is *Gata,* cat in Catalan, in Spanish, in Greek. *Gata,* for her green eyes.

Will you marry me?

IN NANETTE'S LIVING-ROOM again, over coffee, she explains, "Before, it was the parents who decided, and children were promised to one another from the time they were small. But now we have evolved, we have changed. If two young people want to marry and the families are in agreement, there is a great party. The wedding is prepared. The first night is the most important. An old woman goes into the chamber in the morning to check the *mouchoir*—to check if there is blood on the sheets. Si la fille etait donnée comme il faut. If the girl was given as she should have been given. Propre. Clean. This is very important, very beautiful. To have a clean girl. A virgin."

"That still exists?"

Laughing, because I am shocked, Nanette exclaims, "Bien sûr! C'est une chose de la tradition. C'est le plus beau moment de la vie. It is the most beautiful moment of life. An old woman who has held that position for years goes in to check for blood, and the other women, the older sisters and cousins and mothers, wait outside. When the woman brings the sheet out to show the women, they cheer and cheer, and the fathers of the couple embrace, and the brothers, and the men begin to play guitars, then the act of celebrating the marriage begins. Not before."

"Do all the young women agree with this tradition?"

"They have to. From the time they are very young, they know about this crucial moment. We explain to them, we teach them."

"But surely there must be young people who refuse the traditions, who want to have sex before they're married."

"But it's part of our tradition, and our religion. The girl must be clean. It's the most important thing in a woman's life."

"What if the sheet doesn't have any blood on it?"

"Then the young woman is disgraced, and the man doesn't have to marry her if he doesn't want to."

"But they had sex!"

"She wasn't a virgin, though. She wasn't clean."

"But what if her fiancé took her virginity?"

"She should have resisted. If she couldn't resist him, perhaps she won't resist others. It was a test."

"If her fiancé refuses the marriage, what will happen to her?"

"Maybe she will never get married. Maybe a man whose wife has died will take her. An old man or a young man with children to raise. It depends."

"What if a man isn't a virgin before he gets married?"

"It's different for men."

"Why?"

"Because it has always been different for men."

"If a couple gets married, and aren't happy together, what happens?"

"A man might leave and be with another woman for a few months, but he'll always go back. She's his wife. His children are with her. He'll leave but he'll go back. Divorce doesn't exist."

"And if a woman does the same thing, goes with another man, then what happens?"

"Aah, her husband might kill the other man. Maybe he'll kill her, too. A woman can't do that—have another man. It's not the same thing. A woman has to be responsible. That's what a woman is."

Chickens and children

"THERE'S A STUPID question the government people are always asking: Is it racism? Do you think the French are racist with you? Of course it's racism, what do they think it is? Stupid questions. That's why the kids quit school as soon as they're sixteen. And a lot of them quit sooner than that, if they can."

"What happens to them at school?"

"The teachers call them dirty Gypsies. The other kids call them dirty Gypsies, thieves, liars, all of that. Beggars. The bad things. Just like they do with the Arabs. And we have our arguments with the Arabs, too, but we live here together, we both live in this shit. It's ridiculous that the French still believe we steal chickens. Why would we steal a chicken when we can go to the supermarket and buy one, plucked and clean? Be good, little boy, or the Gypsies will come and take you away. Be good, or we'll sell you to the Gypsies. As if we would buy one of their brats!"

"Do you think Gypsies will ever integrate into French society?"

"But we don't want to. We are Gypsies. My family doesn't travel now, but we are still Gypsy. It doesn't change. We don't want it to change. When friends and relatives come through, travelling, we go across the river to the camp where they have their caravans, and we sit and talk and have a fire. Just as though we were all travelling together. But that's a hard life."

"Some Gypsies still do it?"

"Yes, many do. But it's very hard. There are Gypsy camps in France, in Italy, in northern Europe. But it's hard to make money. No more silver or copper work. Big companies collect the scrap metal now. Iron work is done by machines. Not very much horse trading. Less music. And it's even harder to get labour and harvesting jobs. So all the traditional work we used to do is dying out."

"That's happening to everyone. That's the world now."

"We don't refuse the world but we still love what we are. You should talk to the old women here. Then you would understand. I'm in the middle. When I was little, we travelled for a while, but my father came here and became a mechanic. And he trained my husband to be a mechanic. But when my husband was young, he sold contraband liquor and cigarettes from Italy and Yugoslavia. Illegal, yes, but there was nothing else, there was no other work to do. But you should talk to the old woman because they can tell you what that life was all about. You can't imagine it, when you see all this, the doghouses of Montclar and all the poor people here."

"You weren't poor before?"

"When you live in the caravans, you don't need very much money. We never had much money. But we didn't need money, then, to be rich."

Three old women

THREE OLD WOMEN sat on the couch in the late afternoon light of Nanette's house, ready to tell me about *le voyage*. Nanette asked them to come for my benefit; they would never speak to me otherwise, because I am a stranger and a *paille*. They were formal in their nervousness, and their nervousness was contagious. For fifteen minutes, I was dissatisfied with my one-line questions and the women's one-line responses. I hate interviews, and there I was, conducting a particularly awful one. At first, we only managed skeletal facts.

One of the women, Bijoup, seventy-five years old, was originally from Yugoslavia, but when her husband died ten years ago, she decided to come to Avignon; her niece, her sister, and two brothers live here, married to Gypsies of French and Italian origin. When she was young, she and her husband travelled by horse-drawn caravan all over Yugoslavia with trained bears, sometimes working for circuses or simply setting up in the streets and putting on shows for passersby. Bijoup's eyes sparked with humour sometimes (or was she just making fun of me?) but it was hard for me to understand her French, which was full of Catalan and Croatian words.

Of the three women, she was physically the most striking. A hunchback. Eyes the colour of old moss. Dark leathery skin. Large, arthritic hands. She was a very old, gnarled grapevine grown into a human being. Her voice rose from a throat ravaged by time and cigarette smoke. When I asked if I could take her photo, she replied, "Bien sûr" with a gravity that made me smile. The tight black-on-gray knot of wispy hair loosened and fell around her shoulders. When she fluffed it up with her wrinkled hands, pretending to "do" it, the other two women smiled. The shared memory of a ritual passed effortlessly between the three of them: each one was a young woman once, with beautiful hair to be brushed, plaited, undone.

I was glad I had the camera to play with because I was suddenly embarrassed by my own youthful presence. As I chattered and clicked away, all I thought was, I should leave. I really should go. What am I doing here, intruding, with all my presumptions?

Sophie's white hair hung down to her shoulders. She had a fleshy face, a big, soft body, clear brown eyes, lighter skin than the other women. Born seventy years ago near Marseilles, she travelled all over France and southern Spain with her husband, who went to factories, bought the cheap remains, and sold them at a higher price. They travelled with a horse caravan until the late 1960s, when her husband bought a car. Of their seven children, two died in infancy: one of an unknown illness, the other of meningitis. Her husband died two years ago. Three times she said to me, solemnly, deliberately, "That life was better than this one."

Sophie is well-known in the Gypsy and Arab ghetto for being able to cure fever and sunstroke, and heal burns. She discovered this power after the fever-death of her own child. Every year she travels to the holy French city of Lourdes to get water from a certain spring there. Although she wouldn't describe to me *how* she does it, the other two women and Nanette confirmed that she uses this holy water to draw the fever and burn-pains out of dozens of Gypsy and Arab children.

Jeanne was the oldest woman, at seventy-nine, but she seemed the youngest. She smoothed her dark orange skirt over her knees and giggled. Her gray hair was parted in the middle and held away from her face by two gold barrettes. Her family and Sophie's often travelled together, again collecting the remains at factories to sell at a higher price, but her husband is also a guitarist. During the summer months, they lived off his earnings at festivals, then came back to Avignon for the winter. He is ten years older than she is, "and still very much alive!" she told me, laughing in a high-pitched voice. She leaned over to nudge Bijoup in the side. I expected her to blush. I would have loved to see a seventy-nine-year-old woman blush.

Jeanne primarily wanted to make jokes and get her photograph taken—she wasn't interested in talking about her past as a travelling Gypsy. (Why should she have been, really, especially with a nosy stranger?) But her unforced laughter and her coquettishness relaxed everyone. Her humour was the door that opened the conversation. Soon the women were talking about their husbands, arguing, trying to remember certain details of their lives, how different it is now, how different the world is. Every thread of the conversation wove itself back to that, the one solid fact of modern existence: life is different now, life is changed, life is changing. They used to travel cross-country for months in horse-drawn caravans; now the TGV will get them to faraway Paris in four hours. They used to cook daily on open fires; now Jeanne proudly reminded everyone that her son bought her a microwave last month. Sophie said microwaves make you go blind. Bijoup said microwaves should only be used by businessmen and astronauts. I couldn't tell if she was joking.

Sophie insisted vehemently, "That life was better than this one."

"No," Jeanne replied, shaking her head with a school teacher's firmness. "I like having a house that doesn't move. I like being in the neighbourhood, with friends around all the time. It's easier this way."

Bijoup took a more philosophical stance. "Nothing is easier with cars and televisions. Life is still very hard. But it's more difficult to say why it's hard. It's more difficult to understand the world."

I stayed with them for almost three hours, asking questions but mostly listening to them. We drank tea with milk and ate chocolate biscuits. They were occasionally curious about the scribbled notes I took, though only Jeanne knew how to read. She made her husband teach her. "If he refused to read with me, I wouldn't go under the covers with him." Enormous laughter rose in the room.

As the women spoke, shadows began to darken

the crucifixes and paintings. Nanette was in the kitchen, cooking supper; we smelled the frying garlic. The temporarily quiet house threatened to fill again with Nanette's younger children and grandchildren, with her husband, who would soon come home from work. Her son Louis, wearing a shirt this time, walked in the front door and halted in the living-room. He glanced at me suspiciously, greeted the old women, then marched past us, right out the back door.

I shook hands with Bijoup, with Sophie, with Jeanne. They wished me luck. They asked me to come back and visit them again. I could not say "Je vous remercie" enough times. They walked out the door one by one, slowly, careful of the cracked concrete steps. Bijoup's hunched back, more deformed than I thought, made her lean over the ground. Again I thought of the twisted cords and thickness of an grapevine. In the narrow street between the houses, Sophie took Jeanne's left arm. Bijoup, the smallest of the three, took Jeanne's right arm. Then the three old women walked slowly down the darkening lane. I watched them until the sound of their voices disappeared.

A story begins at night

BIJOUP ESPECIALLY STAYS in my memory. I think of her for days. The strange, growling voice full of words I didn't understand. Her old-moss eyes and knotted fingers. After walking for two hours by the dirty Rhône, I wind my way home in the dark, carrying the old women with me. I avoid the underpass where the beggars sleep. I avoid the abandoned housing project, another jail for the Arabs.

Abandoned buildings are dangerous at night.

Night. Bijoup's voice, "An old woman cannot voyage alone." Sophie, with St. Bernadette's holy water, drawing the pains out of burned children. Jeanne, a seventeen-year-old in a seventy-nine-year-old body, a woman who wanted to read, and did. I'm exhausted, exhausted by them, I'm carrying around two hundred and twenty-four years of presence inside me, three old women.

Night in Avignon, dear city of thieves and assassins. Walk along the city walls. Through the next underpass, singing. Don't forget to sing at night, don't forget to leave your own thin echo here, with the pigeons and the waking rats and the car exhaust.

Night in Avignon, past the silent fruit markets and the Algerian butchershop. Past the shoeshop and the small grocery market where a man once gave you a chocolate bar. Past the *boulangerie* where they know your name at last, and actually use it. The house with the ceramic snail on the roof. Who lives there? Surely, if something bad happened to you on this street, if you cried out "Aidez-moi!" whoever lives in the house with the ceramic snail would come out, they would come out and help you.

But nothing bad will happen tonight. The wind has changed. The mistral has blown itself away and now, what do you smell on the faint breeze? The hidden gardens.

I smell the gardens. Lilac. Bigger, more ornamental blossoms than we have in Canada, but lilac, unmistakably. (Summer at the Pallisters', white and purple bouquets in the old house, around my feet on the sun roof.)

Night, and the erratic blue dance of bats below the streetlights. What did Bijoup say about bats? "If things are going badly for you, put a bat's wing under your pillow. A bat can see in the dark. It will fly after your good luck and bring it back." Bijoup and Jeanne and Sophie. Sleeping now, or getting ready for bed in their nightdresses and slippers. Bijoup, who told me that she once loved a bear. Bijoup. A bat's wing.

A story.

The Day Mandori Died
a Yugoslav Gypsy tale

WHEN DUHA WANTS me out of her way, she always tells
me to go and knit with the other women at Stojan's,
the only big house in the quarter, with a good wood-
burning stove the old man rescued from a dump not
far from here. "Mama, you haven't been out of the
house for days, you just sit there at the fire, staring
like a scarecrow. Aren't you tired of it? At least if you
went to sew with the other women, you could talk to
them. The days pass too slowly for you here. Mama?
Can you hear me?"

I've taken to not answering her when I don't want
to, so now she thinks I'm deaf. Why did my son marry
such a stupid woman? All she thinks of are perfume
and a velvet dress she saw two years ago in the city.
She paints her fingernails. He wanted Duha because
she was pretty, like a little doll at fifteen. I admit I liked
her then, too, but I'd never lived with her, had I? My
husband Rajko talked to her father only because he
was rich. The wedding lasted four days and five

hundred people came, even relatives we'd never seen before from Romania, but that was seven years ago. Now Nebosja tires of her more than I do. He's always off in the city or travelling to Italy, thinking I don't know what he does there. Of course I do. People like Nebosja and Duha are wrong to think they can fool children and old women. We learn the truth in ways that my son and his wife are both too old and too young to understand.

DUHA THINKS the days pass slowly for me, but she has no idea how quickly time slips away now. Sometimes it seems I've only drawn a few breaths in the morning when I look out the window and see the sun dropping red down the sky. All day long, the grandchildren and their friends are in and out of the house, chasing dogs around the tables and chairs, slamming the door until it rattles on its hinges. For a while, Duha sent them to school, but they hated it. Not only were the *gadja* children cruel to them, but their teachers called them dirty Gypsies. They're better off learning what they can at home and staying away from *gadjas*. Soon the boys will be old enough to voyage with Nebosja, and he will teach them his trade. He smuggles all kinds of things out of Yugoslavia and in from Italy. I knew before he did that he would end up living that way. At least he feeds his children, and his old mother.

When he was born, I prayed he would take after my family, and go to Zagreb to work with horses. Rajko wanted him to learn the bears, of course, because that had been his work before the accident. But Nebosja disappointed us both. We voyaged all during his childhood, from Kosovo and Montenegro, along the

Dunav to Beograd, through the heart of Croatia, where Rajko worked with my father and brothers for three years. But even with so much *Tsigane* voyaging in his blood and memory, my son became a city Gypsy, living on the outskirts of Sarajevo like a leech sucking an ox in a swampy ditch. Yes, he goes to Slovenia and Italy, but without a caravan—not even one pulled by a car!—and without his family. He considers this hovel where he leaves us a home. His children will never know what it means to be truly *Tsigane*. They will survive—*Tsiganes* always have—but they will grow up with the ghost of what their people were inside them. That spirit will give them no rest unless they learn to make the journey their home.

My grandchildren are still too young to know about that. They play with the dogs, track dirt through the house, and joyfully torment Stojan's donkey, who lays back his long ruined ears and tries to bite anyone who comes near. Winter treats us like a pack of animals, killing the weakest among the old and the young. While the snow outside turns to mud before it hits the ground, men in the dirt-floor bar drink as much *slivovitz* as they can buy with money pilfered from their wives and daughters. All of us have pulled our bodies through knee-deep mud, enough mud to last a pig ten lifetimes. My skin has turned gray after so many of these winters. Even the whites of my eyes are gray. It's an ugly way to live, but when Rajko died I had no choice but to come here. An old woman cannot voyage alone.

I WATCH THE fire so much now because I see other fires inside it. Once, I made roaring fires with my own hands, fires outside, in the mountains. I have not always lived here. Sometimes when night rolls over the quarter, the children come to me and ask for stories about voyaging. So I tell them the world I remember, I paint pictures with my voice. Even Duha sits near the fire like one of her own children, wrapped in brown woollen blankets. A strange thing happens then, as our small kitchen fills with people from the quarter who've come to listen. I rarely speak during the day now—I have nothing to say—but when the children ask at night, my lips move so easily, I forget I am telling stories. My lips take me farther and farther from the fire-shadowed faces before me, to the green places and times when Rajko was still alive and we lived with the bears.

YEARS AGO, in one of the *Tsiganes'* many countries, a young girl woke before dawn after a strange dream, put her hands to her round belly, and knew she was pregnant. Sick with shame, unable to understand how this disaster had happened, she slipped out of her family's tent and went down to the riverside to drown herself. She stood in her night skirts at the edge of the water, weeping. Knowing the most beautiful possession a *Tsigane* woman owns is her virginity, the girl realized someone had stolen hers, although she had no memory of the thief. She cried and cried at the edge of the water, afraid of throwing herself into the fast current, but unable to stand the thought of shaming her family by giving birth to a bastard. As the sun rose beyond the trees, she filled her skirt with heavy stones from the bank and began wading into the icy river.

She stared down into the water as it came higher and higher up her legs, freezing her skin and drowning out the sounds of her weeping and all the calls of the wakening birds. Just as she was about to let herself fall into the strong current, she heard someone's voice. She backed towards the river's edge a few paces, slipping on the slick pebbles. Her eyes ran along the shore of the opposite bank, searching for the one who called her name, but no one was there. The bank behind her was empty, too. When she heard her name called a second time, she looked down, sure the voice had risen from the river. It told her not to kill herself. "Return to your family's tent and tell them a miracle has taken place. You will give birth to a creature who will become a great friend to your people. You will call it *ursa*, the bear."

SOME OF OUR OWN clan don't believe that story, because the new ways from the city make them forget the magic hidden in the mountains. But I know it's true. That is how the *Tsiganes* became bear-keepers. Hundreds of years ago, we voyaged with bears from village to village, town to town, where they danced to our music, amazing the *gadjas,* who thought we were very brave and clever to have trained such savage beasts. The whites paid in gold and silver and fine Turkish cloth to watch our spectacles and tricks. Of course, we never told them how gentle the bears really were. We have always fooled *gadjas*—anything is permissible with a *gadja*—and the bears helped us many times by roaring and rising up like giants to scare the pale-faced crowds.

But the *Tsiganes* became greedy. We began to

forget the bears were our brothers, born of a *Tsigane* woman. We stopped teaching our children the language of the bears. Soon the young *Tsiganes* treated them like any other animal, even chaining them up and whipping them to work when they were tired or sick. Betrayed and angry with us, the bears left the caravans to live freely in the forests. From then on, if we wanted them to help us, the men had to hunt out she-bears and steal away their cubs. Because we were foolish and treated them like any other wild animal, that is what they became.

"STUPID BEAST!" Rajko shouted. He spat over his shoulder towards me, and gave the carcass a powerful kick. Shivers ran over my arms when the net of black flies lifted noisily into the air. Only the middle of August, and Mandori was dead. We still had two months' journey ahead of us, but our bear could not work for us now. Rajko grew angry when I tried to tell him that Mandori's death was an omen against us; I held my tongue. Sometimes I thought my tongue should have grown out of the palm of my hand, because always I was holding it.

I knew that if an animal died of a strange sickness, bad times were ahead. Great swathes of Mandori's hair had fallen out, the holes in his skin seeped yellow blood, and he'd grown thin as an old woman. My husband was born with only a small jar of kindness. It seems the first two children drank most of it up, like thirsty kittens, because when the third child, Mina, was born, Rajko forgot how to laugh. If we were travelling alone, and he started drinking, I would take the little ones and some blankets and sleep in the forest. I carried a bat's wing to help us find a good path through the dark. I made marks on the trees so we would be able to find our way back to the camp. He still beat me when we appeared in the morning, but not for very long, not as badly as he did when I stayed through the whole drunk night. *Slivovitz* made him forget how strong he was, or how soft my bones were. Even now, an old, old woman, I have a bump in my nose and a crooked arm that aches when the rain comes. When I was married, my mother told me I was allowed to run away from my husband if he beat me too much, without a reason. I thought I was very kind to Rajko because, although I left him, I always returned.

THE DAY MANDORI died, my children and I slipped into the woods to hide until Rajko's anger went away. When he left the camp to fetch water at the base of the hill, I slung Mina in a blanket against my chest and called the other children to follow me. In the beginning, when I went off like that, I was always very frightened of *gadjas* and wolves, but the scents of the rocks and mushrooms and moss calmed me. I learned to trust the way the darkness turned my feet into eyes. The night after Mandori's death, we had the moon to guide us. In that silver light, bushes and stones became animals, but none of them hurt us. After walking through ten songs and a prayer, we made a leaf-bed on the grass and wrapped ourselves in our blankets. The trees we slept under pointed out faces and animals drawn in the stars. I told the children stories so we would not be afraid, and gave each of them a piece of hard sugar because they had been so quiet when we left the camp.

When I fell asleep, I dreamed of running through the forest. All I could see was the earth rushing beneath me as fast as any mountain stream. Stones and twigs and the gnarled ropes of tree roots blurred as I ran. My breath rose and fell faster and faster until I thought my heart would burst. I stared at the swirl of ground with my hideous feet pounding over it, crushing leaves and grass, my blackened nails digging into the earth. In the dream, I was terrified, fleeing from torches and vicious voices. The faster I ran, the more dangerous the forest became. They were everywhere, everywhere, the running fires and naked, tall-as-tree animals, coming for me, their howls slicing through the dark.

A cry woke me. Sweating despite the cold darkness, I reached out to make sure the children were still there beside me, then I threw my blanket away from my legs and tried to kick off my shoes, angry because they clung to my feet as though nailed. Finally I knocked them away and tore off my wool socks. I was so relieved I began to cry. They were still the same; nothing evil had happened. I touched the children's faces and lay back down in the dark. For a long time, I watched the glittering walk of the stars across the sky, wondering about the truth inside my dream. I had dreamt that my feet were like Mandori's. My feet had become the paws of a bear.

A WOMAN'S CRIES woke us in the morning. It sounded as though her heart were being torn out of her with a meat hook: I had never heard such noises before. Every tree caught her voice and threw it down to us. The children began to cry and crowd around me, thinking a monster was coming to devour them. "No, no, it's not a monster, it's a woman, somewhere in the trees, near us, and she must be in terrible pain. We'll go get Papa and help her." My heart pounded in my throat as I gathered up blankets and tied Mina to my body. I imagined thieves murdering a woman, coming to murder me and my children, torture us, make us suffer like the owner of that voice. She seemed to be everywhere in the forest, so powerful were her cries. I wanted to run but knew the children couldn't keep up, so I forced myself to walk, checking the marked trees carefully, worried my fear would confuse me and make me lose the way back to Rajko.

Frightened by the screams, Nebosja and Kali whimpered, following so closely behind me that twice I tripped and fell into the wet grass. We walked more slowly now, because I knew our path was leading us towards the cries, not away from them. I couldn't see through the green forest wall, but I heard how close we were to the woman. When she stopped screaming, we stood still, listening for the sounds of men or dogs, but there was only silence. Even the birds were hushed.

Beyond the small clearing and two fallen spruce trees, we would have to climb a small, steep embankment. A deer trail rising up the other side would take us to our camp very quickly. When we came to the edge of the clearing, the woman suddenly began to roar. I thought, A demon is borne inside her. She was very close now, somewhere on the hillside we needed to climb. We skirted the clearing's edge and began walking upward through the thinning trees. She was alone, I decided, she needed our help. Now Mina began to howl against my pounding chest. Nebosja and Kali quickly joined him. I had to pull them along behind me.

By the time we reached the top of the hill, the voice was silent. There were no more cries. Had the woman fallen into a fever? Had she died? I was sweating, biting my lips to keep my fear in my mouth. My heart pounded so hard I could feel it in my tongue, in the backs of my legs, in my hands. As we hurried along the crest of the hill, I looked down through the poplars and glimpsed movement just above the fallen trees, the ones I'd climbed over with the children the night before. I made them wait while I went down the hill a few paces, trying to see clearly.

When I saw her I remembered my dream, and understood. I crossed myself and prayed quickly, touched a tree for strength, and wiped the sweat from my face. I ran up the hill to Nebojsa and Kali. "Quickly, quickly, we have to get Papa, we have to run." And they jumped up like rabbits and followed me down the deer trail. We ran all the way back to camp. "Rajko," I shouted when I saw the caravan. "Rajko! Wake up, wake up! There's a bear on the hillside, a she-bear in a trap!"

When he woke up, ghoul-eyed and stinking of *slivovitz*, he grumbled, "You liar!" He crawled out of the tent with his trousers undone. "You're just afraid I'm going to hit you for running away again!" The moment he took hold of my arm, Nebojsa and Kali screamed. Nebojsa said, "There's someone in the forest who needs help, Papa, quickly." Rajko narrowed his eyes against me for three seconds, then turned and stepped up into the caravan. He came out with his gun and spat on his hands. "If you're lying . . ."

When we found her on the hill, we feared she was

dead. The fur on her leg and chest and all the grasses beneath her were drenched in blood. After Rajko chained and muzzled her, he prised the steel jaws away from her front leg. The paw fell crookedly against the earth. The flesh around the teeth-marks of the trap was swollen and torn, raw, like badly quartered meat. I looked up and down the hillside many times, checking for the small cuts I'd made the night before on the trees. I could not understand how we had passed the same way as the bear without meeting the trap. We must have stepped in the very place where she now lay.

Rajko was very happy. From her teeth, he knew she was young, just a yearling. If she did not die from loss of blood, we might be able to train her. We bandaged her up and wrapped both front paws in thick leather, in case she grew angry. She did not struggle against the chain after Rajko poked her awake, but he insisted I use some of the sleeping herbs to keep her weak. These I sprinkled over her head and all around her body, singing the old Romani chants. Then I began to walk up the hill with the children. Rajko led and sometimes dragged the young bear. She whimpered through the thick wooden and leather muzzle. Seeing her blood-matted bulk limping behind Rajko made it hard to believe that I'd mistaken her voice for a woman's. I pulled the children close against my hips. Perhaps if she heard me in pain, I thought, she might think my cries belonged to a bear.

We broke camp that day and travelled for many miles with the she-bear in the caravan. Rajko laughed often through the groves of chestnuts and oaks, clicking his tongue at the white horse between bars of the songs he sang. When we stopped late in the afternoon to water the mare, he burst out laughing at the back of the wagon. "By now, the *gadjas* have gone to their trap and found Mandori's miserable carcass, his chewed-up hide! We tricked them out of this fine monster!" He thrust his stick into the wagon, waking her. She lifted her big head with a growl and swung it from side to side. "That's it, my beauty! Wake, wake up!" He poked her again. I brought a bucket of water from the stream and leaned into the caravan.

"Can she drink through the muzzle?" I asked.

"Of course. Even if she couldn't, what would you have me do? Undo it? She'd bite my head off."

"Bah, her mouth isn't big enough." But I was thinking that the bear had finer taste; she would never choose to eat a man like Rajko.

"She's very strong, you know. She's not so big as Mandori was, but when she gets well, you'll see what she's really like. We have to file her teeth and get a nose ring in her as soon as we get to Maretko's camp. By then she'll be well enough to start working on."

I watched her drinking from the bucket. She did not look down into the water as other animals do, but stared at Rajko with her small black eyes. He was gazing in the other direction, towards the children. When he glanced at her again, he noticed she was staring at him. "What pig-eyes she has." He coughed and spat at the caravan wheel. "Take the water away from her now."

"But she's still drinking."

"She's had enough."

I touched the fur below one of her ears before I lifted the bucket out.

"You aren't afraid of her?" Rajko asked.

I poured the remaining water into the grass. "Only a little. There's the muzzle." I rubbed my fingers against my wrist, remembering her fur. Much softer than Mandori's coat, it shone cinnamon brown, like a deer's. I don't know why I lied to Rajko; I wasn't afraid of her at all. Even without a muzzle, even without the leather wraps on her paws, I would not have been afraid.

RAJKO THOUGHT IT would take two weeks to arrive at Maretko's camp on the outskirts of Pozarevac, where many *Tsiganes* owned bears. In Pozarevac, he could find the help he needed to pierce Paskanini's nose and file her teeth. As we travelled towards Maretko's camp, through the mountain passes and shallow green valleys, moments from my childhood woke up behind my eyes. While I was small, my father worked in a circus, with our horses, but the other trainers often asked him for his help.

Once he and the other men wrestled a bear to the ground. First they jammed a stick between the bear's jaws, as though strangling a horse with its own bit, then two others roped its legs and heaved it down against the ground. The camp children came to watch this event. My father, who shod his own horses and aimed well with the hammer, was given the task of pounding a spike through the bear's nose, then pushing a ring through and soldering it shut. I watched him do this. On the first strike of the hammer, the bear, even through its muzzle, screamed, and a thin streak of red suddenly appeared on my father's neck. At first I thought it was his own blood, then I saw that all the scarlet marks on his face and shirt and hands came from the bear. After the animal's first fury of pain died away, it howled and groaned like a sick child. I went to my mother and asked, "Is there a boy inside the bear, crying?"

My mother told me, "No, of course not. The men ringed its nose, and it cried."

I said nothing. I stood sliding my fingers around the rim of a wet cooking pot. She looked at me impatiently and wiped the dirty tear-streams from my cheeks. "None of that, my child. Men must be stronger than animals. Go play with your sisters."

RAJKO STRUCK his switch against the side of the wagon. "What are you staring at?"

"Nothing." I bit my lip. "The trees."

"Well, wipe that fortune-teller's look off your face. Didn't you say you wanted to knit Nebosja a sweater? You've been sitting there doing nothing for two hours. What's in your head?"

"I'm just thinking about the bear."

"The bear is my business." Pursing his lips, he flicked the willow switch at the horse. "But it's a good thing you came for me. That was a rare piece of luck. What shall we call her?"

"Paskanini."

"Paskanini? Why?"

"It was the name of a bear my father ringed when I was a little girl."

"Paskanini." Rajko tasted the name in his mouth. "Do you know what it means?"

"Name of a river near Zagreb."

"A river." He tapped his stick against the wagon. "All right. We'll call her Paskanini."

I hid my smile until nightfall, then spilled my joy into the children's games. Preparing camp that night, I sang like a girl in love. I had lied to my husband. Paskanini was the name of a crow I kept as a child. At thirteen, I learned who my future husband would be. My father also told me that when I left home, he was going to kill the crow. I let Paskanini's clipped feathers grow in secret. When they were long enough, I cut the leather string from her leg and gave her to the sky.

AFTER THREE DAYS, we knew Paskanini the bear wouldn't die from loss of blood, but Rajko was angry because she would not eat. He gave her bread and the dry skins of cheese, but she did not even sniff these offerings. In the mornings when he went out to hunt, I tried giving her an apple. She lowered her head over the fruit, looked back and forth like a secretive child, and bit loudly into the red skin. I gave her another one. She ate it in three bites. Rajko would have been angry because the apples were for us. Animals ate only leftovers and what they managed to forage for themselves. He had been very cruel to Mandori, too, feeding him nothing through the winter months but dried bread. Already Paskanini was much stronger than Mandori had been for a long time. Her paw was still too raw to walk on, but she could stand up on three legs now. Often she became very angry at the chains and muzzle. She tried to roar, but the muzzle ruined her anger. She constantly tried to slip the heavy chain off her head, but it was much too tight. After a week in the caravan, a collar of raw skin showed around her neck where the metal had rubbed away her fur. All this time she ate almost nothing but some berries and a few smuggled apples. Leaner and quiet and accustomed to my voice, she let me wash her caked and dirty fur.

While she was still well-chained and muzzled, I cleaned the wound in her paw. She lost a toe—it just came away by itself, rotted—but the deep cuts were closing over and didn't bleed any more. She would always limp, but by the time we arrived in Maretko's camp to have her teeth filed, Rajko said she would be ready to start training. "We'll spend a month there and then move on to Skadarlija. She'll know a few tricks by then." He laughed and stretched his arm behind the log we were leaning against to pick up the tambourine. When he shook it, Paskanini, sitting beside the wagon, and the children, eating apples in the dirt a few feet from the fire, all lifted their heads at the same moment and looked towards him. The children began to laugh and begged him to sing.

THE TAMBOURINE'S bright rattle made me remember how Rajko trained Mandori. The bear was sick for weeks after his teeth were ground down to his gums. He could not eat. Just when he started to get better, the men heaved him down again and pierced his nose and pushed the ring through. Then a rope was tied to the ring. The other end of it was tossed over a tree branch and I pulled it tight, forcing Mandori to lift his bloody nose and head. Then Rajko came forward with a long hot iron from the fire and poked it at Mandori's paws while I shook the tambourine. The bear stood up on his hind legs and turned circles, stretching his paws in the air to escape the pain of the burning iron. We did this so many times that soon

Rajko did not have to burn his paws; as soon as Mandori heard the tambourine's rattle, he stood up and turned around. Rajko taught him other tricks in similar ways, always deceiving him with pain. Soon after Rajko and I married, I refused to help him train the bear. I could not stand the animal's cries. My refusal marked the occasion of my first beating. Afterward, I obeyed my husband unless I was sure I could fool him.

The tambourine brought the children over to play. I scolded Nebosja for jumping over the fire. Paskanini turned her head from side to side, trying to understand the new rattling sound of copper and beaten leather. The fire barely reached her now; she was a tawny ghost sitting by the wagon, like an old woman wrapped in a mountain of blankets. Her eyes caught light and glowed red with the flames. I kept myself from rising and going to sit near her. On the long travels, I missed the voices and ears of other women. When Rajko was off hunting or doing work for the farmers, I often talked to the dog and the horse. They listened to my worries about my husband and children, my songs, my memories of my family in Zagreb. The horse's ears danced as I spoke, and the black dog watched me carefully. The dog, I knew, wanted very much to speak, but he could only bark and thrust his paws in my lap.

Paskanini watched me in the same wise-eyed way. She was beautiful. The thought of Rajko ringing her nose and burning her paws made me wish I had never found her in the trap. She would have died if we had not saved her, but her time with us would be an ugly time, more difficult than dying. By keeping her alive, who knows the heaven I denied her? That night by the fire, watching her, I secretly whispered, "Forgive me."

FIRE WAS THE first and last gift of the day. The smell of smoke always slept in my skirts, clung to my hands. At five in the morning, when Rajko and the children were still asleep, I inhaled the smell of my husband's back, sweat and warm skin, then my own hands: smoke, from the night before. The wind pawed the caravan as I rose.

Outside, the small clearing was full of white mist and the smell of damp flowers, like a green bowl full of sweet milk. Fog hung above us, too, obscuring the forested hills and mountains, pierced now and again with sharp birdsong. As soon as I stepped down from the caravan, I heard Paskanini groan. Before we had gone to sleep, Rajko had chained her to a tall, thick oak tree. I peered around the edge of the wagon. She stood and heaved all her weight against the chain until there was no more breath in her, then she fell back, found her strength again, and tried once more to pull herself free. The raw skin under her collar was bloody now.

Motionless, I watched Paskanini pulling herself towards the trees for a long time. I willed the chains to give way, but they were too strong. When I heard the children stirring, I began gathering witch's hair from the trees, a few small twigs, then took one, never two, of the thick wooden matches from Rajko's tin box. In a few seconds, flames danced under my cold palms and Paskanini collapsed, exhausted, at the base of the tree.

When the fog lifted that day, the sun roared down

on us and burned every wispy cloud out of the sky. It was the hottest day we'd had all summer. Rajko tied the horse near the river. We decided not to travel because it was so hot. Nebosja found a deep pool down the river and took Kali for a swimming lesson. I spent the day mending and washing clothes. Rajko complained it was too hot to go hunting. He had already caught fish for the evening meal, he said, and he had no interest in taking a nap with the children when they returned from swimming. He repaired his saddle and a pair of reins. With nothing else to do, he began to drink. When I came up from the river with a wet bundle of clothes in my hands, I found him poking Paskanini with his walking stick, talking to her as though she were an idiot beggar. She was still muzzled but he'd undone her chains because he wanted her to move.

I began hanging clothes, my back to my husband and the bear. "Why don't you let her be, Rajko? She's hot like the rest of us and wants to rest in the shade." He was not so drunk that my voice would infuriate him. Already taunting Paskanini, he was uninterested in me.

"I want her to move because she has the best tree in the clearing. It will be hot tonight; we'll sleep outside. I'll bring out the beds and I want to get her smelly carcass away from here. She must move!" He heaved on her chain, at the same time protecting himself from her with the sharp end of his walking stick. Paskanini would not budge, except to bat away the stick and shake her heavy head at Rajko. He laughed and poked her in the belly. She growled.

I turned away to hang up my husband's trousers, biting my lips in anger. Fool, I thought, cursing the man I was forced to share a bed with. Paskanini's growls came louder now. Rajko bellowed laughter. When he banged the stick down on her back, I kept myself from watching, but I could hear the blows thudding against her body. He taunted her into swiping at him, as he had done with Mandori, then he beat her. Her groans and growls deepened his laughter.

Clenching my teeth, I hung up the rest of the clothes. Just as I drew my arm across my damp forehead and began to turn around, ready to fight with him, Rajko's voice flew up as though his mouth had been torn open.

Silence swept down in the clearing. I didn't see how she had knocked the sharp stick from his hand, but when I turned around, Paskanini stood tall, taller than Rajko, swaying slightly, and he looked up at her wide-eyed, his jaw fallen open. In that moment, each of us and every tree and all the grasses in the clearing knew what was going to happen. I was not surprised when her heavy paw cut quickly through the air, surely, the way Rajko hit me sometimes, with a fast open hand. But her hand was clawed. When she struck Rajko across the face, all the strength of her mountain-born body flowed into her like a deep river. My husband's body followed the sharp twist of his neck. His head struck the earth before Paskanini lowered herself, still growling, to the ground. She pulled on the chain as I had seen her do in the morning, but now she fell into a few heavy steps, and lumbered around Rajko's body.

I stood absolutely still, watching her smell my husband's knees. "Paskanini," I said.

My voice frightened her. She backed away from Rajko. Mina whimpered from inside the caravan.

"Paskanini," I said again. I had spoken the name many times, whenever I gave her food or water. Paskanini's chest rose and fell with her deep breaths. When I took a step forward, she growled deeply. She growled again and lumbered towards me while I reached into the food sacks in the caravan and felt the apples under my fingers. "Let me give you an apple," I said.

Then she looked at me. Because a bear's eyes are small, Rajko always said their brains were small, too, but she understood me. If Rajko awoke to find me feeding her apples instead of chaining her up, he would beat me senseless. In a terrible, shameful way, I didn't care if he were dead. I was glad Paskanini had stopped him from hurting her. She was braver than I was. Both my hands drifted forward, slowly, slowly, one holding the apple, the other moving to unhook the muzzle. When her mouth was free, she quickly lifted the red fruit from my hand. While she chewed, I undid the collared chain from around her neck. Her nose and lips were wet with crushed apple and juice. When the heavy chain fell down, she stretched her head back into the air and swung it from side to side. Then she stopped, remembering I was still there, watching. She looked at me again. I gave her another apple and stood up very slowly, gathering the heavy muzzle and the chain in my arms.

I had not yet seen Rajko. He had fallen away from me, onto a flat outcropping of stones. A pile of dry branches hid his head and upper body. Now, walking past the kindling, I saw the torn-away side of his face. Paskanini had peeled him like a red-fleshed orange. His blood painted the stones and the green blades of grass. I hurried past him into the trees, farther down the river, to the place where my children had been swimming. A basin of deep water eddied behind an outcropping of boulders. Not a single stone was visible in the depths. Standing on a high rock on the bank, I looped the chains through the leather muzzle and tossed them into the deep pool. The splash was silver-blue and high and broke the green silence like a shout, but the water sewed itself together very quickly, until it seemed as though nothing but a small fish had jumped and rippled the surface. I slid down from the rock, tripped on a tree root, fell heavily, and came to my senses. Freeing Paskanini had been a dream; now I awoke.

When I ran into the camp, the bear was gone. Nebosja and Kali were still quiet inside the caravan, but Mina had begun to cry. His voice shrilled in my ears as I shook my husband back into this world and cleaned the vicious wound his face had become. He drained his last bottle of *slivovitz* before letting me sew his cheek back to his jaw. For three days he writhed in a black fever, moaning, crying, while his head swelled like a rotting carcass. I wondered if he was going to die there.

He didn't. When he was well enough to squeeze the words from his lips, the first thing he said was, "I curse you for letting the bear get away, chains and all!"

"How do you know she ran away?"

"Because I heard you tell Nebosja, you stupid woman!"

"What did you expect me to do with a wild bear and my children to protect?" I demanded.

"And what do you expect me to do to feed us this year?"

"You can go and work with my father and the horses."

"Ah, yes, that is fine for you, and your mother will nag me into madness, and your brothers will borrow money from me every holiday."

"We will not find another bear, Rajko. What else can we do?" He threw the wash basin to the caravan floor with a groan, and refused to speak another word.

Paskanini ruined my husband's face. For a long time, he tried to make me suffer with him. But in my heart I continued to love the bear's anger. My people still capture bears and school them in pain, as Rajko did. We pass on the wounds of our history not only to our children but to the animals we love. The *Tsiganes,* too, have been captured many times. Now we are prisoners in a world we once owned completely because we claimed none of it in particular. Near every road was a place to eat and sleep and work. But it is difficult to live the journey now, in this world nailed up around us.

Rajko changed after Paskanini hurt him. We went to Zagreb that fall, to work with my family at the horse fairs. My husband didn't want to work with bears any more. It's bad luck, he said, when an animal pushes a man so close to death. For a long, long time, nightmares haunted him: Paskanini came back to kill him; her great claws tore out his heart and she ate it, sitting in his place on the front of the caravan. I thought, Bah, she prefers apples. In the nightmares, she told him that the bears would come for him. Then one day, my father embraced my husband and declared him a good horseman. After this unexpected blessing, Rajko's nightmares subsided.

BUT THE TRUTH inside dreams is great. My mother and her mother and the mothers before—all of them believed this. I have tried to pass it on to my children, my grandchildren, the young ones of the quarter, because their lives are riddled with lies from Sarajevo.

The truth inside dreams is great. Years after Mandori died, years after Paskanini escaped, age and weakness softened Rajko. Gentleness grew in him like a mould. One storm-torn night, he woke beside me in terror, crying, "Again, again, I dreamt of the bears!" His body trembled in my skinny arms while I soothed him, whispered away his fear, just as I had comforted my children after their bad dreams. Now an old man with a scarred face was my only child. I stroked his thin gray hair until he fell asleep again.

At dawn I woke in confusion, surprised to feel stones in the bed chilling my back. But it was Rajko's body, cold against mine, every warm breath finished.

A woman without a face

TONIGHT, A DELICIOUSLY warm evening, I attend an exhibition opening. Marie from La Poésie dans un Jardin says the painter is famous, I will love his work. She promises that Shaquil won't appear because he's visiting his children in Lyon. The reception takes place in the inner courtyard of a monastery that has been converted into a cultural centre and gallery. The paintings hang in a long room with white walls and a vaulted ceiling—perhaps a dining hall one hundred years ago. In the centre of this beautiful room we find a feast of melon and oranges, four different kinds of good wine, six kinds of cheese, breads and biscuits, and several small mountains of olives, pastries, grapes, chocolate-dipped strawberries. All on white linen table-cloths. Real linen serviettes are handed out by the waiters, three good-looking boys with longish dark hair slicked behind their ears. Each of the black-suited waiters walks around with a tray of drinks and spare serviettes draped over his shoulder.

So far, I have seven serviettes, six of which are stuffed into my knapsack. If I collect enough of these little linen treasures, I will be able to make a great jacket.

I meet them again, all the cultured wealthy people of Avignon, the people who have converted the old stone farmhouses and churches into grand houses, people who actually buy paintings, judging from the busy fingers of the slim, blond man behind a delicate, blond table: he flips rapidly through the price-lists, telling people which paintings have already been sold, what the prices of #35 and #21 are, who has put in offers for what. He says, "Yes, those details are for sale, and so is the gorgeous drawing in the entrance way, have you seen it? Oh isn't it so full, so rich in details? Such a painter, but the drawings are worth as much as the paintings, really, don't you think so too? The larger one beside the picture window? Is that the one? I think it is 50,000 francs, but I will check. There is also a smaller one there—" he points without curling any of his other fingers; a ballet dancer by day.

I wander out of the exhibition room, chocolate from the strawberries melting in my hands. Shall I lick the chocolate off my palms and fingers? Shall I study the artwork of a courtyard in spring? Observe and listen to the music of water falling into itself, splashing the stones below. The fluid body of a gray cat glides from one courtyard wall to another; its eyes flash blue when it swivels its head to regard the invaders. Emerald moss grows between the stones and an entire wall is hidden beneath a carpet of ivy. My eyes search out what is alive. The diamond slice of sky above us is blue, blue, impossibly deep blue, blue becoming darkness, the colour of my future bedroom.

I stay outside as long as I can, pretending to be fascinated by the printed sheet that gives us the artist's history and biography. But if I could do what I really wanted, what would I do? I would run into the gallery and scream, Come outside, look at the sky, see that colour! Let the paintings hang! Come and look at the bats like black brushes sketching the first lines of night. Stop looking at those paintings, don't you see they have no life of their own?

Every painting is the portrait of a nude woman. The title of the exhibition has the word *femme* in it. There she is, in oils and a few watercolours, in pencil and ink drawings, with her shoulder-length black hair and her long-limbed body: she lies in bed, sits in a chair, stands beside a vase of flowers or blue bottles. Every painting languid, without tension. Slow paintings in subtle tones, mostly white, gray, gray-blue, ochre, dull red. Every painting is opaque, as though viewed through the misted glass one sees in washrooms. The woman is, apparently, the artist's wife.

The artist's wife—oh, most wearisome of titles—has no face. At first I am stunned. An entire exhibition of portraits of one woman—and this woman faceless. And I do not mean that she lacks sharp features, a vague line of nose and unformed mouth. I mean *no* face: a blankness: white or gray-white paint.

In the information sheet about the exhibition, the artist claimed to be painting "all women, the universal woman". Why did he only use one model? Does he suppose all women are indistinguishable? Does the universal woman have no face? Doesn't he know *how* to paint faces? Is the exposed body of a woman her identity? Often enough, it is; but I do not believe that the artist intended to convey this depressing message.

What a relationship he must have with his wife! Imagine yourself taking photographs of a lover—a hundred photographs. Now imagine yourself developing them, and carefully whiting her face out of every frame. Why are you doing this? What makes a man erase a woman's face? Or, worse, be blind to its existence?

I am raving.

People push their silk-bloused elbows in front of the paintings, in front of the ballet dancer who is taking cheques and writing down phone numbers and agreeing, always agreeing about the beauty and "subtle power" of the paintings. I do not spot a single ironic expression in this room stuffed with people wearing fine cologne. To a middle-aged woman standing next to me, I remark, "Isn't it interesting that all these paintings are faceless?" Without looking me in the face, she coolly replies, "He has gone beyond faces."

Instead of laughing out loud, I return to the trough, eat another chocolate strawberry, and try to look transported by the subtly powerful art around me. It doesn't work. I get another glass of wine. Despite the cheeses, the tiers of green and purple fruits, despite the almond and raspberry pastries and wines from the *cotes du Rhône,* despite the subtly powerful paintings, I know I will leave the gallery feeling hungry. Perhaps every one of us will leave hungry. Some of us will know it, some of us won't. But not one us will mention our hunger.

We can't really speak to each other while putting black olives in our mouths.

One Room in a Castle

I want the moment of your touch
to become marble

If from inside a poem
you can win time
then I know what I have lost

Come to me
Come to me naked

—Fotis

Where the island begins

THE CAPTAIN OF Homerus brought me here. I stood with him on the bridge of his ship while he fed his twenty canaries. Red, orange, yellow, and dappled canaries. A flurry of singing birds around seed-filled hands. Later, in the dark, he said, "In Greek we say that when you know how to control the stars, you will be ready to learn our language."

This place begins with poetry.

You ask, "Why can't you keep your poetry in obscure journals where it belongs?"

I simply can't. Poetry becomes depressed and often suicidal when it languishes in obscure journals.

Besides, there are no obscure journals here. Nothing is obscure here: the world is highly visible in every direction. If I stand on a low mountain, I see the hills of Turkey jostle beneath the clouds like a purple caravan.

I'm speechless, awed by this place in a way I wasn't expecting.

Poetry is the only sound I can make.

Arrival

Days, taste the milk of a goat.
Haul cool water at dawn.
Dusk, crush green sage in a clean palm.
The old man wades through sheep to greet me.
The old man tells me the earth.
This is chamomile, he says, thick hands
pummelling the yellow flowers.
And this, peppermint, he points with his stick.
And here, oregano, sweetly ravished by bees.

So much earth.
So many waking rocks
and flowers that grew
beyond Eden, they are nameless and pure,
like the first blood singing in the first child,
splashed symphony of scarlet.
The field outside Talloni
bursts into a million burning poppies.
Sheep swallow petals of fire.

Words cannot contain living flame.
I cannot tell the passion-whirl of butterflies by the well,
nor dusk's honey dripping from the olive trees,
nor the stone on the road hissing into a turtle.

Why didn't you warn me of this place?
So many years sanding language smooth
only to learn and relearn that mystery
resists finished edges.

My tongue is a tentacle of the octopus
groping in the sand, probing
a ruin of purple shadow.
Mystery, these castles of stone and coral.

Living whispers run over my shoulders
as mice pillage the stone house,
as mighty ants ransack the peaches.
When darkness frees the constellations,
shining animals graze on heaven.

How to memorize the names for such brilliance, Libby,
when all I see here burns?

Sappho

THANASEE DRIVES THE vegetable truck from the harbour city to the small hillside village where I go to do my shopping. Leaning out the back of his great green truck, swiping wasps and wiping the sweat from his brow, he sells a large variety of seasonal vegetables from both the island and the mainland. If you are a foreigner and less than shrewd, he will cheat you blind. He is a very fat, affectionately sleazy man with a boundless smile, a whirl of white hair around his big head, and an enormous, boring repertoire of jokes about cucumbers. I don't speak Greek yet. But cucumber jokes are not hard to understand.

I like Thanasee for a number of reasons. He gives me free grapes and, occasionally, free melons. (Oddly, I do not feel compromised by accepting food from him, so he can't be as lecherous as he seems. Or am I blind?) His great belly-laugh and colourful exterior are accompanied by such obvious materialistic slyness that seeing him jolts me out of the dream of this place. Although as soon as I take away my fruit and vegetables, I forget, and effortlessly re-enter the dream.

But I like Thanasee most of all because he has a lovely twelve-year-old daughter. She is a funny, energetic girl with black, curly hair. Round-faced, eyes like coals, she sometimes accompanies her father on the weekends, helps him set up the truck, then sells fruit while he goes to play cards. She and I have developed one of those half-quirky, half-magical communications that sometimes become possible between people without a common language. She is teaching me the names of all the fruits and vegetables in the truck, as well as anything else that happens to be around: bottles, the ditch they're in, fields, birds, old shepherds on donkeys, children on bicycles, motorcycles, dogs, starving cats, clouds, hills. The names for the face, the names for the body. And, thanks to her, I now can count to one hundred.

Because she always forgets my name in English, she is the first person here to call me "Katerina". I call her by her real and true name, the name her mother chose for her when she was born. Sappho. The first Sappho was a great poet who died before Christ was born, a woman who lived in this land. She also knew the names for the land and the names for the body.

Names for the land

SOUNDS EMBEDDED IN silence like snails whorled in stone. Sounds that ancient: shepherds' voices rising behind the sheep, the sheep's bells ringing, ringing their passage, the donkeys' brays, the whirr of wasps and bees in blossoming oregano. And silence around the din as solid as rock, born in the horseshoe of low mountains beyond the house. *Spiti*. And, for this house, the diminutive form, *spitaki*. The *spitaki* is a one-room structure the size of a child's bedroom, a shepherd's day dwelling. A hut with a new pine roof and three small windows. The walls are made of stones carried from the low mountains I mentioned, just as the fences around here and the whitewashed bench I sit on were also born in those rocky hills. They look like temples, faces, enormous broken shells thrust from the sea before them.

The metaphors of poetry promise that everything is connected, everywhere. That is why this place begins with poetry. Because here, on the island, the bonds between objects and landscape, between people and history, are visible and overwhelming. I am the blind woman who wakes one morning and sees, for the first time, her naked feet; then realizes in astonishment that the curved, delicate prints appearing behind her in the dust are linked to her own bony toes. So I wade, amazed, through the union between trees and stones and their shadows, between air and sun-fire. I inhale air that contains twenty different scents. From the high places, and even from this whitewashed bench, I raise my head and gaze past the parched trees and wounded field of poppies, observe the silver-green hills of olive and apricot orchards, the stone huts almost identical to the one at my back. They say a poet was born on the slope of rock and thistle that rises above the smaller hills. Both slack and tight around the edges of land loop an indigo ribbon of Aegean water, an open-ended azure length of Aegean sky.

One thought occurs to me repeatedly. I walk through the field bleating at sheep, scrutinizing red-shelled carrion beetles, laughing at nervous lizards. One fact makes me pick up handfuls of dry, gray soil to rub and rub between my hands. Despite the shimmer of sea, sun, and beauty, this is not a postcard. This has never been a postcard. This is a day, and I am alive.

The shepherd Andreas

THE SLEEK BLACK donkey is called Marcos, and the old man who rides him is called Andreas. They appear early one morning while I am sitting outside, my back against the wall of the *spitaki*, a cup of tea cradled in my hands. The gate is on the other side of the house, out of immediate view. I hear hooves knock against the stones that mark the threshold of the gate. To give me warning, the old man shouts some unintelligible greeting that scares me out of my wits. I spill tea on my lap.

"Kaleemera," he says gruffly, with a cautious smile.

"Kaleemera," I return the greeting, and reach for my dictionary.

He pulls his cane from its resting place in the ropes of the saddle, manoeuvres Marcos to a stone, where he aims the cane, then slides off the donkey's bank. His lower left leg and foot are deformed; the foot fits into a black boot cut open to accommodate its dimensions. How to describe Barba Andreas, the old shepherd? A yellow piece of cloth is wrapped around his head of white hair. He has a big white moustache, blue eyes, a dandy's flower stuck in the lapel of his green army jacket. Hands. What will I love most here, what will I dream about years later, to return me to this place? The hands of the islanders. Their thickness, their roughness, their ugliness. Nails broken below the quick. Scars. Missing fingertips and lines full of dirt.

Barba Andreas names the plants for me, pointing with his cane and leaning down to pluck off the chamomile blooms. Sitting on a milk crate, he lifts his bad leg up to rest on a stone. I remain sitting against the house in the shade. We both take in the view before us: slender Marcos, eating my melon rinds and shitting in what is, effectively, my front yard; poppies; olive trees; the curved and plummeting body of the land, its shapes of green, sage-green, yellow, almond; rose and purple and gray shadow. The sky opens over everything like wide blue hands. And all around us, lassoing the entire island, the sea.

A bearish sound comes from Barba Andreas' throat. As though bored with the view—how familiar it must be to him—he turns back to me and says something I don't understand. He points in my direction with his cane. Is he pointing to the low table between us? I look at the table. Is he pointing to my books on the table? I offer him a book, which he wisely refuses to touch. He pantomimes a motion, but I don't understand. Once more, he directly asks for something, and pokes his finger against his chest. I don't understand. Finally, smiling but clearly frustrated, he grabs the tea-pot with one large hand, pours tea into the palm of the other, and raises it to his lips. "Ena poteeri!" he cries, and bangs his cane on the ground, demanding a cup.

Embarrassed, I jump up and into the little house for another cup. I come out, pour tea, hand it to him. He waves away my apologies. He drinks the tea in one go. How many Greek words do I know now? How many? Not enough, never enough. To learn another language one must re-acquire the greedy hunger of a child. I want, I want, I want. Every desire begins and ends with a word. I want to ask a thousand questions. Where does the path behind the house lead and who lived here before and how do you make cheese and are the sheep in the neighbouring field yours and what is this place, truly, and how do I go to the mountains behind the house? Because there is a gate closing off the field that leads to the mountains, and I am afraid to walk through it.

He understands my last, garbled question. "How do you go to the mountains?" he parrots back to me, almost shouting. It is an international assumption that when people don't hear and understand our language, we think they can't hear at all. "How do you go up to the mountains?" Now a slow laugh rumbles in his throat. "Me ta podia!" he cries. Every line of his face proclaims laughter. He slaps his knees, guffawing.

How do you go to the mountains?

Me ta podia. With your *feet.*

Open the gate, go through it, close it behind you. And *walk* to the mountains.

A meditation on baling-wire

BEFORE I OPEN the first gate, I study its construction.
I ignore the barking mutts and the disturbed turkeys
and the hopeful goats. From the gates I have studied
here, I discern something of the nature of the island,
something of the nature of Greece itself. This particular, rather wide gate was made of anything at hand.
Flattened hubcaps, flattened olive tins, three old bed
springs, fig tree sticks, oak tree sticks, olive tree limbs.
Baling-wire, packing string, many rusty nails and an
ingenious weave of materials hold everything together. Three blue plastic bags are knotted to the
jagged top edge. Why? To warn you that the gate is
there (as if it could be missed)? To frighten away
birds? To make a billowing susurrus on windy nights?
The gate opens and closes with a thick twist of
baling-wire.

Baling-wire. The wire my door is held shut with.
The wire wrapped around Andreas' donkey saddle.
The wire Panagos (who lives down the road) fixed

his sun-porch with. The wire that replaces tape, rope, nails. The wire I regularly trip over in the field. The wire that holds together hay, straw, and tar-paper shipments. The wire that holds Greece together. Did the Greek empire fall because baling-wire was invented?

No. But baling-wire is a clue to the ephemeral nature of modern day Greece. Untwist all the baling-wire in this country simultaneously, and a national disaster would be declared. Luckily, it is hard to untwist, especially when rust sets in. Baling-wire (and other junk) is also a testament to the stubborn resourcefulness of the peasants here. They use everything. When I see them, see how ancient and worn they look, I know that even their lives are being recycled. They are becoming their mothers and fathers before them, attached to the same land, in an almost identical cycle of work and seasons.

In Canada, when I manage to recycle my tin cans and newspapers, I imagine I am being progressive. But I am just beginning to learn what recycling really means. Here, on the island, it is quiet enough to hear what the wind says when it blows: your body will make *fabulous* fertilizer.

Silicon implants, scalpel sculpture, liposuction. From this perspective, the modern dream of eternal consumer youth looks very strange. Absurd, even, to the point of hilarity. Here, everything is old and used and reused. Rampant imperfections are inseparable from the beauty of the place because they are a *part* of that beauty, which is distinctly unmodern. Even the young people who've stayed here, resisting or refusing the temptations of Athens, seem to have walked, stubbornly, out of another time. The time of this island.

The connections, the cycles, the thousand fibres that bind people to seasons and seasons to earth are everywhere apparent. Andreas slaughtered a goat two days ago: a crimson spray of blood shot over the knife and its handle, over Andreas' hand and arm, down, sinking like ink into the earth. Then half-wild cats from neighbouring farms came around to rub their backs against the trees and skulk in, closer, closer to the blood. This morning, one of the last spring lambs was born at Panagos' house.

Death and birth stand beside each other here. Sometimes, when they turn and look one another in the face, we know they are siblings.

An apple in the dragon's mouth

SO I LIFT THE baling-wire latch and go through the gate. I close the gate behind me and begin walking. The animals are thoroughly disturbed. This farm belongs to another shepherd, one I haven't met. Like most of the shepherds, he comes down from the village twice a day to feed and water his sheep and other animals. But we have never attempted to speak to one another. Other shepherds come and go on the little road behind the house—I wake up to the hoof-beats of donkeys passing on the narrow, dust-beaten track—but none of them is as friendly as Andreas. Besides Panagos and Maria, who live three fields away with their children, the shepherds are the only people who come here.

The goats call to me as I walk past, demanding food. The turkeys run away in stark terror. The sheep pause in their cud-chewing and stare, ready to bolt if I scare them, prepared to stampede towards me if I have some vegetable scraps. "He will separate the sheep from the goats," says the Bible, suggesting that sheep are superior in goodness to goats. Nonsense. The goats, insulted by such close association with their woolly, dirty cousins, always separate themselves from the sheep. Sheep are sheep: wide-tailed, huddled, made dumb and slow and manageable from centuries of domesticity and inbreeding. (Sounds disturbingly familiar to me.) The goats, on the other hand, retain an air of wild independence, impetuosity, a certain disdain for human beings. Goats still know, for example, how to use their horns.

I pass through the fig orchard (the unripe figs like tiny green bells). Thistles sting my sandalled feet. In the space of weeks, the land has lost its spring lushness. A hundred spiny plants grow here on the edges of the olive groves and the few abandoned terraces of figs. I walk up, and up, my ankles getting warm and wise, my knees awake now, my chest thumping. Through another gate, into and out of a small, steep-sided ravine, through another gate, over a fence. Another shepherd's enclave of sheep, stone and corrugated tin manger, a lonely chained dog barking maniacally. Once past this last level of fields, I am on the hillsides where nothing is cultivated but stone. Thorns, purple-blossoming thyme, and great bunches of oregano grow here. I close my eyes and breathe in the perfume. I open my eyes: a green lizard runs over the raw earth. Following the lizard, I am suddenly distracted by a small gray snake a few paces ahead; it disappears beneath an oregano bush. What to do? Trail the lizard or wait for the snake to reappear? Or close my eyes again and return to a world of pure scent?

I look up. There are the mountains. Not real

mountains. High hills scattered with massive out-croppings of volcanic stone. The boulders are massive, heaving and caught one under the other, split from the earth, piled in the manner of broken columns. From a distance, some of the ridges are like ruined temples, especially the one hill closer to the sea, terraced rock rising to an altar peak. The one directly before me, the one I'm going to climb, is more like a dragon with its mouth open. A jagged length of tail grows into a monstrous body. A ledge of snout juts beneath two shallow eye-slits. Despite decidedly menacing, narrowed eyes, I heave myself up.

(But imagine the fairytale: the dragon's stone skin, in slow degrees, begins to crack and tremble to life. The woman doesn't notice at first. Her back turned, she gazes out to sea. The dragon's massive skull blushes a deeper green. His slitted eyes open wider, wider still when they see her below, standing on his folded knee. Suddenly the heavy tail rises off the earth and crashes back down like the beginning of an earthquake. Dust and songbirds rise in a cloud. The great stone haunches flex and twist. The dragon raises and pulls back his head, then drops it down with an open mouth. CHOMP. Down goes the woman, bones and all. She is never heard from again. But if you aren't afraid to walk up the mountain, you will find a mound of stones echoing the contours of a woman's body, and one smooth stone shaped like a woman's face.)

Lichen scales, thorn claws. How wonderful it is to crawl on rocks, find handholds and places for the feet, feel something so hard under the skin, even feel the skin give way to the rougher skin beneath it. The higher I go, the more I get scraped, scratched, sanded like a piece of balsam wood.

I am so small. So appallingly *soft*. How much more practical to be stone in this world, you live so much longer. Live? Well, not in the sense we usually think of. In another sense. I take off my shoes and put my feet on the back of the stone in front of me. Sun-warm. In some inexplicable way, can it feel my feet on its reddish mineral back? Stones, like butterflies and goats, are as physically present as you or I.

I sit down in the dragon's mouth and eat the apple Thanasee gave me yesterday. This is a shallow, cool cave full of dust and its scent, full also of the hard, green scent of lichen. My legs hang over the dragon's jaw. Chewing like a horse, I look out at the expanse of land below me. The green valley, irrigation sprinklers turning even now. The hillside village gathered into itself like a sleeping cat. The small beach town, stretching its feet into the sea. The sea herself, calm and resolute, a blue queen reclining in a blue-ceilinged room. Farmhouses down along the village road. The ruins of shepherds' huts in the olive and fig groves. Sheep like grains of rice tossed over the hills and fields. The red roof of the little house where I live. Panagos and Maria's house, not so far from mine, peering out of the trees.

This is the place.

This is the place.

These words sound and resound, like a heartbeat.

Orpheus' head is buried here

THIS MORNING, AFTER swimming at the far end of the beach, I walk to the small restaurant called the Aegean to have a plate of feta and bread. Because it's still early in the season, most of the bars and restaurants along the beach are empty of tourists, and the people who work in them will chat if they are not reading the newspaper. Fotis the waiter comes and sits at a neighbouring table. He sips ouzo with water.

Fotis is a strange character, not loud and flamboyant like most of the men around here. He is quiet. Secretive, though he tells me some of his secrets, some of the secrets about this place. Certain people possess an intelligence that is, in essence, frightening. Fotis is one of these people. Fotis, of the blackest eyes and eyebrows. When I see him, I think: I am not in Europe, this is a separate continent. And he says as much, like most of the islanders. "The E.E.C. can go fuck itself, Greece is not a European country." A common sentiment. "All the E.E.C. has done for us is raise our prices, lower our standard of living, and make us feel stupid. Gamiseta! You know gamiseta? Gamiseta means 'fuck them!' Greece is not Europe. Look at this place," he waves his hand to the *kafeneio* across the square, where fifteen old men sit drinking ouzo or coffee, eating cucumbers, and arguing. Not a woman in sight, except for the one who serves them. If we could extend Fotis' wave further, we would see the entire agrarian culture of the island at a glance. We would see people who only recently acquired electricity. Most still live without telephones. We would see thousands of gates made of baling-wire, tonnes of hand-mixed cement, countless women working in kitchens and courtyards, superstitions born thousands of years ago still alive and breathing. We would see the evil eye.

Is this island part of Europe? Or part of the Middle East? Or part of Asia? Fotis tells me that the people of Crete sing and dance with an African spirit. Where do the borders really begin and end?

Where am I?

Fotis whispers, "You are on the island of Orpheus' head."

"I beg your pardon?"

"Remember Orpheus? I don't care if you are Canadian, I hope someone made you read the Greek myths as a child."

"Well, I read them, but it was a while ago. I don't remember exactly. What about Orpheus?"

Fotis rubs his hands together, he is so happy to be able to tell me this story. The Aegean laps the beach below the restaurant deck. The rock island half a mile offshore raises its dark head higher out of the water to listen. Fotis moves to my table and begins to speak.

Sometimes I have to lean closer to him when the wind shakes the grass-thatching of the roof above our heads.

"Orpheus, son of a Muse, was the greatest mortal musician of ancient Greece. He played the lyre so well that the stones turned to face him, and listened, and the trees leaned down to be closer to his music. By drowning out the lovely, treacherous songs of the Sirens, Orpheus even saved the lives of Jason and the Argonauts.

"Then he fell in love with Eurydice. She was bitten by a snake and the poison killed her. Orpheus was so miserable that he decided to go and find her in the Underworld. That is how much he loved her. And Orpheus was such a great musician that he charmed the gods of Hades with his music. They said, Yes, Eurydice can return to the Upper World with you. Under one condition. When she follows you out of the caverns of death, you cannot look back at her until both of you are out, in the sunlight.

"So they began to go out of Hades, closer and closer to the Upper World. Orpheus stepped out of the dark onto the warm earth. But, like the man Lot in our Bible, he couldn't resist looking back at his treasure. He needed to make sure Eurydice was there. He turned. The moment he saw her, she began to disappear, crying, drawn back into the deep of Hades.

"Orpheus was mad with grief. But unless he died, the gods refused to let him into Hades again. He went to Thrace, his birthplace, and wandered the wild hills in despair, playing for no humans now, only the stones and rivers. But it was very dangerous, in ancient Greece, to go wander alone through the hills. The Maenads lived there, worshipping Dionysius under the trees and sky, sleeping on leaves and pine needles. The Maenads were madwomen. When they found Orpheus playing alone on the hillside, not even his music could save him. The Maenads went at him with their bare hands and teeth, tore his legs and arms from his body, and threw his head into the river Hebrus.

"His head was washed up on the island, the sanctuary of the gods. In antiquity, this was the jewel-island, because the gods and goddesses came to play here. The Muses found Orpheus' head on the beach and buried it here."

"Where?"

"Out there." He points to the northern end of the beach, where a stone mountain with steep cliffs rises over the water. At the top of this mountain is a small white chapel called Profitus Elias.

"Where is Orpheus' head buried?" The skepticism in my voice insults Fotis.

"*Where, where, where?* Just like a foreigner, all these goddamn questions. How do I know where, exactly? Leave the story alone! Can't you see? That's the beauty, no one knows exactly where. Up the mountain. Down the hill. Under the chapel stones. Who knows for sure?"

He seems so genuinely angry that I apologize. "It was a beautiful story."

He growls in a small but ferocious way, like a Tasmanian devil. "It's not over yet."

"Oh. What else happens?"

"Nothing else *happens*. But there is an important detail."

Instead of saying anything, I cautiously put the last piece of feta in my mouth.

"We know that Orpheus' head was buried on this island because the nightingales here sing more beautifully than anywhere else in Greece." He gives me a significant look. "Because Orpheus was a great musician. You see?"

"Yes, I see. You don't have to explain that." We exchange almost angry glances.

"Don't they tell stories in Canada?"

"Yes."

"Then you know you're supposed to believe the storyteller, right?"

"Yes. I suppose so."

"No *suppose*. Definitely. If I tell you another story, you can't say, Is this true? Is that true? And if you're going to stay here, learn Greek. It gives me a headache to tell stories in bloody English."

The house of the sea, and song

A WOMAN HAS left her ghost in the little house. A woman with red hair, blue eyes, large, clay-loving hands. A woman who knows how to make a fire, a fish, a goddess. A woman who communes with mermaids. Do you think I'm telling stories?

Believe me.

The walls, inside and outside, tell of her sojourn here. When she found this field of olive trees and sky, the *spitaki* was falling in on itself. She rebuilt it. She banished the mice. She fixed the roof, reframed the windows, and replastered the walls. She was, and still is, a sculptor. The little house became her sculpture. You can see her handprints in the white plaster.

She also pressed shells into the walls. I know nothing about shells, and there is no book here to tell me their names. Whorled, spotted shells for crabs. Flat white, fanned shells for slippered mollusks. Scalloped shells rough with grit on the outside, shining inside with mother-of-pearl. Years later, they are still here, telling the story of her love for the sea.

I met her once, very briefly, in Toronto. She said, "I read your first collection of poetry in Greece, in a little house I have there. How I laughed when I came to the last page of the book: you ended it with a quotation by Sappho. I went to Greece to find her. A sublime coincidence. If you do any travelling when you go back to Europe, please go. Go and stay in the little house. It's been empty for too long."

Years later, here I am. Reading Libby's house as she read my poetry. What I will learn here, she already knows. What I will love here, she already loves. And Sappho sang it, perfectly, centuries before any of us were born.

Sixteen hooves and a shirtless man

MORNING LIFTS UP out of the hills like a woman rising from a bath, so much clean air and coolness on skin. I am tying the clothesline tighter between two trees when I hear a bell, *clank-jingle*. A man has appeared on the road as if by magic. He swears and pulls on the rope that stretches taut from a goat's halter. He: a quick, spare man of medium height, shirtless, a shepherd's yellow cloth wrapped around his gray-and-white-haired head. Goat: clean white, bell-jingling, slow-walking, reluctant to follow, clearly superior. Occasionally she halts, cries her discontent, attempts to turn back. The growling man heaves forward. She lurches behind.

One goat. He hurries away, returns ten minutes later with another, who is less stubborn. Then two together. Over the course of the morning, sixteen cleft hooves clack on the flat rocks and scallop dust out of the road. The last two goats come much more easily than the first, no doubt lonely for their two companions. The man tethers them all in the field across from mine, each close enough to an olive tree to benefit from its shade but not close enough to eat its leaves. A house like mine, a shepherd's hut, also stands in this field, but it is far too dilapidated for a human inhabitant. The man couldn't possibly *live* there. He checks each goat, making sure the tether spike is set deep enough into the ground. Then he disappears the way he has come, swinging his bare arms long and loose, like a boy.

The Greek Bedouin

AFTERNOON. I AM washing clothes in a small blue basin, fifty paces away from the small house, up the road where a faucet sticks out of the stones like a clawed hand. Land of miracles: the faucet spills clean, earth-chilled water, even on the hot days. I carry my drinking water in an earthen jug and leave it in the stone house. In the morning or late evening, after the shepherds pass by, I take a bucket and bathe in the road, scooping water over my head, speedily lathering soap through my bathing suit, rinsing it off, towel close by in case anyone—any man—appears without warning.

He appears without warning. Again. Above the sound of the water splashing stone, I suddenly distinguish the clatter of heavy hooves on rock. And the man is there, a short distance down the path. This time, he balances on top of a red table like a misplaced sultan. The table is ingeniously roped to a big black horse's back. In fact, the table is bound to a heavy saddle, but I don't see this until I turn off the water, back slowly away from my wash basin, walk down the road to get a better look. Variously hooked and hung from the saddle and the table and their complex tangle of knots are a red chair, a small trunk, two empty rabbit hutches, a burlap sack of animal feed, two rolled-up rugs, and a basket brimming blackened pots and pans.

From the top of the red table on top of the tall black horse, the shirtless man with the shepherd's cloth around his head becomes a stunning cross between Lawrence of Arabia going to battle and Genghis Khan going to bathe. When the goats smell him and the horse, hear the rattle of pots, they begin to bleat and bellyache and cry out in joy. They've been alone all afternoon. "How we've missed you!" they proclaim. I go through my gate and step back even farther, watching him pass.

A curious potion of fear and fascination works in my blood. What is he doing, this Greek Bedouin, in the small field across the road, why is he disturbing my solitude? Peering over the tops of my underwear and t-shirts as I pin them on the line, I watch him unload the giant black horse. Several times, absorbed in the knots of wet laundry, I glance up, thinking his voice calls me. But no. He talks aloud to the horse, who has laid his surly thick ears against his surly thick head. The man shouts greetings to the goats, then he whistles.

Two dogs appear at the base of the road, one gray fur-ball and one white snowflake. They grow larger and larger, running toward us, until finally I see their heads and their dog-grins trained on the whistler. "Skeera! Faleetcha!" he calls in a high, playful voice meant to excite and please them. They hurl their small bodies up the short bank into the field across from mine, and he bends to greet them, repeating their names. "Skeera! Faleetcha-mou!" So I learn the names of the man's dogs before I learn the name of the man.

A Greek lesson

EXO. MESA.

Out. In. *Eime exo. Eime mesa.* I am out, I am in.

Thelo na eime mesa. I want to be in. *Eime mesa.* I am in. The Greek expression to denote belonging, intrinsic understanding of a given place, event, or situation. *Eime mesa.*

Neró. Water.

Thálasah. Sea.

Ouranó. Sky.

Animo. Wind.

Fotiá. Fire.

Vouná. Mountains.

Hóma. Earth.

Anthropos. People.

Psomí. Bread.

Cardiá mou. My heart.

Cardiá mas. Our heart.

Starlight

AT NIGHT, I lie awake and watch the candle shadows on the white walls of the *spitaki*. I make shadow puppets of my fingers, a game I have not played since I was a child. There, on the wall, above the small burlap weaving of the fish:

a barking dog
a rabbit
a slightly deformed horse
a cat with abnormally large ears
a butterfly (or a bat)
two open hands

Then, restless, I go outside, carry the gray wooden chair to the middle of the field, and sit down. I wear a t-shirt and my underwear. All the shepherds have gone up to the villages this late at night. Even Panagos and Maria's house, ten minutes down the road, is invisible. Two fig trees stand behind me. Olive trees stand all around, their very small white blossoms releasing a subtle sweetness into the air. Now, a susurrus of wind through the silver-backed leaves. A trio of crickets near my chair (in the fence-stones) and a symphony of frogs farther up the hill (at the shepherd's water trough). I lean back in the chair and wait.

One. Two. Three. Shooting stars. Meteors. Four. Andreas told me today what they are called in Greek, but I didn't write it down. I've forgotten. If stars are people, are shooting stars people who return? Five. This must be a meteor shower. Or is it just so dark here that I see more shooting stars than I've ever seen before? I stare up at the night sky until my neck begins to ache. Then I lie down in the grass, my vision blurred with tears. For a moment, after my skeleton collapses, the crickets pause in their song. Then, satisfied that I am not going to eat them, they begin to play again.

How can it be this easy?

I don't know. I don't understand. Grace like this is unfamiliar. What am I supposed to do with it? The island temples have fallen to ruins, but on the narrow dirt road that leads to the sea, I say prayers, I sing "Holy, holy," I learn by heart the contours of the hills like the contours of a body I love. Yet I know almost nothing about this place. I cannot remember the order of the alphabet, for example. Andreas brings me fresh feta and eggs every day. The woman at the bakery opens the oven door to show me the fire, the immense orange glow inside. The old man at the *plateia,* the village square, talks and talks to me in Greek, until someone tells him I am Canadian, I can't understand. Then the old man looks at me, touches my face in disbelief, and starts to laugh. The captain said, "We say that when you know how to control the stars, you will be ready to learn our language."

I am ignorant of stars. I know only a handful of constellations and the heat of the sun. With this scant knowledge, I embark on my Greek lessons with the savage delight of a child catching grasshoppers with her bare hands. I sprawl dazed in the field under a lake of stars. I swim through Greek verbs, through a vision of the Greek Bedouin, through my memory of sunlight when it penetrates the sea and sinks glittering columns into the white sand twenty feet below.

Though my backside is cold now and the night dew has soaked my shoulders and eyes, I remain on the ground. I fall asleep here, earth below and a bowl of light above.

The Bedouin plants a garden

HE HAS DUG up the earth. Now he is sowing seeds.
When a man digs a garden, you know he has come
to stay for a while. After he unloaded the black horse
two days ago, he went away and returned with a white
one. It was burdened by a dark blue trunk painted
with red flowers, Greek words. I remembered a circus, a medicine doctor. Another sack of animal feed
arrived on the back of the white gelding, two more
fold-up chairs, numerous leather bags decorated with
bright beads, and a white door, which has been set
up on a pile of stones to make a large, wobbly work
table.

So. Whoever he is, he has arrived. With him he
has brought a family of goods and animals: the black
stallion, the white gelding, the four goats, a bay colt,
a fluctuating number of donkeys, two dogs, a diminishing litter of puppies, one lovesick rabbit, many
tools, bags, buckets, and a bed that hangs from the
branch of an olive tree.

This morning, I speak to him for the first time. I am washing my hair at the tap when he materializes on the road about five feet away, carrying water buckets for his horses. He begins, hesitantly, in French. "There isn't very much water, is there?"

I lift up my wet head to look at him. "Enough."

"You are Spanish?"

"Spanish? Where does that idea come from?"

"Maria said your name was Carmen. A Spanish name."

"Karen. In the village, they call me Katerina. I'm Canadian."

"Ah, French Canadian?"

"No, English Canadian."

"You speak English?"

"Of course."

In English, he bursts out, "Gamoto, why are we speaking French then? My English is much better than my French. Easier. English is a poor language. All of its words come from Greece. It's easy to learn. A dog could learn to speak English if we cut its tongue."

Wrapping a towel around my head, I stand up straight. What a charming fellow. "And what's *your* name?"

"Yiorgo. George in America. But we're in Greece, so my name is Yiorgo." He steps past me and begins to fill up his water buckets. I step past *him* and walk back to my little house.

Greek dog, Canadian woman

WE LIVE BESIDE each other now, separated by a road on which I find turtles, snakes, lizards, and, this morning, a sheep's skull, still being cleaned by ants. As I come walking up the road, index and middle finger hooked in the leather-skinned eye sockets, my neighbour looks up from his garden plot and squints. "What is this thing in your hand?"

"A sheep's skull."

"Manoulamou, holy mother! This is dirty. Picking up pieces of the dead sheep. This is a habit of Greek dogs, not Greek women."

"Eime kanadesa," I reply without blinking. I am Canadian.

Three hundred sheep equal marriage

TWICE A WEEK, on an old bicycle, I ride up to the village in the hills. It takes me just over half an hour to get there. The beach town down the road, Skala, is also awake and buzzing now, full of merchants and small shops and half-naked tourists. How odd it is to see these sun-starved men and women when I go down for a swim in the evenings. I indulge in the luxurious snobbery of someone who eats homemade feta cheese and takes Greek lessons from a white-haired shepherd: I do not believe I am a tourist. But when I go up to the village, I realize what I am. A freak. A tourist who hasn't left yet. A tourist who is learning Greek. A tourist who should get married.

"Why are you still here?" the man I buy my lamp oil from asks me. He winks and leans over the counter of his crammed, unlit shop. "You must be in love!" The old men in the *plateia* stare and stare at me. The women stare also, though Vaso and her husband Nikos, who own one of the *kafeneios,* have claimed me as their impossible daughter-in-law. Vaso says,

"How I wish I had a son, so you could marry him!" And, after accomplishing the linguistic acrobatics involved in understanding this sentiment, I think, How lucky I am that you have no son!

I gather from my little forays in the village that marriage is very often a commercial transaction. A family's money is a big consideration when contemplating marriage. Although traditionally it is the woman who has a large dowry, who is "worth marrying," I think I could easily sell myself to a bachelor for a couple of donkeys and a motorcycle. And sex! Sex is something Greek men anxiously try to get from foreign women, because Greek women have to answer to their jealous fathers until the old tyrants are six feet under. The great majority of people I see in the village are men, old and young; I cautiously asked Maria where all the women are. She answered matter-of-factly, "The women are at home, working. And the lucky ones are at school in Athens. They'll be back soon, for the summer, but then they'll go away again. It's hard to be an island woman."

Maria and I are on speaking terms, but like most of the younger women I've met here, she is still reluctant to get close. Generally, the men here are flamboyant, noisy, vital, while the women are withdrawn, watchful, quiet. It is hard to speak to any of the young women because I can hardly ever find them. The village women are isolated. Isolated from the rest of the island, the rest of Greece, the rest of the world. Isolated from their men by their sex. It seems they are even isolated from each other, because most of their time is spent caring for their homes and families.

The men have their famous *kafeneios* of coffee and

ouzo, those open meeting places to discuss politics, village life, ideas. It is no longer a punishable taboo for women to enter *kafeneios,* but they never congregate there. The women have no open forum. So I learn the lesson again, in a new language: to have a voice is to have power. Isolation is a kind of silence. It breeds fear, jealousy, suspicion, all the stunted children of weakness.

I don't have to answer to a tyrannical father or husband. I smile often. I pick roadside flowers on my way to Skala and give them to various shop keepers and cafe owners. I am, after my long deadlock with Avignon, deliriously, obnoxiously happy. It's sobering to realize that, more than anything else, my freedom sets me apart from the island women. My happiness makes me a foreigner.

Other foreign women live here, although all of them are in relationships with Greek men. I am alone. This is what astonishes. This is the big joke. The villagers who know me are dying to get me into bed with a nice, lonely Greek boy, a good village son who rides an expensive motorcycle and owns two hundred and fifty sheep. That's what I hear from Vaso, and the baker's daughter. Already! And I can't even bake baklava. "That one has three hundred sheep, and his own house. Now he just needs a wife." And Irini elbows me in the ribs. "That one owns a store in Skala. Isn't he beautiful? But he smokes too much grass. Never mind." Over half a dozen German, English, and French women have come here, much like myself, and fallen in love with the place. Then they have fallen in love with one of the men who live here.

Even now, this early on, I understand the way in, I recognize the surest road to enter this place: through a man. Preferably, through one of these men, one of the men born here, not an outsider from another island or Athens. I look at the men around me, who dazzle with their humour, their enormous characters, their generosity, their love. They are people who are full of love, that much is clear. And, like the Spanish, they know how to laugh.

But I go to the village to pick up my mail, to meet, brashly, the stares of the old men, to try out my new words on Vaso and drink a coffee at her *kafeneio*. I go up to the village and then I return to the hills, alone, with fresh bread in my knapsack and a song in my mouth.

The children

Cliffsides seduce us.
Craggy spines of earth
arch jewel-white against darkness.
July wind in olive trees gone wild.
Wild, we watch the eagles pivot above
orchards of figs and apricots, fields of melon.

The square in Skala
is inhabited by sunburned fauns
and eight-year-old muses eating ice cream.
Who has ever seen so many children running
breathless among blue chairs?
They gallop like ponies over the cobblestones,
dash away from the flying beetles, breathless
with the joy of fear.

Fire dances farther down the beach,
glances off boat-glass.
We find flames in the stones,
live sparks in the eyes of Norway's children.
How could anything so gold be human?
They rush past the old men,
prowl like scouts among the benches,
shoulders still hot with sun,
faces like ripe cherries.
What will they take away with them,
these children who have reached the island
with such ease?
What will they remember?

The galaxy in a milk pail

THIS MORNING, AFTER milking his goats, Yiorgos appears with a small bucket. I am sitting on my stone bench, back against the house. I look up from my notebook. "Théleis gala?" Do you want milk? "Gala is milk, right? And galaxia is the Milky Way, in Greek," he generously explains, peering up at the blue sky as if the stars show themselves to him even in daylight. He hands me the bucket of belly-warm milk and clicks his tongue against his teeth. "Galaxy, gala, galaxia. You see, so much in English was Greek first. You know you have a very poor language, don't you?"

I smile, put down my notebook, accept the milk. "Put it in the house to keep it cold," he says, moving to return to his side of the road. Within a couple of minutes, I can smell coffee boiling in one of his small, blackened pots. That's how close together our houses are. "Théleis kafedaki?" he yells over to me, but I have read his mind. Already standing, I gather my notebook and Greek dictionary, then pad barefoot across the road to his table and chairs under the big olive tree.

From where I sit, I can see the hanging bed he sleeps in. I can see his loyal, cantankerous goats. The dogs come to greet me, sniffing, cold-nosing my knees and hands. Although the white dog Skeera is dainty, I know Faleetcha is the favourite, for good reason. She has Yiorgos' own wild, gray and white hair, the same wide face, wood-coloured eyes. Ever since I saw her running up the road that first day, I have wanted to ask him how he came upon a dog that looks like his sister.

But I don't want to insult him. I am carefully polite, even when he happily insults me. "What were you doing over there at your spitaki while I make my garden and saddle my donkeys and sweat in the sun?"

"I was working," I say, indicating my notebook.

"Working! Is that what they call work in Canada? Who digs toilets in your country? Who makes the bricks?" He snorts, not allowing me a space to answer. "Théleis kafedaki?"

Do you want coffee? is becoming a daily question now, a common pleasure on the verge of sliding into habit. Yiorgos makes thick, sweet coffee, talks, and occasionally shares cigarettes with me. (Like vegetarianism, my status as a non-smoker slides when smoking becomes a cultural experience: you can't get cigarettes like these in Canada.)

I sit across the crooked-legged table. His hair is a wilderness, a white and gray and copper briar, shoulder-length. It makes him look older than he is. Above the moustache, an upturned, sunburned nose gives way to wide cheeks, hazel eyes, a wide forehead. A young man, despite the white hair. Yiorgos sits and rolls delicious cigarettes, licking the papers without catching any tobacco in his moustache, a detail which still impresses me. He speaks one-quarter in French, one-quarter in English, and half in Greek. I learn many new words during these long mornings. Under his tutelage, I am now the proud owner of a memorized Greek alphabet. He is an impatient teacher, but I like him very much. At the beginning, I feared he was going to be a bothersome neighbour, a sarcastic, difficult man whose animals would attract flies into the vicinity of the little house.

He *is* a sarcastic, difficult man whose animals attract flies into the vicinity of the little house. But he is also funny, intelligent, and generous, although he owns almost nothing. I must stop being surprised by this paradoxical truth, which I have experienced, consistently, on three continents: very poor people are usually more generous than very rich people.

Odd, isn't it?

Rock'n'Roll Trekking

WE ARE DISCUSSING paper. "Katerina, I need some sheets of clean white paper, because any paper I have is full of skatá. You know *skatá*? Shit. Skatá. And I need this paper because I have to make posters for Rock'n'Roll Trekking, my donkey company. So. You are a writer, no? Can you give to me some paper?"

Together we make small posters with bright felt pens, advertising Yiorgos' business. Using his donkeys and horses, he takes tourists up into the hills. "And *tak tak tak*, I cut grass every day down by the river, I feed the donkeys, I feed the horses, I run like a madman to give them water. Then at six I go down to Skala and pick up the people. Sometimes I take them to the old monastery, sometimes to Profitus Elias, above the sea. This is a crazy job, this trekking business.

"And now the town hall don't want me to do trekking, they say they take back my business permit. Skatá. They say the donkeys make dirty everywhere.

Dirty, you know, skatá. A good word, you see? What dirty? I say. I have a bag for the donkeys all day long! I pick up everyone's donkey dirt because if the town hall sees it they will say, 'Ah, Yiorgos' donkeys do that.' Somebody doesn't like me! Afto eine to provleima. Somebody's going *blahblahblah* against me. These people, they live to gossip."

"So, what does it all mean?"

"Oh, my child, pedi-mou, you are an innocent. It means they screw me blind, and I already wear glasses sometimes."

"You wear glasses? I've never seen you wearing glasses."

"Only sometimes. I don't like. Anyway, they screw me around. You know what the problem is?"

"What's the problem?"

"I'm not from here. I came here ten years ago. I'm from the Peloponnese. I'm a foreigner to them. This morning I have a lot of skatá with the travel office about my bookings."

"Why?"

Yiorgos looks at me with one eye, the other eye closed to block out the sun. He rubs his forehead hard. "The problem? The problem is that they are office people and I am Rock n' Roll Trekking." He pauses to slurp coffee. "The travel office don't want to do my bookings. They don't want to. . . ," a momentary pause as he searches for the correct English word, ". . . to . . . CO-OP-ER-ATE. That's the word, right? They don't want to co-operate. Well, that's good for me. I don't want to co-operate either. Actually."

He pronounces the word "actually" with such enunciated finesse that I have to laugh.

"Why do you laugh?" he snaps, twisting his head sharply.

"Eime haroumenee," I reply. I am happy.

"Very nice for you to be happy, pedi-mou, tra-la-la. You a writer, you don't have to worry about town hall this and travel office that." But he leans forward, slurps his coffee. "Ahh, gamisou, I have my garden. I'm happy, too."

The fortune

THE DAYS RUN together like something slipping through our fingers, not sand or water but a living creature, impossibly quick and green-skinned. A lizard, perhaps, or a snake, camouflaged by stone and night.

It is peculiar to have Yiorgos living so close by now, because I am constantly aware of him. He is always there, or will be there. I look up more often now, to the road that drops toward the valley, because I know he might be coming home. Yiorgos, with his wild hair, riding the white horse called Kamari, trailed by Faleetcha, his sister from another time.

Months ago, if someone had told me that I would be living in an olive grove and eating tomatoes, feta, and cucumbers to stay alive, I would have rolled my eyes in disbelief. If a Gypsy fortune teller had whispered, "You will love a man who repairs saddles, makes leather shepherds' bags, and speaks to goats," I would have asked for another fortune.

Sometimes in the evening when I go swimming, just as the sun sets and the light above the horizon settles into bands of peach and mauve, I close my eyes. I count for ten seconds. When I open my eyes, I am still here. Astonishing, but true. It never fails to make me laugh.

Driftwood

The men are talking
(always the voices of men)
about boats, mice on the ropes,
storm-eyes and horses.
The men are talking
while the sea begs for the shore
and your mouth becomes a hard word
carved in olive wood.

You ask me again
    When are you leaving?
And I answer
    Why do you always ask me
    when I am leaving?
    I keep telling you
    I will come back.

Can you keep time
to a song without music?
Do you have a scale
to measure the weight of winter?
When am I leaving?

I harvest these questions from fourteen olive trees.
You watch these questions ripen with the almonds.

Night, a garden of darkness.
I walk home on the narrow road,
my twisted backbone of earth.
Thinking of your mouth,
I neglect the stars.

I walk up to the house.
It knows where it lives.
The house never leaves.
I kill a scorpion on the patio
and remember the stars like a prayer.

Still you sit near the harbour,
remembering boats, storm-eyes,
horses stamping in the holds.
The sea, you said, bears us away,
then brings us home.
Our bodies are driftwood.

I fall asleep in the field,
the gauze of salt on my limbs
saved for your tongue.

The highwaywoman of apricots

DID YOU EVER read "The Highwayman" in school, that long, romantic poem about the doomed thief and his lover? A line still loose in my brain:

The moon was a ghostly galleon tossed upon cloudy seas.

One of the first metaphors of my reading life, and I saw it last night, walking home from Skala. The moon slid down the clouds as though they were waves. I stood on the road with my head up to watch the roiling, rising, and falling light shine in the mirror of the sea.

I walked backwards for a while, watching this storm of moon and cloud. And walking backwards, I saw the apricot tree.

An abandoned mansion stands away from the road to Skala. Or, rather, a very large, two-storey house, rainworn blue. This house has a face: green-shuttered eyes, eavestrough eyebrows, grinning-veranda mouth. Next to the house grows a great apricot tree. I've seen it many times. Every day, walking or riding the old bicycle down to the sea, I've passed the tree and thought: the apricots will be ripe soon. But last night, the apricots under the moon *glowed* with ripeness. They were tiny orange beacons winking in the dark. I couldn't resist. I untwisted the wire from the old iron gate and snuck into the yard of the empty mansion, heart beating "*Thief, thief.*" I crept through the overgrown brambles and the pink oleanders and the fragrant night flowers. Fruit fell as I approached the tree. Orange jewels dropped off when I touched them. Apricots thumped me on the head and joined a hundred other apricots already melting into the ground.

I grew still and tense whenever a car or motorcycle drove by. Shhh. Shhh. Then, in the silence after their passing, I heard a rustling sound on the earth: ants and other insects, feasting, munching, moving aside leaves and twigs, dragging bits of apricot away.

I plundered until my knapsack began to overflow. My sandals were sticky with apricot jam. A dialogue played in my mind: *You're a thief, you're a thief, what if someone catches you?* But look, they're all over the ground anyway! *Yes, but they're not yours.* The branches are still heavy with fruit, no one will even notice you've been here. *Except for your footprints in the apricots, you thief.* Thief? *Yes, in some countries they'd chop off your whole arm for stealing so much fruit.* Look, you moralistic dimwit, all the fruit I've picked would have fallen off the tree by tomorrow morning anyway. And look at these branches! There's still enough for two hundred jars of jam. This is Christmas, really, the tree all lit with orange bulbs, and I was supposed to come in here and collect my gift . . .

A trail of apricot stones followed me home.

Are you telling the truth?

ANDREAS THE SHEPHERD was away in Athens for a month, recovering from an operation on his bad leg. Now he is back, and he is irate. With me.

The problem is Yiorgos.

Many of the village people are afraid of Yiorgos. I was a bit afraid of him, too. One of the men from the town hall cast about unsuccessfully to find an English word to describe him. "May I borrow your dictionary?" I handed it to him. He looked up a word, closed the dictionary, and pronounced, "A savage. The people of the village think Yiorgos is a savage."

Yiorgos doesn't wear shoes very often.

During the summer months, he lives very close to his animals, outside, sleeping just a few feet from his goats and rabbits.

He has long hair.

He spends a lot of time alone.

His clothes are holey. Or is that holy?

He is a hippy.

He wasn't born here.

The island people often refuse to rent Yiorgos land to pasture his animals. He asked if he could keep Kelis, his big black stallion, in my field. Before Andreas went away, he sometimes grazed sheep in my field as well. Yiorgos told me that Andreas had sold his sheep. So Kelis is standing in the field even as I write, swishing flies off his massive hind-quarters and laying his ears back on his head. He is a very bad-tempered horse.

Now Andreas is out of the hospital, and his half-a-dozen sheep are with him. It's only eleven in the morning and already he has caned up to the house three times to indicate how angry he is that this big, ugly, mean stallion owned by that dirty, conniving hippy is now pastured in the field where his sheep used to graze. "You can't graze a horse and sheep in the same pasture. It is never done. Sold my sheep! I didn't sell my sheep! Why would I sell my sheep? I was just having an operation. I'm not dead!"

Yiorgos has already given up the pasture where he was boarding Kelis. Having heard Andreas rant and rave, he came over to explain that it would be very difficult for him to find another field, especially after Andreas goes to the village and tells everyone what's happening down here in the valley.

Yiorgos says Andreas is a greedy man who gossips.

Andreas says Yiorgos is a liar.

It only occurred to me this morning, after Andreas came over, that it was indeed Yiorgos who passed on the incorrect information that Andreas had sold his sheep. Yiorgos says a shepherd in the village told him that. Is it true? Who knows? If I ask him,

"Are you telling the truth?" he will be terribly offended. Andreas says that he doesn't have any other place to graze his sheep, which I don't believe, because I've seen him grazing them in other fields. But if I ask him, "Are you telling the truth?" he, too, will be terribly offended.

But someone isn't telling the truth. The problem is that I know nothing of the history of this place. I am ignorant of who has had feuds with whom and which families refuse to speak to other families because of a sin someone's grandfather committed. Initially, this ignorance was blissful: everyone seemed so generous, kind, caring. And, to me, generally, they are generous, kind, and caring. That is because, as Yiorgos repeatedly says, I am a child. In this place, I am a child. The people here have no history with me. I haven't done anything to offend them yet.

But as I learn more and more Greek, the possibility of my offending them grows. As I understand more Greek, I wake up by degrees to the reality of the people who live here. Their politics. Their rivalries. Their jealousies. I wake up to the contradictions and complexities of this world, some of which I can't even properly articulate yet. It is like being a child: I live by my senses here, I comprehend the islanders' world by intuition, understanding nothing completely,.

I still don't know what to do about Yiorgos and Andreas. When I ask, no one will tell me anything straight out. When I try to get the opinions of the other shepherds, they avoid my questions or answer me with words they know I will not understand.

Andreas does own two or three different fields. Yiorgos owns nothing but what he came here with, that first day I saw him.

So I think the big black stallion gets to stay and swish its long tail in front of the little house. I acknowledge this may be a mistake. But whatever I do now will be a mistake. I will insult, offend, or injure someone's pride.

Why are fucking up and growing up so closely related?

Philosophy is a Greek word

NOTHING EQUALS THESE fields at night when the moon is coming round, when every stone is a diamond with its own velvet pouch of shadow. There is a time between dusk and moonrise when the sky ascends into itself; each time you blink another star appears. Then, slowly, the light of the stars is drowned by the greater brightness of the moon. Luminous, unearthly blue floods the sky. The edges of the hills and broken stones shine like scythes.

I sit outside in this bright darkness. Yiorgos' goats have turned into unicorns. I can see the words I'm writing here. Squinting, I can even read the dictionary.

"Philosophy" is a Greek word.

So is "chaos."

With the air of a sage, Yiorgos declares, "You go blind if you read in the dark."

"I'm reading in the moonlight."

"Yeah, well, stop this reading. Why you reading? Look at the moon."

We stare at the moon like two cats. Two real kittens purr, loudly, in Yiorgos' lap. I sip my wine. I take in the blue and silver tumult of light in the olive groves, the fig and almond orchards. Each tree stands in a black pool of shadow.

"Philosophy is a Greek word."

"Of course philosophy is a Greek word. The Greeks invented philosophy. Plato and Aristotle and Herodotus. All Greeks."

"What's your philosophy?"

"My philosophy?" He looks at me with a raised eyebrow. "The moon does not make a Greek philosophical."

I laugh. "Come on, Yiorgo, I'm serious."

"Katerina, you are a funny one. *You* ask *me* my philosophy? You the writer. My philosophy is to have a very good life, a nice life, a life with my animals and my garden and olive-picking in Yera in the winter. With good smoke and good friends and good food. And clean. A lot of people have dirty lives. I want to live very clean. With church sometimes."

"You go to church?"

"Yeah."

"What do you do there?" I find it difficult to picture Yiorgos in church with a dozen widows dressed in black, all the young women of the village, and a few grumpy merchants.

He sips his wine and gives me a surprised look. "What do I do in church? I listen. It's a church. What do you think I do? There is a priest talking, I listen, I say Yia-sou, I go home."

"Oh."

"I worked for a long time at Mount Athos. I was a wood-cutter for one of the monasteries. And if you live for a long time at a monastery, it changes you, even if you are not a monk. That's why I go to church. I worked for monks. Sometime I tell you that story."

"I know you don't want to talk about philosophy but tell me, because I'm curious about what you think. What is life? What are our lives?"

"You know what I think? Canadian girls read too many books. And all that writing. Your brain is fried."

"Yiorgo!"

He laughs. "Life, life, what's life? Life is a very serious business. This for sure. Which is strange. Because life is also very funny: there is nothing funnier than being alive. You know it, you're laughing all the time over there, even by yourself, I hear you. But you know it's serious business. Life is . . . a mystery. Mystery is also a Greek word, you know."

"Give me a metaphor."

"Metaphor is also a Greek word. You see? I tell you, nothing original in English. Boring language."

"Just give me a metaphor!"

He becomes mock-serious, and leans over to put one of the gray kittens in my lap. The kitten purrs under my hand like a small generator. "Life is a mysterious blue animal. Big as a mountain. Small as a flower seed." There is a package of petunia seeds on the table in front of us.

"And what is death?"

"Death? Gamiseta, where is your sense of humour? We have a full moon! We should run around naked and go swimming." He pauses. "Death is a sea urchin."

"And the world?"

He smiles a satisfied broken-tooth grin. "This I know from a fairy story. The world is a castle." He turns his head away from me to look over the valley, at the craggy, silver-carved hillsides, at the sea. "A castle with a big garden, lots of big tomato plants. Good cigarettes." We both look at the garden beside us, slowly filling with more red and fuschia asters, more greenery. The sunflowers are waist high now.

"If the world is a castle, what is the little house?"

Yiorgos screws up his face and turns his head to look at the *spitaki* where I live. "That, Katerina, is just one small room in the castle. Your room. Full of mice and ants!"

"And a scorpion last week."

"See how lucky you are? Now!" Slapping his hands against his skinny knees, he stands up. A kitten drops to the ground. "No more philosophy. It's a full moon. Let's put away the dictionary!"

A chair, a flower-pot, a garden

EARLIER THIS MORNING, Maria called out to me as I was passing by. Her husband, Panagos, is usually friendly to me, but I'm never sure of her. Sometimes I think she likes me and we will be friends. But not yet. Other times, after inexplicably cool meetings, I think she distrusts me. We are like two different animals. She is slow and serious. I am too quick to laugh.

So I was happy when she invited me up to the porch for a coffee. We sat under the shade of the sprawling grapevine that grows above the patio, exchanging the daily news of neighbours. She asked, "Do you or Yiorgos want eggs? My chickens will not stop laying."

"If you have extra, we'll eat them."

She flipped a tea towel from the top of a basket on the table and counted out half a dozen. With their rich orange yolks, these eggs bear no relation to the ones you buy in a supermarket. These eggs squawk when you crack them open.

"Who can I give the rest to?" She peered thoughtfully into the basket. "It's good to have chickens."

"It's good to have anything here."

She looked up. "What do you mean?"

I wasn't quite sure myself. I hesitated. "I think I would like to *have* something here." I don't know the verb "to own" yet, but my meaning was clear. I was slightly shocked by my words, spoken for the first time, not in English, but in Greek. Maria waited for me to go on. "I would like to have . . . a chair. For example. Or one of the big clay flower-pots Doukakis sells. I would like to have a garden." Only this last sentence satisfied me because the verb was right. You cannot own a garden, not really, but you can have one.

Maria had a curious expression on her face. A small smile threaded the corners of her mouth and eyes. "You mean you want to have a house." The word "house" in spoken Greek also means "home." I sat in silence for at least a minute, considering. The *spitaki* up the road. Four stone walls. Fourteen olive trees, three fig trees. Mice in the roof tiles. Ants in every edible thing. No electricity, no plumbing. A wide view of the Aegean. Hills that keep the village like a secret. A dolphin skull in the flower bed.

Maria repeated, "You want a house. That's it, isn't it?" She has few words, this woman I don't know, but the ones she has are true.

"Yes," I said. "That's it."

"You want to live here. Not just for a few months."

"I think so."

A donkey brayed loudly, gracelessly, farther down the road. Cautionary advice or celebratory agreement? Maria and I laughed. We drank our cooled coffee. I asked her about the whitewash—I want to whitewash the *spitaki*. When her children, Jeremiah and Iris, came out onto the patio, sleep still in their eyes, she said, "I have to get them breakfast. Do you want to come in for another coffee?"

"No, it's time for me to go." She folded my eggs into the tea towel. As I got up to leave, she said something which initially puzzled me, "Don't think about it too much."

Now I know why she said that. Because I've been thinking about it all day. Every moment and movement weaves itself into the larger question. I walk across the field to see how ripe the figs are. Could I see how ripe the figs are this time next year, the year after that? The Meltemi wind rises high and wild in the afternoon, knocking the olive leaves over on their silver backs and tearing the clean blue sheets off the line. As I run after them across the field, I think, The wind will be this strong next summer. I could be standing here, right here, holding this same blue tumble of clean cotton.

I will whitewash the house, as I have seen the country women do. According to the village custom, the house ought to be whitewashed every spring. Could I stay for the winter?

Am I out of my mind? The old women say, "The winter is cold gray sea and wind that knocks your heart back against your ribs. The winter, we stay home, with the shutters closed, the stove full of wood, yarn in our laps." The younger women say, "Wait until you find out everything you don't know yet. You'd die during the winter." The men say, "Stay, please stay. It rains in the winter, the grass turns green and beautiful." They get so lonely that they even notice the beauty of the grass.

I write this with my back against the wall of the *spitaki*. A small, apple-green lizard with a very long tail comes over the stone fence toward the water basin I always leave in the sun. Because I've just filled it, the surrounding grass is jewel-wet. The lizard licks water droplets from single green blades for two minutes, as he often does after I fill the basin. Then he pivots his keen head one way and another, glancing up at me when I make a clicking sound with my tongue. He flickers over the dry ground like an errant green flame and disappears, extinguished between stones.

The green lizard will live in the stone fence until he dies. I could watch him drink water droplets for years. He will grow to be a foot long.

I look up now at the road. Yiorgos won't be coming home for hours. I look up at the road again. Why? Who or what am I waiting for? No one, nothing. Slowly I realize the road itself is a presence, a possibility. And I live at the end of this dust-filled, stone-backed road. Beyond the *spitaki* are Nikos' fig orchard and flock of sheep, then the wild hills. There is nowhere else to go.

The labyrinth

Hills so hot the husks
around the almond shells blush.
Yiorgos names one of his goats
Heeonati—Snow White.
When I bend to give her water,
she licks salt from my collarbones,
nuzzles corn around the tins.
I toss hay to the rabbits,
who are in love and demand feeding.

The rocks on these roads
and the horseshoe of mountains beyond
let me come as close as I dare.
Swallows careen under a pure azure burden.
The roads guide me like the woman
with her blind man in the morning.

Nights, I watch the moon, patient sculptress
gathering light from a quarry of darkness.
The millennium collapses, fire in a corrupt temple,
and still her work is unfinished.
She gathers and carves, again fills
and starves her contours.

Mornings, I sing myself down from the hills
for lessons in the village.
Meet the tongue's blade, the Greek sword,
unwieldy, every word a thrust of history.
The villagers pull me from blue rain
to bloody ruin, send me
beyond silence, into
the throat's labyrinth.

What is a mouth but a pearled entrance to the waters?
What is a mouth but a speaking grave?
Accompanying the lutes under the plane trees
and the night-haired women turning by the sea,
I learn the harsher village music.

The seamstress stabs pins into fresh silk.
Your foreign hands cannot touch
the island's true face.
Our mysteries will never be yours.

After comprehending these words,
I detect eyes less than generous.
In the taverns, in the shops.
Eyes jealous of their secrets,
jealous of the treasures here.

A Gypsy camp at the salt flats

THE GYPSIES, WHAT of them? *Tsiganos,* they are called here, the word from Romani, their own language. In the eleventh century, Greece became their gate into the West. Like everything and everyone else here, the Gypsies of the island are an older version of the people I've met elsewhere in Europe. And I have not met them yet, besides the odd greeting in the city, where they sell carpets and kitchenware. They hold their silence like a talisman. I will wait for my Greek and my confidence to improve.

Sometimes they come in large groups to eat and drink on the beach. They carry firewood, mandolins and guitars, children. Music rises, then, from a distance, human voices whirling around a small orange fire. What music do I hear? Greek, Turkish, Oriental, North African? I can never separate one strain from the other, nor the dissonance of the women's voices from the instruments, nor the moments I watch and listen from the moments they sit on the cold night sand and sing.

I see them camped out in the immense, barren salt flats near Talloni. The morning sky thickens with gray clouds; pure light becomes smoke. I stand on one side of the rough highway. They are encamped on the other side. Dark-skinned women in colourful, layered skirts and beaded headscarves lean over cooking fires. Tent openings flap in the wind. Farther away, half a dozen men cluster around one man who holds the reins of a jumpy gray horse. Black-haired children run after a dog. Younger children sit by the fire and rub smoke from their eyes. Older children watch me watching them. Sea wind from the wide Gulf of Talloni almost tears the hair off my head as I stand beside the old bicycle, my jacket billowing like a sheet. The women around the fire glance up.

We look at each other for a long moment, across the width of road and salt and sand.

Only this staring through the wind. The children wave, but the women make no sign. They gaze at me as though I am a ghost, or a tree, suddenly grown in the saltiest earth of the island.

I get back on the bicycle and continue my ride to Talloni.

Isadora at Talloni

TALLONI ON A Saturday morning! After the quiet of the valley and the village, the small town of Talloni is Istanbul to me. I walk dazed and giddy through the bustle, the surge of people, the fish markets and street hawkers, watching out for the honking trucks and swerving cars and motorcycles. Watermelon pyramids fill the street, a tonne of tomatoes, a truckload of walnuts and red peppers. I wander around the hot, crowded lanes, eating a piece of watermelon, eating a piece of almond cake, eating fresh walnuts. It's market day. I have only a small knapsack and bicycle; what I need is a donkey to help me carry home my treasures of food and paper.

Civilization has its perks. There are women out in the streets here, even young women! Later, in the evening, I will go to Koula's house and take a hot shower. Right now, I go to the bookstore: good notebooks and paints and pens that do not explode in two days. I go to the shop with the best almonds where the shopkeeper's daughter and I practise our French. In the blue-walled bakery, a heaven made of flour and warmth, I chat with the baker about his peach trees and children. This is a true measure of progress in my Greek studies; the first time I met the baker, all I could say was "Thelo psomi." I want bread.

For lunch, I eat souvlaki from a charcoal grill and drink beer with a woman named Isadora. She sells jewellery and her boyfriend, Gavrilo, sells the souvlaki. After closing her silver boxes and draping a scarf over her jewel cases, she asks me if she can sit and eat at my table because the few tables with sun umbrellas are full. I am happy to have her company. Perhaps what I miss most here is the company of women. There are plenty of tourist women on the island now, but I want to know Greek women—not an easy thing to do. In her late twenties or early thirties, Isadora has long, dark brown hair, an aquiline face, thin arms. She wears a faded red dress and a light, quick smile. Hers is a rare face for a woman, because it never decided if it was beautiful or not; it abdicated from beauty altogether and decided to be striking, unignorable. Almost immediately, I like her very much. Why? Because, unlike most of the young women here, she speaks freely. She does not whisper.

"I cannot imagine your life. You see? You are the lucky one, because you see me here, today, and you know what the peasant women and village girls are like. But I have no idea what it must be like to live in Canada. No idea. The Greeks are so in love with Greece, you know that. And so was I, until university. In university, with the history and the professors and all the shit, I got sick of Greece, sick of patriotism, sick of politics. And now, even more disgust, because of the E.E.C. Now we will be like the rest of Europe! And Europe becomes like America. And isn't Canada America? You're brother and sister. You're lucky to be a Canadian woman, maybe, all this freedom and not the same history. Your grandfather didn't sell his daughters for a fucking olive field, right? But America scares me. Money and murders, that's all I know about America. America of the fucking television. Five years ago, you couldn't find a television in a Greek bar— and now! *Plaff!* They are everywhere, everyone thinks television is God. Everyone wants to buy a television. What's happening to these people, they losing their brains?"

She leans across the table to me, her brown eyes wide and sparking. "The peasants are all dying, you know that. Soon none of them will be left. And they don't even know what's happening. They don't know they are the last ones. Just like animals don't know when they're dying out." This last sentence, uttered so quickly, seems to surprise and sadden her, as though it is the first time she has articulated something she has long understood. "And the new island people, the new young people, they are shits. They are the tourist babies. They don't know how to live without sucking on the tourists. You know what we say? Tourism came to Greece and the gods left."

Discussions like this always put me in an awkward position, because what am I? I am not a tourist, am I? I am a traveller. This is what I tell myself. I am actively engaged in the life of this place. But who ever admits she is an ugly, grasping tourist? I ask, "Why did the gods leave when tourism arrived?"

She takes a swig of her beer and looks at me as

though I am remarkably stupid. "Because it's all about plata, lefta, drachmas. Money. The tourists come with their money. In the beginning, it was okay, the peasants don't mind the foreigners, the kafeneio owners learn a few German words, a few English words, everything is okay. The fishermen put up the visitors in the spare rooms. Fine. Very nice. But then more and more come, to take the sun, take out fishing boats, take pictures, take home souvenirs. Take take take. Anything for money. That's the only thing they give. Their stupid, fucking money."

"But the Greeks want tourist money, right?"

"Of course. This is the problem with money. It's a disease everyone wants. And then they go sicker and sicker with it."

"I notice, in Skala, that the kinder business people are usually the older people. The younger ones are distrustful, less likely to be friendly, more business-like."

"Of course. The tourist babies. They don't know any other way of life but tourism, the money trade. They don't care about the olive harvest or fishing or any of the things their parents did. They don't love the island. All they want to do is set up shop and make cash off dumb tourists." She leans over the table to me, almost whispering. "Do you know, they hate the tourists? They hate them! So many Greeks hate tourists. Despite all this nice exterior, these smiles and this hand-shaking. It's all shit to get their money."

"Why do they hate tourists?"

"Because we always hate the ones we can't survive without. What is this word in English, to be without help?"

"Helpless."

"Yes, we always hate to be helpless, to need someone to free us from helpless—"

"Helplessness."

"Yes. It's a fucked system, this tourism. Pure capitalism, and what does the best capitalism make? Polluted seas, people who love nothing but money, air thick as shit. That's why I'll never live in Athens again. Millions of people living in little apartments like chickens, just to get by and have a stupid car. It's crazy." She drains her beer and asks Gavrilo for another souvlaki.

"So if you see all this, and think it's wrong, what do you do?"

"I used to believe I would be an economist, I would be political. Studying economics made me decide that money was shit. That, and my grandparents—"

I have to interrupt as quickly as she talks. "Your grandparents?"

"I lived with them when I was a teenager. They had pistachio orchards. That's all I remember them talking about: pistachios, and the olive harvests. They *loved* those trees. I learned how to cut and harvest and where to take the pistachios for processing, all that stuff. And they lived off their trees, that's how they made their money, but it had nothing to do with getting rich. It was about the trees. Everything was about the land." Here Gavrilo interrupts by calling her and handing her two more souvlakis. She gives one to me.

"So what happened with the pistachios?"

"My grandparents died five and seven years ago. First my grandmother, then my grandfather. And before my grandfather was even cold, my father sold the orchards, because neither of my parents wanted to do the work."

"And you?"

"I was still in university. This is my big regret. That I didn't stop university and go to work on the orchards. Then I would not be selling jewellery and picking somebody else's olives every November."

"That's how you stay alive?"

"In Greek we say, Whatever your ass can grab. This is what I do. Whatever. I've done everything. I've done every kind of work you can imagine, and other kinds you cannot imagine. I know about getting money. This is the funny thing, you know. It's easy to get money, it is very easy." She pushes my souvlaki towards me, and takes a bite of her own. "But I don't believe in money. I will live how I want. I will pick grapes or olives or work in a kafeneio, but I will never go back to Athens and live like a chicken again. Here, even the chickens do not live that way!"

Isadora and I talk for a long time. When business drops off, Gavrilo joins us, eats a couple of souvlakis himself, and drinks a beer. His black hair is tied back in a ponytail and his shirt is covered in yoghurt and pork grease. Gavrilo is very quiet, though twice he teases Isadora for talking so much. "You see why I don't speak much, eh? She says everything. There is nothing left for me." Both of them laugh, and she leans across the corner of the small table to kiss him. The souvlaki is mid-way to his mouth; it collides with her face, smearing yoghurt on her cheek and nose. We all laugh again.

Together they close up shop while I write here. I am calmed by the rare, gentle way they talk together, discussing the business of the day and touching each other, lightly, whenever possible. Sometimes, it is impossible to know when a man and a woman are together here, because they seldom touch each other in public. Often a man will speak to his wife or girl-friend as if he were speaking to a casual acquaintance.

But not these two. It comforts me to be around people who love each other. We spend part of the evening together, then Gavrilo leaves us to visit a friend. Isadora and I begin the long walk to the beach of Talloni. Fields of fresh-cut alfalfa spread away from the road, filling the air with the scent of honey and hay. We swing our bare arms as we walk. We watch the bats and the slow march of stars into the sky. All the while, we talk like old friends who haven't seen each other for a long time. We have our whole lives to tell.

Isadora of the Red Dress   a story

NEVER LET ANYONE tell you, "Don't run away from your problems." Why wouldn't you run away? My advice is: Run hard with your eyes open and do not stop until the scenery turns to paradise. Even there, nothing will be perfect, but it's better to have problems in a beautiful place than an ugly one. That's how I ended up on this island.

EVERY ISLAND is the end of the earth. Freaks and lepers in spirit quit the world and go to islands. The people who have lived and worked and died on *this* island for centuries claim that no outsider can ever understand its mysterious power. Its secrets.

They have a passion for gossip, the villagers, so I can't say, "I've got enough of my own secrets, you old goats, I'm not interested in yours." If I said that, they'd lean towards me, wide-eyed, whispering, "Tell, tell . . ."

No, I didn't come here for the secrets. I wanted good olives and a house in a field. I came for the summer sea, to hold me in her blue arms. And quiet. That's why I stay. Silence. The silence inside stone, in the skin of growing plants. Every farm in the valley, every house in the village has a garden, not only of vegetables and fruit, but of flowers, sharp yellow and fuschia splashing out of painted tins. The land around spreads and rolls from silver-green to rose to amber tones, brilliant green in the wet winter and spring. The sky is azure and the water sky-deep.

The water's quiet. If you swim long and far, your heart starts to beat in time with the currents lifting and rippling the sea's sand floor. You go into the water, a weighted blue door opens, closes. And you know you belong to the sea.

MY NAME IS Isadora. In the village, they sometimes call me "Isadora of the red dress". It's true, I own a red dress. Not because I want to be glamorous, no, and not because red is my favourite colour. I came by the dress innocently. One of the German tourists who stayed at the hotel last summer gave it to me before she left. She said she didn't like it any more, but the fact is she drank too much ouzo and ate too much oil cheese and moussaka. The dress fit her like a sausage skin by the time she went away.

Now I have the dress, my only nice one. I burned everything else when I came here three years ago, and I don't have the money to buy clothes any more. I don't want the money: I want to dress simply, like the people who live here. But this dress came to me so easily, accidentally, and it *is* beautiful, so I've kept it.

It has a low but not too low neck with a fitted top and waist and loose skirt. It's made of thin, tightly-woven cotton, the kind that looks like silk from a few feet away. I often wear it to the dances in the village, but sometimes I wear it just because I want the feel of it on my body, the skirt dropping from my hips like water, the smooth-fitting waist. The old men sitting under the plane trees at Koula's *taverna* say they wish their wives would buy red dresses.

They tease me a great deal, the old farmers and shepherds, because I am from Athens. In their minds, Athenian women are loose and untrustworthy. "Isa! Isa of the red dress!" Mikhaili said to me the other morning when I went up to the village to buy bread. "When are you going to marry my son? All winter long you sleep alone, and now it's spring! My boy is going crazy. He loves you more than life itself!" They always talk like that, these goats, everything is exclamation marks and melodrama. When I stuck out my tongue, they all laughed aloud, and thumped their canes and empty glasses against the table. I walked down towards the cheese shop; their eyes rolled after me like grapes. Horny old men with rotten teeth and goat-leather hands. They're narrow-minded, backward; they gossip and drink all day. They took a wrong turn at the seventeenth century and ended up here, rubbing their gums in the twentieth. But they're good people, mostly, and their wives have the hearts of giants. A few of them would break their own bones to keep you from harm.

I'M BRINGING the red dress to Solinos for the weekend. Nikos' jaw will drop when I put it on, because he hasn't seen me wearing it before. In fact, the few times he's seen me I've been at work, in an old t-shirt and shorts, hair in my face, hands stinking of blue-grit bathroom cleanser. It didn't seem to make any difference, though. He still waited around and brought me a drink, bought me supper, suggested a late-night swim. An offer I declined.

I would like to have a good reason for Nikos, but I don't. I'm not hungry: the garden's blossoming into food and the work at the hotel brings in enough money. Certainly I'm not in love. A dozen times I've told myself that lust is not a good reason, although it's better than no reason at all: I only have weak twinges of lust for Nikos, nothing spectacular. There is no purpose. As I fold my red dress and find my silver earrings and toss my lipstick into my stained leather bag, I say to myself: I must remember what I am doing now, so that I will not do it again.

But I'm afraid I'll do it again anyway, because the habit stays with me even though everything else is finished. Like the blood-filled belly of a tick. You can yank it off so easily, you think it's gone, but the head is still buried in the flesh, drinking, turning the blood it sucks to poison.

SOON NIKOS will come to pick me up. I clean toilets and make beds at the hotel. Nikos eats and drinks here when he happens to be on this side of the island. That's how we met. He was spearfishing one afternoon and came by in the evening to have a drink with Dimitri, my illustrious boss and benefactor. Dimitri is always trying to get the women who work here into bed with his friends because he can't have us himself.

He's married and scared to death of his father-in-law. When he introduced me to Nikos, I smiled and chatted about the fine weather and glanced at his Rolex watch and could not help noticing the BMW key chain on the table. This is just a habit for me from before; I can't help noticing these details and making certain calculations.

For a couple of weeks, Nikos seemed to turn up at the hotel on weekends, once even during the week, and finally last Friday, he asked me if I wanted to go "away" for a weekend. He owns a camera shop in Solinos. Solinos is a very picturesque town, built on a hill, with a castle fortress at the summit. Naturally, everyone who visits wants to take pictures. It's only June now, not many tourists, not many cameras gobbling up rolls of Kodak and Fuji film, so Nikos has a little time "to relax and enjoy the beauty of the town and the nearby beaches." He often speaks that way, like a tourist brochure. He talks about the sky, the sea, and the beaches as though he owns them all and would like nothing better than to sell them to you, not because he's greedy—never!—but because he wants you to own them, too, so you can feel the way he feels, expansive and free and unselfish.

I've known a lot of people like Nikos. Nice people. Generous because generosity means nothing to them. They have the well-oiled grace of money, good looks, good cars. They possess impeccable style. In fact, they eventually possess whatever they want. Possession is their talent and their code.

You might think I despise such men and women on principle, like a good socialist. But nothing is simple. It's possible to understand someone's mind in such a way that you admire it even as you despise it.

Don't we admire what we dream of being? Don't we despise what we are afraid of becoming?

I don't ask these questions for effect. I ask them because I don't know the answers. Sometimes I am glad of that.

HE IS NOT a big man, although he is bigger than me, and getting a little fat. But good-looking enough, full-mouthed, with small greenish eyes, hair dark as mahogany, healthy brown skin. Healthy, and kind. The sort of man mothers wish upon their daughters, with an easy laugh and a gentle but strong character. Strong but gentle hands: a gold but not gaudy ring on his finger, a thin gold chain around his wrist. Another looped round his neck, a small cross dangling there, often hidden under white cotton. Some chest hair, hair on his hands, on his fingers, but not too much, he's not a wolverine.

His face is smooth and unlocks into a radiant white smile. Great teeth. That's really where you can see the money in a Greek. Every time Nikos leans over, smiling, to adjust the volume on the car stereo, or turns to tell me a joke or point out a field of poppies, every time he laughs, a million drachmas gleam in my direction.

I DO NOT think like this when I am with my friends from the village. Sweet Koula at the *taverna* tells me all the gossip, makes me rub her neck after she feeds me supper. When Yiorgos comes to visit me, he works away at his jewellery or rolls joints while I drink coffee and watch the tomatoes grow, or read a book. Gavrilo, the anarchist alfalfa farmer, rages to me about government corruption whenever he comes for a visit. They are misfits, leftover hippies, come to this island for reasons similar to my own. Although I know them well, know their faults as they know many of mine, I don't dislike them or regard them cynically. After three years, we are real neighbours. Friends. Gavrilo and I had a lightning-quick affair last summer—one of his old girlfriends showed up howling, put a stop to it—but we're still friends. I love them, I think. Imagine. I love them. When they laugh, I hear laughter. I don't even notice their teeth.

"A GORGEOUS mouth," Nikos says. "Why don't you smile for me?" I glance up. Something about his grin reminds me of a dog. That eagerness. The camera shutter clicks. "You are the most beautiful woman on the island." He changes angles, knocks the sea behind me now. *Click. Click.* We are on a beach called Eftalou, seven green and rocky hills behind us. He continues taking pictures, although I don't believe in photographs and ignore his camera. He took pictures of me on the journey here, too, on the cliffsides, at the broken-down altar of one of the ruined temples. Each time the shutter winked down, I gritted my teeth.

"Niko," I say, dropping the "s" as we do when addressing people by their first names—"Niko. I am shy. Don't take my picture. Please." I smile. He smiles back. Still squatting in the sand, he slides his black sunglasses back on, transforming himself into an insect with great oblong eyes. I lie naked on my belly, a book open in front of me, sand already shivered between the pages.

Few people come to Eftalou so early in the season. Except for two couples and three Scandinavian women, we are alone. The Scandinavian women are far down the beach, playing paddle board. The hard ball strikes the wooden paddles regularly, *tock-tock, tock-tock,* although that sound and the sound of the women's laughter seem to come to us from far away. "Isa, once you see how beautiful the photographs are, you'll want me to take more."

I make a sound deep in my throat. "I read some-where once that Chinese peasants used to believe photographs were made from the eyes of dead babies."

Nikos sits down heavily on the towel beside me, and leans back to put the camera in his canvas bag. "Really?"

"Yes." I look up from my book into his insect eyes. "Tell me, is it true?"

"Isadora!"

"Well, it could be true. Maybe that's why I've never liked having my picture taken."

"Of course it isn't true. You're crazy." Laughing, he stretches his arm over my back for the mask and snorkel, black rubber imitations of what he doesn't have. The bottom of his forearm grazes my waist. "I'm going swimming again. The kamakee must be ready by now."

Earlier, after we had crossed the sand and re-moved our street-clothes, Nikos assembled his *kamakee* and dropped it into the water so it would be ready to use later, the same temperature as the water, smooth-shooting. He hopes to spear fish this after-noon. "And we'll take them to the Horizon, a restau-rant a friend of mine owns. Beautiful place overlooking the harbour. Lanterns and flowers and mandolins at night, the best cooks on this side of the island. They'll do something extraordinary with whatever I catch."

KAMAKEE IN Greek means "speargun", that pronged, devilish device made for killing sea creatures. *Mee mou kaneis kamakee* is a phrase well known to Greek women. Although people might argue about exact word usage, it essentially translates into, "Don't use the speargun on me." We say this when we don't want a man's attentions. When we don't want him to come on to us. When we do not care in the least where he comes, as long as it isn't near our bodies. "Don't use the speargun on me."

Every time Nikos spears a fish close to shore, he throws it: sunlight glimmers and flashes off the scales as the catch flies through the air. It thuds on the sand near me like a big silver medallion. Nikos has told me I must gather them up and deposit them in the netted basket he has anchored in the water, very close to shore, but I ignore his instructions and continue to read my book. If the fish are not already dead, pierced by the *kamakee,* they flop and twist until their glistening lengths are sand-coated, almost invisible, part of the beach. But you know they're there because of their gasping mouths and gills. They kiss the useless air until they die. I try not to look at them.

BUT NOTHING is simple. Almost night now, the Aegean hour of blue air and bluer shadow, even the low white wall around the restaurant terrace looks blue, like snow too magical to melt. Far below us, the water spreads heavy purple, heaving indigo salt, and men in small boats pull and hoist up their nets. They look like puppet-masters animating underwater marionettes, their hands jerking up and down.

I'm getting romantic about these things because I'm getting drunk. Nothing is simple. When I politely explained that I didn't want to eat his fish, the rich man Nikos leaned over, kissed my hand just below the middle knuckle, smiled with his glorious teeth, and ordered lamb for me instead.

And here I sit, in my red dress, eating every last shred of flesh and sucking on the bones, drifting from romantic to philosophical. I'm so drunk I don't know how I'll make it to the bathroom. On four, maybe five miserable glasses of wine. Because I don't drink an more, you see, I limit myself to one glass, no more than one, just one.

It's dangerous to be drunk with a man who owns a speargun.

At least I don't have to deal with him alone. Thank you, Artemis, thank you Athena, oh, the fierce goddesses, you must still be here, somewhere. Under the table, maybe? Do you hang invisible on the grapevines overhead, shaking your heads as you watch my disappointing performance?

Nikos and the restaurant owner and the restaurant owner's ladyfriend discuss business and Solinos and common acquaintances and spearfishing and a famous Greek pop star, someone I've never heard of. I sit, nodding, smiling, making useless but occasionally clever comments, listening, not listening, not listening, hearing the music so well, too well, it's vibrating and dancing up and down my back, the backs of my legs. The *bouzouki* player has a stool in the corner of the terrace, but occasionally he stands, takes slow strides, legs scissoring against his loose black trousers. Black eyes half-closed, he steps and turns near our table, stroking and plucking fine strings of the instrument. Turkey stretches toward us in every tortured chord.

Nikos rests his hand on my arm. "You're so hot. I was about to ask you if you wanted my jacket, but I guess you're fine. . . ."

"Yes, thank you."

"More wine?"

"No, no really, please, I'm fine." But the liquid already unfolds and folds back into my glass, warm burgundy silk.

The woman across from me smiles without exposing her teeth. A patient, condescending smile. She has black eyebrows and perfectly blond hair pulled away from her face, neatly secured with a gold clasp. Her bronze skin glows against cream linen. Elegant, with lush make-up, like a movie star approaching forty-five. "So, Isadora, Nikos tells us you're working on the other side of the island for the summer."

"No. I live there. I live there all year around."

"Really? Even in the winter?"

"The winter is the best time, in some ways."

"Ah, yes, that's what they say, the solitude and all that." She regards me with more cold smile over her glass, summing me up in one sip and writing me off in the next. I wink at her. Her eyes fall to her plate. I want to dance, but must be content with rubbing my thighs together, watching the *bouzouki* player's hands, the long fingers, his long eyes half-closed. The men resume eating. A stack of fish big enough to feed three families still sits on the table, with roast lamb, eggplant salad, calamari, grilled octopus, *teeropita,* and, of course, raw feta and olives and cucumber and fresh bread.

The meat cleaves away from the slender bone as I pick up another lamb rib. I begin to think about arithmetic, a subject I was never very good at. How much is the lamb worth? How much, the olive oil drowning the feta? The mauve handmade plates, the marble table, the snakes of gold around the movie star's wrists and neck? And how much for the *bouzouki* player, what's the price of *his* music?

Then there's the elegant house where Nikos has given me a room with thick pink towels. And what about the pretty balcony overlooking the sea?

Do not forget to take into account the BMW and the endless iced coffee, the eternal glass of orange juice—I never drink orange juice on my own, I have no fridge—the best wine on the island, the sweet morning cakes. *Posso kanei?* How much is it worth, the sun-rays slanting down the white walls of the church like blood dropping through a glass of cream?

If I knew the price of all that, and if I cared to look at a newspaper (the Swiss franc, the Deutsch mark, the yen, the dollar) would I be able to calculate the exchange rate for human skin?

I still don't know what I'm worth. After three years, after coaxing tomatoes and potatoes and peppers out of the ground, after building a fireplace and chopping my own wood in the winter. Now I am dazzled by hot running water, a white toilet, the fluted railings of the balcony, which are still bars, of a sort. But he is so kind, this man, Nikos, so nonchalant about the holes in my shoes and my single red dress, it's clear he isn't just interested in my body.

If there were a chorus in this play, laughter would rise from it now.

LATER, MILDLY drunk, exhausted, we sit on the balcony outside my room in his house and watch the lights of Solinos, the more distant lights of the Turkish coastline. Across the water, headlights swerve and dive along invisible roads. The people inside those cars think and speak and dream in a different language. "But we are so similar." Only when Nikos looks across at me and smiles do I realize I've spoken aloud. Before he can reply, I say, "The Turks and us, I mean. I was just watching their lights."

"Ah." Disappointment. He speaks in a stern voice, "Similar in some things. Very different in others. Don't forget religion." Patriotism, and the cross around his neck. I'd forgotten. "Go up to the castle and you can see how dangerous the Turks are. Bastards. Everything is still there: the cauldrons we kept for boiling oil to pour on them when they tried to break into the fortress, rape the women, the children, burn everything." He takes his feet off the chair, wraps his hand around the top rail of the balcony, leans toward Turkey. He glances at me for a moment, turns away. It would be a mistake to mock him now, in this serious patriotic moment, although a dozen sharp taunts push against the inside of my lips. The invasions he has just described must have happened four or five hundred years ago. "Once," he continues earnestly, "they pillaged the village seven times in a year, but always we drove them away. There's a huge hole in the ground at the top of the hill, in the castle, a tunnel that drops down, all the way down to a sea cave on the shore, a hidden place where we kept boats to escape."

"Is it still open?"

"Of course. There's an iron grid over it, though, to keep the goddamn tourists from falling in." He laughs suddenly, leans back again. "I'll take you there tomorrow, if you'd like. You should see it before you go." He turns his head toward me slowly, purposefully.

My eyes close now, two doors I want to lock, hide behind, sleep inside. But Nikos is sitting close to me, his bare foot touching mine. Behind us is the dark room I am supposed to sleep in, alone. "Isadora?"

"Hmm?"

I open my eyes. He is coming toward me, his hand on the table to keep him balanced.

"Niko, I'm sorry, I don't think—"

"Shhh. Shhh. I want you." He pushes his face into my hair, his hands go loose, run down the red dress, push the skirt up my legs. "This is what I want."

I could push him over the balcony. I could set a price. Instead, I rise quickly, pass into the bedroom. He comes stumbling behind. That's a kind of power. I keep my eyes open. I want to watch it. I want to know why, why *this*.

A LONG time ago, I learned that it's possible to take the brain out of your head and place it on the night table (or the carpet, or the desk, or the tiles) while things happen to your body. If you do it well, the money can be very good. I thought I was a mechanic, for them, but also for myself. The brain is like an engine. You can lift it out of the car, put it back in later, make some adjustments, and things run again.

But you cannot do this with your soul. That was my discovery. When I finally understood, I had to leave. The soul feels everything, knows everything, and never forgets. This is the way the men of my country sometimes describe God.

AFTER FINISHING, Nikos separates himself from me and sits up, almost businesslike, turning his back to peel off the condom, the little wet ghost. Then, quick as a sneeze, he goes romantic again, turning to me on his side, lifting my legs over his. After smoothing the hair away from my face, he thrusts his hand into it, gently scratches my scalp, then pulls downward and wraps as much hair as he can around his fist. If he wanted, he could lift me up like one of those circus girls. He looks into my eyes for a long time. I blink hard to push his gaze away. It doesn't work.

"Isadora, you could stay with me. You could stay with me in this house. Rent-free. You could take a summer off, swim every day, relax. It's shitty work, at the hotel, no? Wouldn't you like to live here for the summer?"

I laugh. A gentle, happy laugh. A lie. I close my eyes. Maybe the problem, the problem of my whole life, has been my talent for lying. They make you these offers, though: *If you lie, you'll get this, a shred of treasure.* Sometimes you shove your soul so deep into yourself that you almost forget it's there. Then you pretend to forget completely. Every word you say shoves it deeper. Sometimes you can't find it again until it's too late, after the lies have grown a skin like truth. You wake up one day knowing you're inside them, you live there. Everyone can see that you live there, it must be where you belong. It's hard to imagine getting out.

"Isadora?" I know he's watching me, waiting for an answer.

I got out, though. I escaped. My first summer on this island, I swam so much that the sea salt ate away the lies. The sun burned through my back, my shoulders, down, clean into the deep.

"Isadora?" My eyes are in the Aegean. His voice comes to me as if from the edge of a boat. I sink farther, away.

IN THE MORNING, before going to swim, I remove my two silver rings and leave them beside his BMW key chain. Maybe a dozen keys fan out bright on the table, heavy, complicated, signifying the car, another house, the camera shop, a motorcycle. I am careful not to touch them. We are at the town beach, where a few local families and their children splash and play in the water. One stone face of the castle rises above us, off the cliff, diminishing the stone houses of the town. *Castro,* we say in Greek, for castle, but really we mean fortress, bastion, citadel. A place of refuge that has nothing to do with a princess.

I want the water now, only the water. There is a difference between me walking slowly across the beach, barefooted, head down to watch for sharp rocks, and Nikos under the umbrella of the beach-front cafe, drinking iced coffee, smoking a cigarette. There is a difference between us. A strange smile tightens the features of his face. It makes me think of some of the peasants I know. Even though he's a city man now, and spends his winters in Athens, Nikos wears the smile of a shepherd who has just bought a new sheep, or a new knife. Or both.

I do not look back at him. I think of the fields I have come from, the almond cases green under the sun, the olives growing even as I walk over the sand into cool blueness, and dive, disappear into the water below the castle.

SWIMMING, I see a blue starfish, and wonder if the crab scuttling below me has a voice I can't hear. Imagine it: the animals in the azure territories might sing, or tap signals on sea-stones, but we never know. We just watch as they crawl and glide over the white sands, or fly, simple sea-hair rippling around them. I once followed a stingray far, far away from shore, wondering where he might lead me, but the water got so deep I couldn't see the sand he wove himself over and under. I lost him and turned back toward land. But I wonder just how far you could go, following a ray or a dolphin or a lone fish. How far away would they take you, and once you got there, what would you become?

NIKOS STANDS in the water now, balancing first on one foot, then the other, pulling on his black flippers. When the water reaches his hips, he falls forward in slow motion. The *kamakee* jabs through the surface of the sea, once, twice, then disappears.

But his snorkel pipes out of the water regularly. I watch him for a while, a stone growing cold in my belly. He wants me to stay another night. Minutes ago, I glided over the same sand and opal floor that he eyes now, gripping the *kamakee* in his right hand. I do not know what to do. I can't read any more. The man in the water hunts.

When he comes into the shallows again, I sit up and shield my eyes from the sun. A young octopus curls and wraps around his hand. Nikos steps over the low-breaking waves. I walk to the water's edge and squat down beside him.

The octopus is mottled gray and small, marble come alive, a fantastic creature from another kingdom. It coils its cool tentacles around, under, over Nikos' knuckles and fingers and thumb and wrist, grasping as he grasps it and flips it over. "You kill it here," Nikos explains, *jab jab,* "in the gills. Or here—" *jab twist,* "—in the eyes." Then he releases his grip and takes away the *kamakee* blade because my hands are going down, open, to touch the octopus.

Its arms writhe and whip around my fingers as soon as I touch them. When I try to pull away, they grip tighter, the suction pulling at my skin. The flesh is muscled and cool, an eight-legged child wrapping its limbs around my hands, sucking at my fingers, searching for the water washing through me.

Just below the octopus' twisting form spread my feet, toes gripping the small rocks. Salt in my hair, dried now, dusting my back, forearms. My lips taste of the sea. And the animal clenching my fingers and wrists so desperately wants to go there, into the water two feet away. "Kill it now or let it go home," I say to Nikos, thrusting my octopus hands against his to make him peel the creature away. "Let it go. It's too small anyway. Give it back to the water."

Nikos casts a surprised look over me now, because my voice is strange, a sound in it he hasn't heard before. He pulls the octopus off my hands as I stand.

I walk up the sand to the towels, where I sit down and fold my arms around my knees. Nikos hesitates at the water's edge, the octopus still suffocating in the air, writhing around his hand. I close my eyes. A few seconds later I hear it, the light splash just past the shallows. He has thrown it back.

When I open my eyes, he is gone again.

I'M NOT SURE why, but I know their terror like a memory. Looking up at the high castle wall, I remember the fortresses I've seen, on this island, on others, on the mainland.

In late afternoon, the invaders gained the main square and market-place of the city. Anyone who was still alive had already surged in a frantic wave up, up, into the stronghold, out of houses and stables and chapels that fell now in flames. The smell of fire, the crush of bodies and braying animals and ash-stained faces made the women think of hell. The very entrance of hell seemed to gape, starving, in the flagstone floor of the fortress.

But it's not hell, a fourteen-year-old boy yelled, his voice huge, frantic above the noise. It will save you, you must go down. So the women tied their smaller children to their bodies with their own torn skirts, and the boy helped them find their footing on the knotted, dancing ropes. They slid down, down the dark lines, through the dripping innards of the earth, below the ovens and mills and olive press in the village. The archers lost above them let go their flame-tipped arrows. Scalding oil streamed through the holes along the battlements, burning, sometimes blinding the enemy men below.

The palms and fingers of the women and older children began to bleed before they reached solid ground, the sea-cave. Red handprints marked their faces, the stone walls, the gunwales of the boats. These handprints remained until the boats gained open water. Then wind-spray and waves loosened the red grips and washed them back into the sea.

NOW FLOWERS struggle out of the chinks in the castle wall. Only sun fires the gray stones, bleaching them such an old-bone white that you have to squint to hold your stare. Strange, I like it, the hurt that sun on a white wall pins in the eyes.

But I look away when the sea urchin wings black and spiny from the water. It lands on the beach three paces away from me, deep in the sand in front of Nikos' towel.

Nikos can't help himself. He just loves killing these things. Nikos thinks voiceless creatures don't speak, but the urchin bristles its purple-black spines slowly, so slowly, in desperate sign language.

Fishermen and sailors will tell you about sea urchins. If you step on one, it's wise to pee on the wound. One, two, three, or thirteen spines might stab and lodge in your foot if you meet up with an urchin, but don't walk until you get each one out. The smooth spines are made for sliding; if you put pressure on them, they break and separate under your skin, working their way so deep into you that they get lost in your blood. A man I knew once fell on a cluster of urchins in a tidal pool. So many spines stabbed into his knee that it looked like a cactus head. He squeezed and pulled as many of them out as he could, but the rest had pushed below the surface of his skin. For years, every spring, when the sap began to drip out of the pines, the man discovered a festering bump on his body, sometimes on his ankle, sometimes his thigh, once as high up as his shoulder. When he opened the blister, the tip of an urchin spine appeared like the bud of a tiny black flower.

Nikos stands dripping in the water, waving for me to come in with him. His wet hair is slicked back off his face, his brown body shines. He's good-looking. But I shake my head. He shouts, "Why not?"

"I'm tired! Why don't you come out of the water instead?" A smile in my voice, a promise. I am shocked at myself, partly. Partly I am glad. Nikos still stands, smacking the water lightly with the flat of his left hand, holding the *kamakee* like a trident in his right. He grins like Neptune, shakes sun-alive wet out of his hair, and begins to push through the water.

The sea urchin in front of his towel has stopped moving. It rests in its small valley, camouflaged by shadows from the sand-peaks and hills, difficult to see from any angle but my own. I turn over now, belly down, and stretch my legs along my towel, toes and the top flat part of my feet in the warm sand. I run my eyes over the beach front. In one of the terrace cafés, a small group of people begins to laugh and clap their hands. They are a good distance away, faces and brown arms and pale clothes without detail, but their strong laughter blows down on the breeze, telling me they are close friends. Sun beats like a heavy canvas sail at my back.

Just half a minute more. It will not be my fault. He threw the urchin out of the water.

His body casts a shadow over mine; beads of

water drop and spray lightly on my calves. My toes are tensed, pointed. He steps to the side, maybe to drop the mask and snorkel down beside his towel. Now he buckles, breath sucked in with surprise, pain. He exhales with swears, cursing aloud, loudly. Mothers and children look over in curious surprise. I am curling to sit as he falls onto his towel beside me, his body so cool and wet he's almost like a wave.

He makes clenched-teeth sounds of pain while angling his foot upward to survey the damage: a bushel of spines pushed deep in the soft middle flesh. He gropes and clenches for a rock at his left and leans forward to smash the urchin. He pounds until the spines are mangled, broken down to a wet pulp, the translucent eggs wasted in the sand. "Fucking thing," he hisses, and spits. Then he pincers his forefinger and thumb together, and begins to pull out the spines.

"NO. I WILL take the bus back, one leaves tonight at six, there is time if I get ready now." I stand at the closet, slipping my red dress off the wire shoulder of a hanger while Nikos sits in the facing room on the toilet lid.

"But it's crazy for you to leave today when I can easily drive you back tomorrow. It's two buses to the other side of the island and an hour's wait in Talloni, don't be ridiculous. Stay the night. We don't have to sleep together, we can wait." I pause at the doorway, the dress over my arm. He winces, dabbing iodine on his foot one moment and frowning up at me the next. A shining pair of tweezers rests on the edge of the sink. "Isadora. Don't be unreasonable."

"I'm not being unreasonable, I just want to go

home." I turn around to survey the room, the wide white bed, the blond wooden night tables, the double doors flung open to the balcony, a blanket of sea beyond, silver-stitched under the late afternoon sun. Then my eyes draw back, inside the room again, the opposite wall, the painting of a boat, the window open to the town, the camera on the dressing table. Its uncapped lens faces the mirror, as if it might try to take a picture of me secretly, by capturing my reflection. I turn and look at Nikos on the toilet, his head bent in terrible concentration, the tweezers glinting in his fingers. I turn and look again at the camera. The camera stares back, its greedy black eye open wide.

"ISA, I DIDN'T know you had a camera." Gavrilo is up, wandering around the room naked, as he often does after making love. Instead of calming him, sex usually makes him more restless. He will chop up tomatoes and cheese for a salad, he will go outside in his undershorts and fix my fence, he will leave me naked and drowsy in the midday heat and charge his bladed tractor through fields of alfalfa like a revolutionary cutting down foes. My eyes are half-closed, sweat collects like warm rain in my belly button, August presses me to sleep.

"Hey, Isa? Hey! I'd like to borrow your camera sometime."

I roll my head toward him. "I don't have a camera."

"Then why do you have this roll of film?" He holds it up near his face and shakes it back and forth, as though trying to hear the trapped images rattle back and forth.

"Oh. That. Those are pictures I never developed."

"Why not?" he drops the tight green cylinder back in the basket of shells and stones.

"They're old. People I left behind." A yawn pulls the last of these words out of shape. I stretch, arching my back off the damp sheet. When I hold my sleepy arms out to Gavrilo, he comes forward in his slick skin, a grin on his face. Even before he bends to kiss me, his hands opened, reaching down, I inhale the acrid, heavy scent from his body, the sweat from the purple-headed fields, the wet salt of our indigo sea.

I read The Guardian

I HAVE BEEN reading *The Guardian*.

Because I live without electricity, a television or a radio are useless to me. The newspaper is my only real connection to the active life of my century. The way I live now is also part of this century, but, as a friend recently explained to me, it has nothing to do with the modern age. "Be careful," he wrote, "you're becoming obsolete as the donkeys around you. You'll never get on the Internet if you stay there. Your life will shrink to the size of an olive." I laughed. If the modern age dictates that beauty of any kind is obsolete, then I will resist it a while longer and remember only the goats, who need water this afternoon because Yiorgos is out trekking.

But like you, like Isadora, like each individual in every separate country, I am the invention of my century. Never mind that I distrust it like a strange animal distrusts the sorcerer who conjured her from another era, another world. There are no time machines here; there is no other world. Only this place exists, this globe of canaries and demons, destruction and hunger, extremes of beauty matched only by violence beyond comprehension.

Do I forget anything I see? Skinned sheep hang in the village butcher shop. Those bulging eyeballs remind me of my beggar in Avignon, the grandfather with the rotting eye. Carmen, the young Gypsy woman, is married now, without finishing high school, and the children of Montclar have not escaped the poverty of their lives like so many David Copperfields. In northern Spain, someone else has lost their hands and arms to an exploding bomb, someone's face has been blown off, and at least fifty heroin addicts have overdosed since I received my last letter from Maru. The sea is heaven, but who knows what goes on in my stone-hard village tucked in the hills? The men used to believe they owned their women and children, like dogs. What do they believe now?

And what of the greater world, the one I've never seen? Once a week, I read *The Guardian*. Once a week, I stop singing and remember that the island is a small place. What of the carpet children in India—so close by, really—weaving away their lives in half-darkness, weaving the carpets we walk on from the thread of their own blood? I remember Africa without ever having been there, a continent of people slaughtered by greed. I haven't read any articles about South America lately, but a friend in Brazil writes to say that she has just completed a U.N. tour of the orphanages there, and she cannot stop weeping. "*You have no idea what they do to these children.*" She says she will adopt an orphan, she will adopt a hundred orphans, she will never have a child of her own.

I read the paper at the Aegean Restaurant. The waiter who looks like Sylvester Stallone sits down and asks me, "What's the news?" I tell him. He rolls his eyes and throws back his head, rejecting the world with his chin. "Don't think of these things." Eyes shut tight, he waves his hands in front of his body like a blind man. "Far away. Invisible." But he is wrong.

The work of pure Greek light exposes the essence of things in seconds. Nothing and no one is far away. The world is highly visible in every direction. The world is here. I am trying to understand what I see, but it is very difficult. My century has not produced a single invention that understands itself.

Time on the island

Music currents play in the ocean.
Swimmers make love with the water.
Rising in tides, even the medusas
are sexy in their see-through lingerie.

The sky dives, spills over the beach front,
lights down blue on the tables and chairs.
Incisor of moon releases the sea. Stars appear.
We do not care what they might be called.

Shall we believe this, then,
the clean cotton grace of summer? Is it true?
Is Greece really a laughing old man with a donkey
tattooed on his chest? Is such happiness legal?

For the children, yes, forever
for the holiday children, who turn brown
on the run and howl through hours,
all day long, forever, I am tempted
to say, forever, the password of faith.

Time grows long on the island.
People begin to suspect Eden.
Fishing boat lanterns flicker far away.
I do not care when Fotis
begins to fold up the tablecloths.
It is very late, he says, drawing
eyes like obsidian stones
over my face, my neck.

Hmm?

I said it's late.

In the evening, in the century,
our lives.

Peace with the shepherd

I'M INSIDE THE *spitaki* getting dressed when I hear the shepherd Andreas yelling at the bottom of the field. Because we are still not on speaking terms, I think his shouts cannot be intended for me. I recognize his powerful wordless yells, whoops, and half-roars. He uses certain ones for his sheep, certain ones for his donkey, certain ones for other men. The call he uses for me is different from all these, somewhat quieter, with the hint of a question in it, occasionally accompanied by a high two-tone whistle. When I hear the whistle, finally, I come out of the house.

Barba Andreas stands at the fence waving his cane. Is he hurt? Does he need my help? "What's happening? Are you all right?" I yell across the field to him, my voice running past the fig trees, through the olive grove, down onto the lower terrace of the land.

He yells back, "I'm fine! Come and drink a coffee!"

He waves his cane in the air again and turns, walking around the corner of his hut.

This is strange. Since Yiorgos started keeping Kelis the horse in my field, Andreas has stopped coming over to visit. I rummage around for some biscuits—the coffee offering of peace—and begin to walk towards Andreas' hut.

He's inside, making coffee.

I say, "Yia-sou, ti kaneis?" Again, he replies that he is fine. I sit down on the stone bench. Look over the garden. Look at the donkey. "How is the beautiful Marcos?" The donkey lifts his head.

"Marcos is a bad donkey. Beautiful but always making trouble. Headstrong." One of the mysteries of this place is how much the shepherds resemble their donkeys, or, possibly, how much the donkeys resemble their shepherds. Down the road, Elias' donkey seems to have barely survived the German Occupation of Greece, just as Elias himself almost died during that ugly time. Both of them are visibly scarred, beaten-looking creatures. Half of the donkey's left ear is missing; two of the fingers on Elias' left hand are mangled and partially paralysed. Elias has round growths of flesh on his arms, some kind of skin cancer. The donkey has strange bumps and discolourings through its coat.

Sleek Marcos is handsome, like Andreas. When he was young, Andreas must have been beautiful, blond and blue-eyed, a living remnant of ancient Greece. Even now, as he comes out of the house carrying two tiny cups of coffee, I see how well-groomed he is: the moustache is carefully curled up, his hair is combed, the shirt, though very old, is clean, with every button intact. (Elias sometimes ties his shirts together with bits of string.) Today, Andreas has a small pink rose tucked behind his ear. As soon as he puts down the coffee cups, he hands me the flower.

I am astonished. "What's happening? I thought you were mad at me." I hand him the package of biscuits.

Looking momentarily flustered, he puts down the biscuits, turns away to the water tap, and washes his hands. Then he leans off the concrete patio and spits under the apricot tree. I know what he's thinking. Just like a foreign woman to bring up a sensitive subject brashly, no grace, before we've even had our coffee. Holy mother.

"I am not mad at you. Victoria says—" Victoria is his wife, whom I've met, very briefly, in the village "—that I am not mad at you. You don't know what you're doing. You don't know how things work here. Victoria says I am mad at Yiorgos. And yes, I am mad at him. He is using his friendship with you to get what he wants."

I argue momentarily with Andreas, but then I let it go. He might be right. I'm not sure. I don't know. I don't care. Yiorgos has become part of my days. I lend him my soap. We cook together. I ride with him sometimes, to the monastery, to the chapel above the sea. I like Kelis the horse in my field.

Andreas drinks his coffee. "You don't know. I watched over the little house while it was empty. I took care of the olive trees. And now, what? You don't even say Yia-sou to me in the morning."

"You don't say Yia-sou to me, either."

Again he grows flustered, and looks around, almost wildly, as if trying to find the words for all this in mid-air. "I wait for you to come here! You were the one who changed the arrangement. I used to come all the time to see you. And when Libby was here, every day we saw each other, every day, to make sure everything was fine."

I sit with my hand under my chin, half-covering my mouth. I uncover my mouth. "Yia-sou."

"Yia-sou," he replies, gruffly, not looking at me.

Sigá sigá. I understand so slowly. I've insulted him. This is why he is angry. Why didn't I see it before? I was upset with him for being inflexible, for being selfish, for being mean-spirited. Because he does have other places to graze his sheep; the field itself means very little to him. But now I see my own stupidity, my own lack of perception. The house and the field are symbols for him, as they are, in many ways, for me. When Andreas grazed the sheep in front of the *spitaki,* he was establishing and re-establishing our friendship, our mutual dependency, our closeness. He always asked how things were, if I ever had any problems with strangers at night, if I felt too isolated. He was *taking care of me.* I suppose I knew this, but I took it for granted. I didn't realize how important it was to him.

I've hurt Barba Andreas' feelings. He may be mad at Yiorgos, but he probably also feels intensely jealous. Yiorgos, the great interloper. Wonderful. Now I have to carefully balance my affections for an old shepherd and a hippy peasant. Andreas watches me expectantly.

"Are we all right with each other, then?"

"Yes, but you'll see. You'll see that I am right, and you are wrong, and you don't really understand Yiorgos' ways. You don't know."

I get up and rinse the fine grounds out of my coffee cup.

"Ahh, it doesn't matter. Victoria asks when you

will come to the village to have supper with us. When will you come? She wants to feed you."

I laugh and grab my stomach. "See this? This is the problem. I'm getting fat. Everyone is always feeding me. Sweets and cheese and oil and goat's milk and almonds—"

"It's good for you. You look fine. Very healthy."

I snort like a pig. "Very, very healthy."

"What do you think? If you go back to Canada skinny, with no meat on you, your family won't let you return to Greece. They'll say we don't feed you." He takes his cane from the ground and stands up. "I have to go and bring the sheep in. So when are you coming to supper? Tomorrow? You should come tomorrow, Victoria wants you to come."

"Okay. I'll come tomorrow."

"At five?"

"At five."

"Bravo!" I am still sitting on the bench, watching him untie Marcos. "Bravo! We will see you tomorrow." In a burst of enthusiasm and relief, he canes back up to the patio and gives me a hug and a kiss on the cheek.

Home

ASVÉSTI, IN GREEK, for lime. It comes in thick plastic bags that you have to cut open with a knife. Inside is a heavy chalk-white mixture of lime and water. It has a strange consistency, like the finest quicksand or a very watery, marble-white mud. *Asvésti.* The base for whitewash, and a major ingredient of cement. You want to put your hands in and squeeze.

But resist the temptation. I did it numerous times, to fish a lost brush out of the pail, to flick insects or pebbles out of the impeccable ivory. Now, after white-washing the *spitaki* inside and out, my fingers are like leather strips chewed by a litter of puppies. The country women told me, "Be careful, asvésti eats your hands," but I didn't know what they meant; I thought it had something to do with giving you a big appetite.

Outside, in the late afternoon sun, the house is dazzlingly, blindingly white. My hands are burning. Seated outside on the stone bench—careful not to lean against the damp whitewash—I hold a glass of

Metaxa and water: my fingers ache. I've washed them with sap and rubbed them with olive oil, but they are still sore, split and raw at the tips.

I'm glad. It makes the work more real. My hands are ruined but the house is beautiful. Every two minutes I find another excuse to go inside. Inside is even better than outside. A child would think: heaven. A warm, full white, like fresh milk, like an undone bale of cotton, a white that invites you to go to sleep and dream. There is nothing on the walls now, no clutter in the small dimensions of the room. Only white walls and a pale blue sheet on my bed.

Whose voice comes to me now, out of the wide sky and the dusk-kindled air? Angela Pallister's. I remember her saying, about the house on Hope Street, "It's hard for me to explain what happens when you love a house. Certainly it's as wonderful as loving a man. Perhaps more so." Angela. Albert. My own mother. My brothers and sisters and friends. They are so closer than I know.

Sheep bells ring above me now. The big flock is coming in from the fig orchard, thirsty and ready to sleep. Yiorgos waits for me down the road with Maria and her husband. They've invited us to eat fish with them tonight. Later we'll go to the sea and drink a bottle of wine together. These pleasures will unfold so naturally, with such random, excellent rhythm, that even their ordinariness will humble me. And tonight I will fall asleep in my perfectly white house. *Spitaki*.

Home. I will fight with this word for the rest of my life. Mysterious and heartbreaking word. Home. Sister to the word "love."

Aphrodite's almonds and the gray snake

ALONE TODAY. Yiorgos has gone to the harbour city for leather and goat bells. No visitors, no chat with Andreas or Elias. Silence. And, to remind us that summer is not the only season, a gray sky stretches above a steel-faced sea.

Columns of light shaft through the clouds. Columns of light fall like spears into the Aegean.

The sun shines, drowns. Shines, drowns.

A woman named Aphrodite was born in the abandoned stone house across the field. A big almond tree stands near the little house, its dark branches overhanging the road. Aphrodite runs a restaurant with her husband in Skala. This year, they have been too busy to collect the almonds.

Every time the shepherds walk past the tree, they stop, pick an almond, crack it open on the stone fence, eat the nut, and continue on their way. Aphrodite laughed when I told her this. "When the almonds come ripe, all the people turn into birds!

Do you have an almond tree in your field?" she asked me.

"Only a small one, gone wild."

"Then if you have time, *you* gather the almonds. You'll need a big stick to knock them out of the tree. And if you crawl up into the tree, you can knock down more, but be careful not to slip on the sap."

I carry a tin pail up to Aphrodite's house. It is like the *spitaki*, one room made of stone, a family's summer dwelling. Yiorgos tells me that ten years ago, all the village people and their children came down and lived in the countryside for the summer. Some people still do that, but as the island economy changes, involving more and more tourism, fewer people have the time to tend a garden and live without electricity or hot water.

Amigthala, in Greek, for almond. I eat almonds every day now, from Yiorgos' trees or this one, even from the bitter tree in my own field. Notes for the almond-feast: Snap off the pink and deep orange husks. On a flat rock, turn the nut on its side, where the two halves of the shell meet. Then, with a smaller rock, crack the nut open. The old men and women can do this with dazzling speed, never breaking the nut inside.

If possible, the nuts should be eaten with fresh figs. Almonds and figs, fresh green *sika* from the slowly ripening trees in my yard. These fruits are evidence of the divine nature of the world. Who but a god and goddess could have planted almond and fig trees in the same earth, knowing how delicious they would be together? A fig is ripe when it bulges inside its own skin, when it's soft under the pressure of fingers. Pick figs in the late morning, when you're hungry, when the sweet, red anemone inside is warmed to its fullest flavour, ambrosia jam. Peel the soft outer skin away. Push half a dozen almonds into the moist fruit. Eat. Very, very *slowly.*

Priests are not allowed to eat fresh figs because to do so would break their vows of celibacy. But I eat the figs every day, as they ripen, at every meal, at night, naked under the fig trees.

Now I will have my own little stash of good almonds, too. Until my shoulders and neck are sore, I knock *amigthala* out of the trees with a long stick. Then I begin to gather the nuts from the ground, tossing them into the pail. Many of them have fallen over the stone fence, in the dusty road beside the field, so I crouch down and send my fingers into the oregano bushes, into the open chambers in the thorns, into the fence-crevices.

Light spills out of the gray clouds. I half-kneel, one knee in the dust, the weight of sunlight heavy on my back. Quickly now, in a light sweat, I distinguish the nutshells from the grass, the stones, the herbs, the earth. *Sshhh-cling!* they clatter in the tin pail.

My fingers are on an almond when I see it. The snake. A hand's breadth from my hand. *Fidee.* My eyes find the motionless tail first and for an instant I think "empty snake skin" but it's not empty. The snake's length is laid upon itself like a coil of folding rope. Shiny dark gray, with triangular black markings down her back. Is she a poisonous one? People die from snakebites here. Silver-gray snake against the slate-gray fence: the black markings are like vertebrae, the backbone of the stone itself. How can such a delicate creature be sibling to stone?

My fingers are still on the almond as the gray skin

begins to slither against itself, so close to my hand that all I need to do is let go of the almond, stretch out my fingers, and touch the living gray leather. . . . My eyes slide back, back over the black markings, to the lizard head and tapered tail, lying side by side. Her head is perfectly still now. My fingers are becoming almond tree roots. Aware of my presence, the snake considers her next move. Slow slide now, and a flicking black tongue. Smooth gray belly glides against the belly of the gray stone. The snake feeds herself into a crevice between two smaller rocks in the fence. The black crevice pulls her in. Lick of the gray tail, and she's gone.

Still the almond touching my fingers. Still the sun leaning like a tired horse on my back.

This is the world.

The almond tree.

The snake.

The stone.

My fingertips on the verge of each thing.

The orchard

EARLY EVENING. How shall we name this light that ignites everything it touches, but burns nothing? Sheet of saffron flung over the land. The gold behind every colour, the gold inside our own skin and eyes. I walk across the field to throw a handful of fig-skins to Andreas' sheep. In this light, even the dusty sheep look brilliant. I see Yiorgos sitting across the road, shirtless, at his small red table under an olive tree, working on Scarlatti's donkey saddle. He seems absorbed in his task, so I don't disturb him. I return to the *spitaki,* sit down on the stone bench against the house, and begin making a few notes on the poetry I've been writing. Poetry ripens and spills out of my mind like the fruit that overflows the valley now.

My concentration strays. I begin this letter instead. I look out at the olive grove, the hills, the sea. I look at my hands. What has happened to my fingers? When I first came here and saw Maria's rough and hardened hands, I thought, "Awful. I will wear gloves.

I will be careful. I will buy good cream and apply it twice a day." But then I learned. Digging an outhouse hole. Cleaning the mice nests out of the *spitaki*. Washing clothes. Feeding and watering the animals. Riding the bicycle. Picking fruit. Climbing the hills. Repairing the trellis, the shutters, the door. Making fires. Re-building the fallen sections of the stone fence. Whitewashing.

My hands are newly scarred. No white nails. Callouses hard as gems on my palms. Feet made of goat leather. Changed hands and feet, and all the flesh in between, changed. Though still nothing like Yiorgos or Andreas. Their hands are the living histories of their bodies' work. Maps unfold in the scars on their knuckles and palms. Fingers, thickened by winter work, tell of axes sharpened with stone. And animals; you see animals in the hands of these men, and every season's harvest.

As though he knows I'm thinking about him, Yiorgos calls out, "Katerina, I make coffee! Stop writing!"

"How do you know I'm writing?"

"Because I smell a big fire!"

I laugh. Yiorgos. Poetry is a country, and Yiorgos lives there. The sunflowers, taller than both of us now, lean down to touch him when he walks by. Snow White, his favourite goat, calls him by name.

"Katerina! Stop writing! Your kafedaki is getting cold."

But how can I stop writing?

How can I stop writing when the sun drops now into the sea, a medallion sinking in slow motion? Night comes quickly. In a few minutes, the pale blue lines will fade into the white paper, spilling words

431

down the page. In a few minutes, darkness will quiet my hand and send me across the narrow road to Yiorgos. While we make supper together, he will say something like, "Eggplant? Why we call this eggplant in English? It does not look like an egg. Or what kind of eggs you have in Canada?"

And I will laugh and smile, as I smile now. Because I am alive. Because you are there, somewhere, on the other side. This very moment, our hearts echo the same rhythm. The great myth of this country, of every country, is the myth of distance.

Darkness falls down, so quickly, a blue-gray hand over these fields I love. Night now, but I dream of giving you another day, a day whole like an apple, something ripe and shining that you can hold in your hand until you're hungry. And when you're hungry, you can eat it, seeds and all, then fall asleep, an orchard sown inside you.